ACCOUNTING WARS

AND REVELATIONS FROM A GREAT CAREER

"THE WISDOM TO KNOW THE DIFFERENCE"

3rd Edition

Written by Mary E. Hallett
from discussions with Charles E. Hallett, CPA, CGMA

Table of Contents

FOREWORD

My name is John Strader. I was fortunate to become a founding partner with Charles (Chuck) Hallett in, Strader Hallett & Co., P.S. Certified Public Accountants (CPA's), Olympia, Washington. Chuck and I formed the firm in February of 1983. This was accomplished over a single weekend at the beginning of the 1983 income tax season - the worst possible time to try to start a new CPA firm. Luckily, I had been in business as a sole CPA practitioner for four (4) years prior to the formation of the new firm. As a result of that experience, our firm began with a very unique computer system for its time, including two (2) fully trained associates and many of the administrative systems in place. This foundation really helped us through our first tax season and year of operation.

I was looking for a partner at the time we met. I had had talked to many different CPA's and CPA firms regarding merging and/or forming a new firm. One of these CPA's, Dave Mackey, called me on a Saturday morning from Chuck's kitchen, and explained that he had talked to a young CPA that just left a CPA firm in Olympia over unusual circumstances. The firm was one of our competitors in town. Dave said that Chuck wanted to associate with an existing CPA or firm in the Olympia area. He went on to say that this CPA had told him about an amazing story regarding the head of the CPA firm that Chuck left. Dave said it was hard to believe the story and I needed to hear it from Chuck. It turned out that I had 2 or three (3) mutual clients with this other CPA firm. I knew that something was occurring inside this other CPA firm but I had no idea what Chuck was about to explain to me - it was mind blowing (Chuck explains what happened in a latter part of this book). My original reason for talking to Chuck was more to find out what was occurring at this other CPA firm than to associate with him; although, if he turned out to be what I was looking for in a CPA, I would definitely consider him as a Partner.

I had prepared a list of attributes that I wanted in the CPA or the firm to possess. My wife and I met with Chuck and his wife. Chuck and I had a long discussion concerning what he was looking for and wanted to accomplish in public accounting and business. The result was that same weekend we decided to form a Professional Corporation and CPA firm. We contacted an attorney. The attorney had the corporation formed. We were in business by the following week. The first 2 months were very hectic as we were constantly setting up new clients that Chuck brought into our firm. We were working almost all night. I can remember concluding many "all nighters" with many breakfasts at 3 or 4 AM. We then had to be back at work the next morning at 8 AM or earlier.

At the time I didn't know that I had just become associated with the "Michael Jordan" of the certified public accounting field. If you have ever seen Micheal make one his spectacular dunks where he takes the ball moves through and avoids 2 to 3 defenders, does a double clutch while hanging in the air for what seems like minutes, and then slam dunks the ball. This is what Chuck could do metaphorically when it came to litigation support, accounting and tax matters. As you read this book you will come to understand my comparison with Michael. I was intimately involved in many of the recollections in this book and others I discussed after they had happened in our office or over a meal at a latter date. I remember all of these recollections actually happened as they were portrayed in this book.

Some of the amazing things he was able to do/accomplish, which are not fully included in his book or only lightly touched on, include some of the following:

> 1. "Negotiated" a recently remodelled 26,000 square foot building for one dollar ($1) in a backgammon game. He sold me half (1/2) the building that same evening for $1 and "got all his money back"!

2. We we able to open 2 additional offices and become the nineteenth (19) largest CPA firm in Puget Sound, according to the Puget Sound Business Journal, within six (6) years of founding of our firm.

3. We never had a problem obtaining clients, our problem was developing the staff fast enough to keep up with Chuck's marketing capabilities and knowledge of the industry.

4. Chuck was "24/7" in the pursuit of serving his clients.

5. Many times during tax season and sometimes after tax season he would work all night. His goal was to get the work done.

6. He became the President of Washington Society of CPA's and he served on the American Institute of Certified Public Accountants (AICPA) National Council.

7. Father to two fantastic sons while managing to juggle his professional schedule.

8. An unbelievable and supportive wife, Mary.

I am sure you will enjoy his many recollections. Even if you are not a CPA or accountant, most of these are applicable to other professional service businesses. Many of the issues unfortunately all to often apply to many of the firms that are in business today. I consider myself to be very lucky to have had the pleasure to work with Chuck for over 20 years. And after all this time, we remain as close friends. My wife and I try to get together at least weekly with Chuck and Mary.

PREAMBLE

I worked in Public Accounting for 33 years and for the Internal Revenue Service (IRS) 3 years before that. I believe that Certified Public Accounting (CPA) is one of the most difficult professions, and, if done properly, being a CPA is one of the most personally and financially rewarding ways to spend your working life. While I was able to work, I met many people from many different walks of life who worked in many different professions or businesses. Some of these people had different personal or political beliefs than I have. Whereas, most were small business owners, many others were still high quality individuals. In my professional life, I always tried to set a good example in doing the "right things"; regardless of the client and regardless of the circumstances. A CPA in public practice is introduced to the most diverse people who have different financial issues and problems. I believe this profession is more broad than any other profession. By far, the number of ethical people whom I worked with far exceeded the others. However, I hope this summary of my experiences can give a broad over view as to what a CPA has to be prepared for while in business. A goal of this writing is to summarize for you, the reader, several of my experiences with some of those individuals during my professional career.

My father first introduced me to what he believed a CPA did in public practice. This discussion ultimately impacted my designated major in college and my decision to try to become a CPA. As background, our family legally immigrated from Canada during the 1950's. My parents had no more than high school educations and believed that the United States would allow them to provide the best place in the world to raise their children. Nonetheless, mom and dad were able to wade through all the immigration documents all by themselves. Previously, my maternal grandparents had legally immigrated to the United States. This helped to pave the way and the manner for my parents to apply for immigration to the United States. Prior to my birth, my parents had applied for immigration and reapplied a few times prior to their application being approved for acceptance to legally immigrate into the United States. My parents told me they knew they had to be patient and persistent to be able to be afforded the benefits of immigrating into this great country.

Finally, 5 years after their first application (and 8 months after I was born), our family was able to immigrate to the United States. In order to qualify for immigration status, I understand that we were required to have a sponsor in the United States, a place to live, my father had to have a job, and our family was required to have health care coverage. By the way, I understand the rules are similar today for legal immigration into the United States.

After another 5 years, we were able to become "naturalized" or be able to become legal United States (US) citizens. This was incredibly important to my parents. I remember them studying for the test to become a United States citizen. And after we became citizens, each and every 4th of July until my parents passed away, our family celebrated becoming US citizens. I believe that it is an honor and privilege to be a US citizen and that honor and privilege should not be ignored.

Along the way, I was reminded by my Canadian family that being a US citizen is not the same as being an American. Anyone who is born on the North or South American continents are technically "Americans". Not all are US citizens. As an example, my Canadian relatives continue to refer to me as a "Yankee". After all, they are Americans also.

We originally immigrated to Southern California and we lived with my grandparents until my parents could purchase their own residence. Finally, after slightly more than a year, my parents were able to buy a home. As economics and conditions changed, they were able to move to bigger and bigger homes. Although none of these homes were more than a thousand square feet, they were all terrific homes for our five (5) member family and better than the living conditions that my parents enjoyed in Canada. The third home that my parents purchased in Southern California was a real find. It was an acquisition that made my parents even more proud of all the hard work they had done to get to that point. At the time, our family moved to a "new" subdivision close to our elementary school so my eldest sister could begin kindergarten. Our home was in the middle of a block and between two similar homes. One of those homes was owned by a Hispanic family and the other owned by a black family. They were born in this country, and accordingly, we immediately learned that we were the "immigrants" in the neighborhood. We all became friends.

As we had some South African friends who were Caucasian (white), we were taught to refer to white and black people as just that. My parents found it offensive to stereotype or profile people from Africa and taught us not to use certain terms or stereotypes. Although we became friends with our neighbors, there were certain hard times because we were the local immigrants. For instance, I remember the day my mother was called a "dirty immigrant" from a white woman in the neighborhood. This is a memory that has impacted my life and my thinking. I learned at a young age to try to get along with everyone. I also learned at a young age that anyone can be discriminated against. Our family certainly was from time to time.

My father explained this as normal and customary. He taught me that many people are afraid of other people, certainly people they did not know. He taught us that color did not matter or ethnicity did not matter. My father taught me to overcome people's fears that I would have to be willing to work harder at everything I did than everyone else to succeed. He reminded me over and over again that he demanded and that he expected great effort from me in all that I pursued. My parents demanded and expected that I would have the highest academic grades in my classroom. They took their time to help me whenever I needed it. My father helped me to excel at all sports. My father counseled me on what my future would be if I worked hard at everything that I did. I am blessed to have had such a great relationship with my parents.

My father taught me that there are only two people in life that you have to get generally along with. Those were the people you worked with and the people you worked for. Pretty simple. True. And that pretty much covers everyone.

When I landed my first job, I remember being so happy that I had a job and was able to make money for the first time. My father counseled me on the importance of trying to be the best and hardest worker in the company, regardless of my assignment. This history and relationship with my father really helped me to do the very best that I could as a CPA later in life.

When people generally hear the term CPA, I have found that they tend to be quick to think of their tax preparer or the company auditor. However, CPAs do many different types of things and work in places other than in public accounting, such as: industry, teaching, government, and not for profits. In my experience, I prepared many income tax returns and worked on many financial statements. However, the most interesting memories that I have were in other areas of public accounting. These include the legal system, the Internal Revenue Service (IRS), fellow workers, and certain clients. These are some of the memories that I want to share with the readers in order to help them gain a better understanding of my experience within the public accounting profession.

Expert witness work and business consulting are types of specific services that I spent quite a bit of time in assisting clients. These types of matters generally allowed me to think at a higher and more creative level. Many times there was not a boiler plate solution. These experiences helped me in many ways. One important way was to help me to understand that people have differences and a key to success can be to quickly identify these situations and try to mitigate those issues efficiently. If those differences could not be mitigated, then I had to try to think of intelligent and creative manners to help settle those differences. I took great pride in trying to look at these differences at a higher level than most.

For instance, it was not unusual for some clients to not pay their bills timely. Accordingly, standard and customary practice for those instances is to simply telephone or contact the client. It is then important to engage the client in some sort of dialogue to discuss the reasons for nonpayment. Sometimes, the client was simply unable to pay and we would simply have to wait for payment. Other times, there may have been a misunderstanding about the bill. It is always in a CPA's best interest to try to mitigate any of those differences in a manner to obtain payment immediately and to enhance future business. Of course, there were some clients that did not pay and we had to pursue other methods to secure payment. For those, our firm may have had to assign the account to collection. Generally, these bills would then be paid. However, after our firm initiated collection actions, the CPA firm that I co founded was frivolously counter sued 5 times for "malpractice" while I was working there. As I explained to my business clients, in the US, people can sue people for any reason, and, sometimes no reason at all. As you will read later, not one of these instances remotely had any malpractice component; albeit, that does not seem to matter anymore. I have learned that our court system allows professional people from all walks of life to be sued for no reason whatsoever. This is sad; however, it is something that professional people must tolerate in my opinion.

In these experiences I met many reputable attorneys and some attorneys who I did not have such high opinions for as a result of their actions. And my opinions from working inside the legal system are simply that; that is, my opinions from working with the legal system. However, I have found the legal system to be inefficient in many ways and I believe that the legal system is broken in certain respects. I believe the legal system allows bad people to perpetuate the system and leverage the legal system to their own benefit. I believe that the legal system is not operating consistent with what a normal and reasonable person would expect. That is, most people want to quickly and efficiently simply resolve conflicts. In the beginning, I believed the court system was about the law, it was about being fair, reasonable and honest. Today, I believe that you can forget all of that. From my personal experiences, I believe that the court system today is based on winning, and, winning at any cost.

And I believe the court system is currently being operated to reward attorneys for bad behavior. That is, instead of working toward a fair, reasonable and honest timely result; instead, an attorney can endeavor to unreasonably delay the matter and those attorneys somehow raise irrelevant issues that only prolong the matter. This is a frustrating experience for most and an experience that not only delays the ultimate outcome of the case, but also, those delays add substantial costs. This behavior has irreparably damaged many businesses and individuals that I know and had represented. Most individuals and small businesses cannot afford to defend a case that is being dragged on by opposing counsel. And opposing counsel seems to know and understand this point. In my experience, most judges are generally slow to award a fair amount of legal fees and other related costs to the injured (or the right) party. For instance, the injured party can incur many thousands of dollars in legal fees. The injured parties are more often than not only reimbursed a portion of what the injured party actually incurs; thus, allowing the frivolity to almost perpetually continue.

I have come to these conclusions based upon experience in both civil and criminal matters in working with clients and for our firm. These included cases in which I was an expert, meeting with clients on their own legal matters together with their attorneys, cases where our firm was a party to the lawsuit and other actions, such as grand jury investigations and criminal fraud audits before the Internal Revenue Service (IRS).

And, in my travels, I have found that the perception of our legal system throughout the world is not favorable, and some may go on to say, uncivilized. For instance, while in China, I had the experience of meeting with one of their communist party leaders. During my visit, we were able to meet and spend a few days together and we spoke of many issues. One of which was our legal system. His observation to me at the time was that the United States is perceived as one of the most, if not the most, uncivilized country in the world by many. This surprised me as I then believed our civilization had something to do with great roads, running water, low pollution, and nice residences. He went on to say that he believes China is "thousands of years ahead of our country". He went on to say that the United States is the only country in the world that allows people to: kill people, rape women, molest children, and sell drugs.

He then said that we reward our criminals with free legal help, free room and board, free health care, and, our victims get nothing.

Right or wrong the perception of others as to the United States legal and justice system is a perception that many share and I was able to experience first hand. And, I believe that the legal system needs to return to the "spirit and intent" that it was founded upon. That is, the legal system has gotten away from the truth (or right and wrong). The legal system seems to justify this by falling back on terms such as "advocacy", "representation", "laws", regardless of what the attorney knows or reasonably should know about the case. And, the legal system seems to be established so that it can not be fixed or that fixing it would be incredibly insurmountable. Instead, our existing system seems to protect itself from doing the "right thing", and accordingly, the legal system seems to perpetuate and condone the bad behavior by many --- not all.

In my opinion, the bad behavior needs to change. In my opinion, too much money is being spent on bad people and on criminals. I notice that many of our elderly are going hungry, that they can not pay their rent and quite often our elderly are in need of medical attention. I believe that our elderly should be entitled to equal or greater benefits than the criminals. This is just one example where I believe how our legal system has become twisted and needs to be fixed.

A local Chief of Police is an acquaintance of my wife and I. I remember one evening while he was in our home he told us different stories. He spoke of different local citizens who could not get medical or dental care. So, he explained to us that they would commit a crime --- not a felony, but a crime to get them arrested "for a night or a week end". Once in jail, the local citizen would complain of a tooth ache or being sick. All of a sudden, the legal "system" that has evolved results in our government having to pay for this care.

I also represented the Superintendent (Warden) of one of our local prisons. Many times he invited me to visit him at his work. Quite honestly, right or wrong this invitation made me a bit nervous. However, one day while I was in his city and had some available time I decided to give it a try. So, I dropped into the prison administrative offices to see him. I had never been to a prison before (or since). Prior to getting to see the Superintendent, I had to leave certain items with a guard at the "check in". Those items included such things as pencils and even my keys and my belt.

The Superintendent's wife also worked at the same prison. She was a prison guard at a men's institution. I found this odd. This surprised me that a woman would be a prison guard at a men's prison. After the three (3) of us met in the superintendent's office, she took me on a tour of the entire prison and its grounds. I was able to see the visiting room, conjugal visit rooms, cafeteria, etc. None of these surprised me at first blush. Then, all of a sudden doors opened and I found myself in the actual prison yard. Frankly, I was scared and very nervous to be in the prison yard surrounded by murderers and felons. I was again surprised that a woman could be a guard at a men's prison and that she was not afraid to be in this prison yard.

Of course, I had my own perceptions entering this prison from my own experiences and expectations from everything I had been exposed to and also seen on television. From watching television, movies and generally my common sense belief about what prisons should be I was surprised as to what I learned inside the prison. I was told that this was not a "violent prison". Later I learned more.

For instance, we visited the gymnasium for the prisoners. I was shocked at the amenities inside this gymnasium. I observed multiple full court basketball courts in this gymnasium plus many weight rooms and other sitting areas. I never saw anything like this at any school or college I had attended or even my local health club. It was both an impressive facility to see and it was also frustrating to me (as I could not afford to belong to such a health club). I understand the use of these "health club" facilities is "free" to the inmates. And, the gymnasium was full of prisoners while I was there. Without exception, the prisoners appeared to be in terrific shape, certainly, better shape than I am.

We then went to the cell block. My expectation of what I was to see when we entered the cell block was from my experience in watching "prison movies". I fully expected to see metal bars, bunk beds, cinder block walls, a toilet with the seat torn off, flies, etc. in each cell. I was shocked as to what I learned and saw.

Each "cell" door was a solid core door, there were no bars. Each door had a small window that has a drapery on the other side. Thus, the guards or other prisoners could not simply look in on a prisoner. The walls were solid. It was like a small apartment complex. I was told that this was to help respect the inmates "privacy".

And the doors to each cell had two key locks on them. One key is in the possession of a guard and the other is in the possession of the inmate. I understand the guard can not gain access to the prisoner's room unless the prisoner allows access under normal circumstances. Once inside a room I noted that each room was a "single". That is: one bed, one desk, one closet, one television, etc.

The showers were community showers as were the bathroom areas.

Frankly, these living conditions were certainly superior to the dormitories at any school, college or university that I ever visited. My son lived in a fraternity while attending college. The rooms in this prison were superior to even the fraternity! I was surprised.

At the conclusion of the tour I spoke about my surprise concerning these living conditions with the Superintendent. I mentioned how great the living conditions appeared to be at his prison compared to what people experience in college or the elderly who need assistance experience. He agreed. He told me that many criminals will get out of prison, then purposely commit another crime and try to get reassigned back to this same prison. He told me that for many of these inmates, they never want to leave. In fact, the prisoners generally know and understand that they can not support themselves legally outside the walls of the prison, so they want to stay and use all the amenities of the prison system where everything is provided to them free of charge.

I also was able to see the "maximum security" prisoners. Those prisoners did in fact have metal bars and were able to be observed in what I expected to see all prisoners living in. This was a very small portion of the prison and the space represented a limited number of the total prisoners in the facility.

Many of the above experiences influenced my ability to work within the legal and court systems. We all initially hope that if we need to use the legal system that the result will be justice. However, what many of us do not understand is that many of the people in the legal system are flawed, and accordingly, there may or may not be an ultimate fair solution to a specific problem. In other words, it is possible to spend thousand of dollars and thousands of hours preparing for your "day in court" only to get a "bad draw". That bad draw can be a poorly trained attorney, a much better attorney on the other side, a judge who did not listen and/or understand the issues, and/or an unqualified judge for that particular case.

We may believe the court system is about what is right and wrong, but I learned that many judges simply try to "create a new law", "make an intriguing decision", or return a favor to an acquaintance/friend/attorney. This is regardless of what any written pre existing agreement or contract between the parties had stated. Bad rulings in these types of matters can be especially damaging to honest people and many businesses that rely on written agreements. More often than not, these people simply want an agreement that they negotiated in good faith to be enforced. More often than not, these individuals and businesses had that agreement well documented by their attorney. Their reasonable expectation was that that agreement would be upheld and enforced. It was surprising to me what "noise" and distractions could be "made up on the fly" by the other party to improperly delay or even sometimes obtain an unfavorable ruling to the detriment of the honest person.

Of course there are appeals and other manners to settle cases, even after the fact. Those also cost a lot of money. And, there are names for the different majorities of the courts, thus there can be greater concerns depending upon the the next forum of resolution of a case. In other words, you may understand that you can not appeal even a bad decision. For instance, many business people fear liberal justices. I have heard many times that these justices tend to make consistently bad interpretations of what appear to be pretty clear facts from time to time. The decisions that are made by these justices can sometimes depend on the area that you live and/or the type of case that you have. In other words, some of the appellate justices are not inclined to uphold certain types of agreements or decisions. I found that fact surprising and sickening at times.

I always tried to do the right thing with respect to cases I represented. It was not about money to me. If I did not like a case or if I did not believe in the case at inception, I would simply refuse the case. Many attorneys criticized me for this. If I believed the party was wrong, I did not believe I could assist them with a clear conscience. I also believed that it would impact or impugn my reputation among the business people who I wanted to represent.

My default action and response to most clients was to consider what could happen if everyone could quickly, fairly and reasonably settle any disputes between honest business people. It was my experience that many of these small business owners worked countless hours. I believed they were entitled to an efficient process to receive what they expected from their hard work. Thus, I often suggested a forum to settle matters outside of the courtroom.

While I was working in the normal course of my business as a CPA, I would be asked from time to time to review contracts and other similar documents that were drafted by attorneys. Normally, those agreements would contain a provision as to how to solve disputes. There are many types of dispute resolution forums and I learned that the court system is only one of them. I found the court system lengthy, frustrating, boring, costly, and too often wrong, in my opinion. Thus, I would encourage our business clients to include a provision that would include a more efficient process within a system that would have an arbitrator or mediator that was more qualified than most sitting judges.

As examples, there are other types of dispute resolution forums. These can include resolution forums such as local arbitration or mediation services to those that are a bit more formal. I was told by the attorneys that the original written contract or agreement between the parties can allow the settlement forum to be binding. I also learned from the attorneys that the original contract can award costs of the dispute. I learned of many different forums to settle business disputes and concluded after many years that Binding Judicial Arbitration and Mediation Services (JAMS) with substantially prevailing party awards of all costs became my favorite manner to financially, efficiently and timely solve disputes.

What this generally means to me is that honest people generally want a forum that is legally binding and not appealable. Then, when the action is over, it is over. Thus, complete preparation by the attorneys the "first time" is imperative. I was taught that "if you don't have time to do it right the first time, when will you have time to do it right?".

Also important is the selection of the arbitrator/mediator. I learned that it is important to select an arbitrator/mediator with experience in similar matters. In other words, the arbitrator/mediator should be skilled in resolving similar and specific types of matters. In addition, the winning (substantially prevailing) party in these types of disputes should be able to recover not only their losses that lead to the matter being arbitrated, but also, the winning party should be able to recover all of their out of pocket costs as a result of the action in order to "put them whole". I have found that these provisions in written agreements between parties, especially dishonest ones, discourage bad behavior by other attorneys in prolonging and frivolously attacking a binding agreement.

Although I have met many good judges, arbitrators and mediators; unfortunately, I have met others who I did not personally believe were qualified to efficiently rule fairly to "once and for all" fairly settle a dispute. Thus, it was normal and customary behavior in these later cases for the frivolous party to just continue and continue through the mediation process, the court system, the appeals process and all the way to the supreme court in some cases. This seemed true if the damaging party believed the "process" would be too costly for the damaged party or if the process would ultimately frustrate the "right" party. I came to the conclusion that the traditional court room process is too financially risky to honest people. Sometimes, you may have a good case and you may get a poor decision by the initial judge because the initial judge in my opinion was not qualified to take the case. Appeals of these cases may then be too costly by the truly damaged party. Ultimately, I found that with an unqualified judge on a particular case, that the cost of a fair, reasonable and honest resolution exceeds what one is ready, willing and able to ultimately afford.

I remember a discussion I had with an attorney general concerning some observations that I had made. At the time, I was told that everything the attorney general's office did was completely legal. I had no reason to doubt that. Instead, I said, "I am holding you to a higher standard than that". I then asked if "everything the office did was fair, reasonable and honest?". In many actions, I represented the attorney general's office and found the office to be "truth seeking". This was a positive in my ongoing relationship with the office. I had this same experience with the Prosecuting Attorneys' offices that I represented.

Instead of "using" the court system, with a group such as JAMS there seems to be a protocol to resolve disputes efficiently. I had experienced the particular arbitrators are normally invited into JAMS via their own personal reputations. Many of these arbitrators are themselves retired judges with experience in the types of cases that you want resolved. Having their final decision as "binding" means that when it is over, it is over. In other words, your attorney needs to be well qualified, ready and your attorney needs to be well prepared as a well qualified and fair arbitrator or mediator will try to come to a fair and reasonable solution.

In my opinion, you should always choose the best attorney for the type of case you have. The "cheapest" attorney is sometimes just that. Be careful and remember, when you are going into battle, you are going there to win. If you could have settled the dispute, normal and reasonable people would already have done that. So, if you disagree and end up in this type of forum, plan everything you do to win. I found that a majority of the times cases would be litigated, that the litigation process was the best result for the "wrong side". In other words, this allowed the delay of proper payments and the ultimate hope that a wrong decision could be granted. As stated above, this behavior is wrong and should not be allowed to continue in my opinion.

In my profession as a CPA, I would be responsible for billing sometimes hundreds of clients in any given month. It was not uncommon to receive telephone calls from concerned clients about their bills. I found it important to be able to reasonably explain to them what the bill was for and why the amount of the bill was what it was "to the client's satisfaction". Frankly, if the explanation did not satisfy them the firm would risk losing potentially a good client. And, if the explanation did not satisfy the client, the client may continue to delay payment or simply refuse to pay.

It was not uncommon in a small portion of these discussions to make a compromise on the bill. For instance, the client knew me and I knew the client. I tried to have a personal relationship with all of the clients I managed and I tried to be fair with all of them.

Although most initial inquiries about the bill would be immediately satisfied with the telephone call explanation, many times for business and other reasons an adjustment would be made to the bill. Sometimes, during the course of the telephone conversation I concluded and agreed the bill was too high. Then I would simply make an adjustment to the bill while the client was on the telephone. My goal was to solve the problem as quickly as possible and concurrently try to maintain goodwill with the client.

However, not all inquiries could be resolved with a telephone call. As an example, if the complaint was from an ongoing "problem" client, I would ask the client to pay what they believed was "fair and reasonable" and told them I would accept that as payment of that bill. When the payment came in, based upon the amount of the payment, I would then decide if we could afford to continue representation of that client. Sometimes I would decide yes. Other times I would then "disengage" from the client if I believed the payment was unreasonably low and/or not fair. I found disengaging easier than arguing about the bill, especially if I believed the client behavior was going to repeat itself. I did this because I believe that once the "foundation" with a particular client is set concerning their ongoing complaining, I found there is little or nothing one could do to satisfy some of them. Thus, I would communicate to the client that they had "outgrown our services". I believe that it is important in the CPA profession to try to be fair to clients. So, if one client demands that you work for free or for a very large discount, this is not fair. I learned that, whereas, you can talk about service, quality and "all the key words", you sometimes have to conclude that it is better to move on.

In other instances, sometimes a telephone call is not enough. In other words, regardless of the conversation, the client simply did not pay for the services rendered. For those clients we would turn their bill over to collection. The collection company we used was a client of our firm. We trusted the collection company and its ability to reasonably collect amounts due to our firm. An overwhelming majority of those bills would then be collected through the collection agency. However, we did end up in court and/or legal actions for our firm with 5 different former clients. For each and every one of these actions, prior to sending the bill to collection, we tried to collect the bill for months, if not more than a year. At no time had any of these clients ever complained about the "professional services". However, in each of these actions, the former client counter sued us for malpractice, after their account was sent to collection and after not being able to convince the client to pay for services through normal and customary channels. Although we prevailed in each case, the amount of time spent on these types of frivolous actions is uncompensated. In addition, it is difficult to explain how a frivolous attack against one's reputation has a lasting impact on a professional. These types of frivolous cases has to impact any professional in any subsequent meeting with a client. However, hard work and professional work is important to any CPA so it is important to persevere.

With all of that said, my original CPA partner and I were able to find an outstanding business attorney. Granted he was one of the slowest attorneys we ever met at completing paperwork. However, he was completely honest with us and we both trusted him. In my experience, most business partnerships generally fall apart. There are many reasons for the businesses not continuing or the partners not continuing to be partners. There will be disagreements. The trick is to how to mitigate those differences. My original partner and I would simply buy our attorney lunch, meet with him or telephone him. Generally, lunch worked the best. We did not take the opinion personal; however, we would each explain what we wanted and let him make the decision. There was a lot of trust between all of us. Each and every time, our business attorney was the straw vote. I believe it is important to find an attorney such as this in any business relationship. He was worth his weight in gold (as long as you did not need a business problem solved immediately).

My goal was to try to be the first person in the office each day. I worked as hard as I could each and every day. This included meeting with various and multiple types of people each day. In addition, each day would bring new challenges. I returned each and every telephone call each and every day that I worked. Quite often I was the last person to leave the office. Needless to say, doing this every day for 33 years was financially rewarding. However, along the way I ran into some questionable and remarkable behavior from former clients and other professionals.

The following are some examples of my memorable experiences and my resultant perception of our legal system as to how the legal system worked for me. Of course others will have different opinions. This is my opinion. Some of the "experiences" have been changed to emphasize the legal system. Here is my rather cynical view of the system based upon my own experiences.

CHAPTER ONE – MEETING CLIENTS FOR THE FIRST AND LAST TIME

Going to Work

Upon graduation, I was lucky enough to begin working for the international accounting firm that is now known as DeLoitte. At the time, there were eight (8) international firms that were referred to as the Big 8. Now, after mergers and years later, there are four (4) international firms. Because of my "resume" during college, I was lucky enough to get job offers from all 8 of those firms at that time.

An accounting student can consider different ways of practicing as a CPA. In those days, it pretty much came down to being an auditor (accountant type) or a "tax guy". I liked the latter. I had interned with the Internal Revenue Service (IRS) for three (3) years in their Volunteer Income Tax Assistance (VITA) Program. In addition, I maintained two (2) other concurrent jobs and managed to graduate before I was twenty one (21) years old. This seemed to give me an edge over many in my graduating class.

I was lucky enough to be hired into their small and emerging business consulting division. This was the closest to taxes at the time. I found that most small businesses come to their CPA for income and/or estate type advice. If their CPA is "engaged" in helping clients, then the results can really enhance a client's tax position.

Upon going to the office on my very first day of work, I was ready to "take on all clients". After all, I had just graduated from college, with honors. What was there left to learn?

The partner in charge of the first international office that I worked at had a slightly different opinion. He simply came in, welcomed me to the firm and then asked if I knew how to use a ten (10) key calculator. At first, I did not know how to answer the question. After all, I was a college graduate.

The partner in charge simply opened a telephone book that he found on my desk and asked me to show him that I could use a calculator. It never dawned on me that in all my time in college, I never had to learn how to use a calculator. I was "hunting" and "pecking" all of the numbers. Needless to say, he had a reasonable expectation of my ability at the time and he had a great way of coaching.

He simply told me, "Your first project is to add the telephone book from cover to cover". He taped over all of the keys on the calculator, except the central or landing key. He provided me a visual guide of each key and told me "Do not look at what you are entering". He told me that he expected me to add the entire book and he was going to check to insure that I had properly added the telephone book.

I spent the next day and a half adding that telephone book. What began as a slow process began to improve. Honestly, by the end of the telephone book I was much more efficient, I had learned the keys by touch and I was much faster.

So, I had sort of wrapped all of the adding machine tapes around me and proceeded to walk down the halls and into his office. He let me in to his office and it appeared that he did not know why I was there. He actually asked me, "Why are you here?". I told him that I had successfully added the telephone book. I told him that I had the correct answer. He then sort of looked at me in amazement as I now believe that no one really added the entire telephone book. I must have looked so eager to please him. So, he did the next best thing. He opened a drawer in his desk, sort of grabbed a paper inside his desk, looked up, and asked me the number shown on the bottom of the adding machine tape.

I carefully read the numbers. He then asked me to repeat the last 2 numbers. I gulped and read the last 2 numbers. He smiled and said, "I guess you are ready for your first job!". I felt relieved to have passed my first job assignment. From his perspective it was simply a lesson that I had to learn.

Over my professional career, I found that the so called easy stuff had to be mastered. Clients did not want to pay you to learn basic things, including operating a calculator. This lesson became so important to me that I had a standing offer to any staff member of our firm. That was, if they could beat me in adding up a series of numbers, I would give them twenty five dollars ($25). There was no downside for them to challenge me. Both happily and sadly, I never had to pay anyone. My lesson was learned!

Today, it is not only important to know how to use a calculator, but also, to know how to use such things as spreadsheet applications and word processing (typing). Grammar is important. This is not only when dealing with clients, but also, when dealing with governmental or quasi governmental individuals and organizations. I would encourage all students to become familiar with these applications.

Depending upon where one will be practicing today, it may also be important to have learned to write computer code. This can be a real plus on one's resume, and also, something that one can use their entire career.

I found that during college, I memorized many tax rules and regulations. Accordingly, I tested high on exams. However, doing complicated research was not something that I believe is emphasized enough during college. I would encourage any accounting student to learn and to practice researching different matters in both accounting and tax while in college. This can be a real plus in the hiring process.

Our firm hired interns. These were generally juniors or seniors in college. This gave the interns a chance to see public accounting from the "inside". In addition, interns gave us an opportunity to observe those who worked well in accounting and well in an office environment. We generally tried to hire (or help place) each and every one of our interns. I honestly believe that my internship through the aforementioned VITA program was instrumental in obtaining the job that I wanted.

The final item that I would encourage a student to learn is the "business of accounting". This goes far beyond the practice of accounting. For an accountant to be successful, that accountant must practice as other successful accountants do. For instance, I did not know that most accounting firms bill their clients at about four (4) times more than they pay the staff accountant. On the surface, this seems high. However, substantial training goes into each and every staff accountant. Not all of a staff accountants time can be "billed" to a client. There may be unproductive time, training time or time that is simply unfair to bill the client.

Thus, staff accountants need to be able to go to another more experienced accountant to ask for professional assistance and guidance. In addition, there are overhead expenses that the firm must be able to pay for. These are direct expenses to the staff member, such as: continuing professional education and training, employee benefits (i.e., vacation, holidays, sick days, etc.) and payroll and related taxes.

In addition, each staff accountant should be contributing to the firm's overhead.

And finally, a goal for each staff accountant is to be able to "show a profit" after all of the above. A good staff accountant should probably return a profit of about thirty three percent (33%) in my experience.

The business of accounting can be more difficult than the practice of accounting. One must learn the basics and use them properly. A professional must all learn the practice of accounting. Your most successful accountants learn both.

A former colleague and former Chair of the American Institute of Certified Public Accountants (AICPA) once told me that there are three (3) types of CPAs: finders, grinders and binders. However, that is for later in this book.

My First Client

Being a CPA in public practice is an honor and a privilege. During college and while studying, a young accountant learns certain skill sets that are necessary to become a CPA. Although this is a substantial amount of "book smart" types of categories: accounting, auditing, income and business taxes, theoretical issues, business law issues, valuations, expert witness types work, and more, to name a few --- many students leave college without any experience in representing real people.

My father taught me that "You can be the best CPA in the world, but without a client, you have nothing". In other words, the most important fundamental issue to learn about the profession is that a CPA in public practice must have a client to perform services for; otherwise, there is no reason to perform any accounting services. Hence, there are different manners to represent clients in public practice.

The normal assumption when you leave college and want to work in public practice is that a student will begin employment with an already existing CPA firm. This is exactly how I left college and began working as a young accountant. The existing CPA firm has its own clients and as a young accountant "new hire" the young accountant goes through a rigorous on the job training program. This program introduces the young accountant to "real" public accounting. And the actual job assignments will vary from firm to firm and can also vary depending upon the time of the year.

Normally, the young accountant does not meet the actual client until the supervisors or the owners believe the accountant is ready. Frankly, the clients are paying a lot of money to the CPA firm. Errors in work product, poor people skills, disrespect, a mistake, and other potential slip ups can cost the CPA firm a client and a friend. Accordingly, it is not uncommon for a client to not meet the younger accountants.

In my experience, I believe I came into the profession with above average people skills. I also maintain that people skills are an integral part to becoming a successful CPA. My background included door to door sales, pumping gas, and selling such things as ladies' shoes, pets, electronic equipment, and life insurance products (all before college graduation at the age of 20). In other words, I was able to meet many people. This was important in my professional development because one wrong word to a potential customer could cost a sale. And if you work on a commission, like I did in college, you would not make any money. Hence, a relationship with a client is a very important issue for CPAs. There is no second chance for making a good first impression.

As a CPA, your firm is like an "at Will employee". In other words, a client can terminate a CPA firm for many reasons. Normally, in my experience a client will terminate a CPA firm for two (2) basic and important reasons. The first reason is that the CPA firm made a mistake. Clients pay a lot of money to CPA firms and they expect to get what they pay for. I believe this is a reasonable assumption for a client. The other is that the client believes for whatever reason, that the CPA does not effectively communicate. This can be a result of many factors, including the client expectation that the CPA "has their back", meets important deadlines and is generally personable and caring toward the client.

Not all CPAs can "pull this off". The proper practice of public accounting takes a lot of energy for CPAs to be able to work at a high professional level and still have the clients' best interests in mind at all times. In the third office of an international firm that I worked for, the managing partner taught me, a client can fire his CPA at anytime; however, a client cannot fire a friend. In other words, if the client perceives that the CPA is generally concerned about their well being, then a client is less likely to terminate a CPA. I found these things to be true, without exception. A client/CPA relationship is special.

Accountants then participate with clients at different levels. The first is the example that was set forth above. That is, a young accountant works to gain experience on client matters without meeting the client(s). Later, the accountants meet the clients. And at some point in time, when the accountant is ready, the accountant becomes the "in charge accountant" on a client relationship. The in charge accountant is not something that can be readily given. Specifically, if the client does not perceive the accountant as "in charge", then the client will either ask that the client is reassigned to another accountant, or alternatively, the client will find another CPA firm. This "hand off" is critical to the life of any CPA firm.

This transition becomes further complicated for different reasons. As stated above, during college, it is unlikely that the accountant had any experience in dealing with clients. Further, many accountants graduate and assume their job will be "8 to 5" and that they will not have to get involved with any of their clients. That was certainly my initial belief. For the first several months that I worked in public accounting, I was content to get to work at 8 o'clock and be ready to leave by 5. I always believed that I worked hard, but I do not believe that I was aware of the much bigger picture when I first entered the profession. That is, once I was done doing what I did, then the accountant in charge had to effectively communicate the project to the client. In other words, although I believed I was working hard, I was not working smart --- until one day.

In the third office of the international firm that I originally went to work for, the income tax partner called me into his office. Although I had been in his office many times before, it was different this time. As I entered his office, he was seated at his conference table with two individuals that I had not seen before. This was a new client to the firm. It was a small business with two owners --- a partnership. These individuals were best friends. I dressed in a three piece suit in those days. These guys were dressed in jeans and one had on a white tee shirt. Up to that time, I always thought of the clients of an international CPA firm as three piece suit people. After all, I originally believed that I was working on the richest of the rich, not these poorly dressed people. These two guys were more than twice my age. They looked like a couple of "red necks" to me. As it turned out, I made a terrible misjudgment with these individuals.

The boss explained his understanding of their business to me concurrently while they were sitting at the conference table. There was a lot of discussion between the boss and the clients and an enormous amount of information was exchanged. I learned a lot about these individuals during that time as well as a lot about their business. This discussion humanized the client/CPA relationship for me. I was able to observe for the first time the client asking the CPA important questions. I was able to watch my boss interview the client to "harvest" the requested financial information that would be handed off to me in order to work on their account. However, I still did not understand the connection between the client and the CPA. At the end of the meeting, the boss instructed the new client to contact me directly with any questions.

I was surprised. I had never had to speak to clients before about anything. All I had to do up to that time was show up and perform the work that was assigned to me. I had no idea what these individuals were going to ask. I had no idea how my world was going to change.

I remember the first question that these clients asked me. The question concerned the acquisition of assets in their business. They were going to acquire the assets and rent them to their customers. Their options were to pay cash, or alternatively, finance the assets over different periods of time, from three years to ten years. They asked me which would be best for their business. I did not know at the time. At the time, I thought that all of the alternatives would be about the same. I did not understand how the different choices could and would result in different possible outcomes for their particular business.

By the end of the discussion, it seemed that these guys were teaching me about finance and business. I could not believe these "red necks" were so perceptive and knowledgeable about business. At the end of the discussion the new clients and I came to a conclusion and a decision as to how to proceed. I then "ran it by" my boss and he agreed. My boss smiled.

These gentlemen owned and operated a rental business. They pretty much rented anything they could get their hands on to the general public. Sometimes the rentals would be over night. Sometimes, the rentals may be over a weekend. In other words, short term rentals. I could not believe that some of their customers would come back time and time again to rent the same equipment. I mentioned this to them (1977). They smiled and explained to me, "The economy is changing. Many people cannot afford to buy the equipment or they would have already purchased the equipment. You will see that over the next few decades people will begin leasing bigger and bigger assets. Assets like automobiles and housing will be leased. That is because the economy is changing due to governmental intervention." I thought that was hogwash. Now I look around and see the number of people leasing their automobiles and their housing. All this from a couple of red necks!

No too long afterward, these guys telephoned me at my office to ask me to a barbecue and dinner at one of their homes. The event was during a weekend. At first, I felt that their invitation was an invasion of my privacy. I believed at the time that early mornings, lunches, evenings, and weekends were mine to enjoy without interruption from anyone at work. However, I accepted and visited them at their home.

Both of their entire families were there when I arrived. They jumped in their pool, played badminton, drank beer and had a good time. I participated and ate their food and as the day went on, I found that I was enjoying myself. I also noticed for the first time how much both of them and their families respected me. As I stated above, being a CPA is an honor. It is not to be taken lightly. And it comes with a great responsibility.

What I learned from this relationship is that when a CPA does work on any project that real people are involved. I learned that what we did had a direct impact on different people's lives. I learned how important it was to make good and proper professional decisions. I also learned that I liked this part of the profession.

Of course, after this client relationship, I was introduced to more and more clients. The job became more of a profession after that. I enjoyed this part of the profession.

Then one day, the managing partner asked me to come into his office. When I entered the office I noticed that the managing partner had a prominent individual sitting with him in his office. This individual was there to request that one of the CPAs from the office join and participate in a local civic organization. The partner then introduced me and told me that I was going to join this organization.

Later, after this prominent individual left the office, the boss called me back into his office. He explained to me how important it was to regularly attend and be a part of this particular men's club. He explained that most of the members of the civic organization were local business owners. I was told that my participation in the club would result in more clients if I was properly participating.

At first, I looked at this assignment as something that was going to compromise my personal time. After a few meetings, I found that this was probably the one thing that kick started my career as a CPA. Specifically, it was not too long after, that substantially all of the club members were using me as their CPA. Here I was, the youngest person in the club and that all of the members respected me and trusted me enough to become their CPA. And by the way, many of those members are still some of the best friends that I ever made in my entire life.

How to Fire a Client

Over the years, I believe I became pretty good at obtaining new clients. My retention rate of existing clients was much higher than the average for our profession also. When I originally joined the profession, I learned that the average business client will remain with a CPA firm for about five (5) years. This did not seem very long to me. However, I understood that by that time, some disagreement may have occurred, a mistake would have been made and/or the client may have felt disrespected in some manner.

Accordingly, I believed that good internal quality controls were necessary in order to help avoid mistakes and disagreements. Common courtesy would help cure the latter. And remember the words from my former boss, that is, clients will not fire their friends, (is true).

It actually got that I could not show up at a club event or a business lunch without picking up a new client. This is because of happy other clients and business people that were known to me and they were referring me new and more clients. I believe an accountant can advertise all they want, and, I believe advertising generally will not bring in "good" clients. I found that good clients were referred from other happy clients and other business people in the community (referral sources). Instead of reading great advertisements or listening to the radio, I found that when a prospect was unhappy, that person would normally ask other business people whom they knew and trusted.

These referral sources only referred to you when they believed that you were effectively communicating and providing top notch services. And, my prior sales background did not hurt either. However, sometimes I found that our firm obtained a client that we did not want. Sometimes, these clients were paying their bills and sometimes they were not paying their bills. For instance, sometimes the client would pay their bills and treat your staff badly. Sometimes these clients would not reasonably respond to our requests for additional information. At other times, the client may try to put unreasonable expectations on you to complete the work. Neither of these situations were good.

Other times clients would complain about their bill. Sometimes the client would simply be complaining with no reason other than they wanted to delay or negotiate a lower fee. Sometimes they just did not want to pay. I believed it was important to "cut the calf from the herd". In other words, if the client were complaining to complain and taking an unreasonable portion of your time to collect the bill, then that relationship was not worth maintaining. In other words, it took time out of the day for your staff or yourself from working on other important deadlines. Accordingly, constantly complaining clients were not good long term clients.

On the other hand, sometimes a client would have a legitimate complaint about their bill. In the public accounting business, there are different manners to charge your clients. A normal and customary billing policy concerned charging your client for the hours or time that you spent on their account. These were typically called "chargeable" hours. One method to evaluate your staff is in productivity. That is, how many chargeable hours do they have versus nonchargeable hours. In other words, which staff were working on client business more than the others?

Just because an account was "charged", that did not necessarily mean the account would be billed. Many times hours could be charged by a professional that were ultimately not "billed" to the client. That is, an "expectation" of the amount of the bill would be known by the accountant in charge or the responsible billing person for that account. If the amount "charged" was different than the amount expected, questions needed to be asked of the staff working on the engagement prior to sending a bill to the client. If the additional time was "productive" and able to be billed, the client would be billed for that time. On the other hand, if the additional time was not productive or "billable", then the CPA firm would normally "write down" the client account by reducing the time charged by the professional. This process of sorting out what can be billed to a client becomes more of an "art" than a "science". And if there were questions concerning a bill, it was imperative that the in charge accountant could quickly, reasonably and efficiently explain any billing questions to the client's satisfaction.

This discussion with the client may also result in additional adjustments to the client in order to compromise a collected balance on the bill. I believe it is important to hear a good client's concerns before making a decision on what to do with the bill. If the client was simply questioning the bill, that is one thing; however, if the client is legitimately concerned about the bill, then that is another thing. On the other hand, if the client is just complaining, the CPA firm may not be able to continue to provide professional services to that client.

In the latter case, it is critically important to a CPA firm to know how to fire a client. This is not easy and the matter has to be handled delicately. Sometimes, it results in explaining to the client that they have "outgrown your services". Sometimes you just have to tell them that their behavior was no longer acceptable to the firm and you were withdrawing from the engagement. In these instances, it would be difficult to later collect outstanding charges on their bill, so the timing of these discussions and the tone of those discussions were critical to the firm's success.

I always tried to refer the client we would no longer represent to another CPA firm. I would go out of my way to try to help with any transition to that new firm. In reality, a small percentage of the client questions generally resulted in stepping back from the client engagement.

There is another type of client that should also be fired. Those are the clients who want the CPA to improperly present an accounting interpretation; whether in financial statement form, or alternatively, in an income tax return, etc. There is generally no upside to this type of a relationship with a client.

Firing clients is one of the least favorable things a CPA has to do. However, if done successfully, both the CPA and the CPA firm will have better long term success. If not done properly, the process can take many hours and may result in a court hearing or tribunal to remedy the situation, even if the CPA took proper action to resign from the account. And, for the clients you fire for non payment, I normally found those clients acted similarly with their new CPA relationship.

One of the things that I learned before accepting a new client was to inquire of the potential new client whether or not they had an outstanding balance on their bill with their existing CPA. If they did, and if I did not ultimately know why, it was unlikely I would accept that new client engagement.

However, to a young CPA, it is difficult for them to know which clients are good and which ones are not so good. And, in a young accountant's career, it is important for them to work on all types of client engagements and all types of clients. In other words, until they have walked the walk, they cannot then identify similar clients in the future. Therefore, and although these types of clients were unfavorable to the firm at that specific point in time, they are a good training experience for young staff to learn about these types of people in the young accountant's development as a professional.

Tom and Jerry's

You never know when or how you will meet a good client. Such was the case with respect to these clients. At the beginning of this story, I was out of town and working with a legal firm with respect to helping to summarize the legal firm's year end books and preparing the resultant income tax returns. All of a sudden there was an electric power outage throughout the entire area. There we were, sitting in the law offices of a small firm in a small community. There was no coffee, no power and the work needed to get done. The partners in the legal firm indicated that we could move our conference to a local restaurant where there were always lights and hot coffee. They said they believed that it was the only place in town with a generator!

So we walked down to a local restaurant. We sat down with our hot coffee and we began to discuss their company's operations and income tax planning opportunities. The meeting seemed to have continued pretty well when this really tall individual stopped by our table and began talking to the attorneys.

The attorneys introduced the gentleman as the owner of the restaurant. The owner was a likable individual and the attorneys told him what I was doing with them. As the consultation with the attorneys was over, the restaurant owner sat down with us and began to talk with us. He also explained his concerns about his own income tax situation. We discussed those issues together with his attorneys. The restaurant owner and I agreed to meet a later time to discuss his particular income tax situation and any potential opportunities that he might have with respect to his business as a result of that consultation.

We later got together to discuss his specific concerns and what, if anything, could be done to help optimize his particular income tax situation. As it turned out, I was able to help enhance his business with general income tax planning services. He was very happy with what I was able to do and subsequently invited me to speak at an investment club meeting that he participated in within that community. I found that these types of "get togethers" could be great ways to obtain new clients.

Other than the attorneys and the restaurant owner, I did not know anyone in the club at that time. The meeting took place around Christmas time and the members were all cordial and in the Christmas spirit. I was given my first "Tom and Jerry" beverage. Everyone there was drinking them and it appeared to be the local drink. It was pretty good! I was asked to speak about certain income tax planning matters to the group. It was not uncommon to discuss income tax planning and there were certain ideas that generated lots of questions and potentially lots of new business. These types of forums, if done properly, can lead to lots of business. However, I had no idea who the other members of the club were at that time.

My presentation was straight forward and rehearsed many times. It is important for a CPA in making these types of presentations to know and understand the issues presented. As expected, there were many questions from the group. There was lots and lots of discussion about the issues presented. And, there was one person in the room who contested just about everything that I presented concerning planning opportunities. He was well respected by the rest of the group and it was clear that he was very loyal to his then existing CPA. By the end of the evening everyone understood that I knew the material that was presented. The result of the evening was that every person, except the aforementioned individual, changed there CPA relationship to me.

I then learned that these were all of the local business people. All of them for the entire small community. This was a resort town and the members of the club were the owners of pretty much every large business in that community: hotels, restaurants, retail stores, hardware stores, contractors, recreational activities, real estate offices, professional firms, mini storage, and other businesses.

Over the following income tax season I completed all of the aforementioned income tax returns. I got to know all of these owners more and more. The more I got to know these clients, the better I liked them. All of them seemed happy with the change to our firm.

After I completed the restaurant owner's income tax returns, I received a telephone call from him. He told me how happy he was and then asked if I remembered the guy in the investment club meeting who did not change to our firm. At the time I did not. He reminded me that the guy was very happy with his CPA, he contested just about everything I presented and he was not exactly nice to me during the presentation. As it turned out, I did remember this gentleman!

The client told me that the other gentleman also received his income tax return from his CPA. He further explained to me that the two of them talk regularly and they seem to earn about the same each year from their respective businesses and their investments. Although he said it may sound odd to me but the two of them generally owed about the same amount of income taxes each year. As it turned out for this particular year, the restaurant owner owed substantially less than the other for the year. The difference was in excess of six figures. In other words, the difference was substantial and he told me that it was very much unanticipated and appreciated.

The restaurant owner indicated that he truly expected to owe quite a bit more than he did after I completed his income tax return. However, he learned what I did in order to help optimize his income taxes for the year. He also indicated that his friend owed quite a bit more than he had expected to owe. The restaurant owner told me that this person's CPA was also one of that person's best friends and also his racquetball partner. Bottom line, I was asked to speak to this gentleman. Prior to finishing, the restaurant owner told me "Do not be nice to this guy. He is one of my best friends and if he can step on you, he will. Be careful".

Although this is not one of the best introductions that I have gotten over the years, I agreed to speak to the guy. And as expected, he telephoned almost immediately. He began the conversation by telling me, "This is the luckiest day of your life, the day you get to represent me!". The guy was not modest and he had a very high opinion of who he was and what he had accomplished. He went on, "And you can't charge me unless you can help me. I already have paid to get my income taxes prepared. I am going to give you the opportunity to help me".

This was not only unusual, but also, arrogant. I thought about what I was supposed to say at a time like this, especially in view of what the restaurant owner had told me. So I said, "Well, I guess that means that if I can help you, I can charge you double!". I figured if I was going to spend my time during the busiest time of the year helping someone, there better be a quid pro quo for both of us. He thought about it and then agreed.

When he arrived at our office, he was accompanied by his wife. I was immediately impressed with his spouse. She was not only an angel, but also, she kept the books for all of their different businesses. I found over the years that successful dominant business people, whether man or woman, always seemed to find a really nice partner. This was definitely the case with this couple.

Their income tax return was fairly comprehensive and involved many different businesses and investments. I thoroughly reviewed the income tax return to the books and the supporting information and I was able to legally substantially reduce their income tax liability. In fact, upon completion, the income taxes owed by this taxpayer was even less than the gentleman who owned the restaurant.

Of course this guy was a skeptic. He either did not believe me or he did not "want to" believe me at the time. He was loyal to his friend and his CPA. He then asked me to write a summary of all of the changes that I made to his income tax return and the statutory support for each position. He said he wanted to read it carefully before making any changes. In other words, upon obtaining the summary, I expected him to take it to his buddy (the other CPA) and get his opinion.

So I carefully drafted a letter to him that described each and every change in detail and with the relevant authority for each change. In those days, there were no computers with great word processing capabilities. So, it was important to get the letter right the first time. And, with all the differences between the income tax return that was prepared by the original CPA and myself, the letter was about fifteen pages long. He drove into town to pick up the letter. I carefully went over each and every part of the letter with him. He left.

A few days later he telephoned me. He asked that I make him two dozen copies of that letter and sign each one. He explained that he showed my letter to his then CPA and the CPA read the letter, looked at his original income tax return and then the CPA apologized to him. Well, I made the copies of the letter for him and he distributed those letters to several businesses and business leaders. As it turned out, meeting this gentleman was one of the best things that ever happened to our business. He became a very loyal referral source and friend.

For your information, I did not charge him double! However, over the rest of my career, I not only charged him "plenty", but also, I charged the resulted referral clients to our firm from him millions of dollars.

This gentleman is about twenty (20) years older than I am. We became friends and have remained friends to this day. We traveled together and also played racquetball together. We went to different sporting events together. And we dined together whenever we were in the same general vicinity with each other.

It was on one of those evenings when we were dining together that we were in a local night spot in downtown Seattle. We were in a popular lounge with stand up tables instead of sit down tables. We had our own table; however, as it works out in that particular night club, it was very busy. Accordingly, it was not uncommon to share a stand up table with others. Such was the case this particular evening.

Two gentlemen in suits joined us. As a matter of fact this was during the NCAA Basketball finals in Seattle. The two gentlemen were the "partners in charge" of the Seattle and Houston offices of a large international CPA firm. And at that time, they seemed a bit arrogant, especially towards me. They did not know at the time that I was also a CPA, that I formerly worked for another international CPA firm and that I was now an owner in a local CPA firm.

Instead, the two arrogant individuals seemed to get along with my arrogant client and friend. I believe the two of them at the time believed I was the adult son of my client. And I already knew that one should not assume anything at a table such as this, as the two CPAs later learned that evening. As one thing led to the next, the CPAs began talking to my client. They asked what he did. My client explained that he owned different businesses: mini storage buildings, reservation businesses, restaurants, hotels, recreational properties, real estate companies and other investments. At that time, the two of them "perked up". They brought out their business cards and presented them to my client.

They explained their CPA firm being one of the largest, if not the largest CPA firm in the world. They asked him who his CPA was. As my client was also "playful", he simply said that his CPA was Chuck Hallett from Olympia, Washington. He did not tell them that it was me at the table. He simply carefully explained to them how happy he was with his CPA relationship and then told them the story of how we met and what I was able to do for him. At no time did he tell them that I was sitting right next to them.

There was alcohol being poured at the table and the two international partners in charge of their firm began bantering with my client about why he should use an international CPA firm and how bad some of the local CPA firms are at preparing income tax returns. My client assured them that not only did I know what I was doing, that I knew all about income taxes, income tax planning and when to speak and when not to. They still did not catch on to who I was and what my relationship was with my client. They proceeded to say more terrible things about local CPAs.

While they were talking to him, I simply reached for my business cards and gave each one of them a business card. I then spoke for the first time, "I guess I pretty much own your entire firm at this time from what you have been saying to my client and friend about me". I went on to say, "Obviously, no one ever taught you how to solicit a good client. Instead of saying what is wrong with everyone else, the potential client simply wants to know "what's in it for them". That is, bring them a solution, not a problem". Then I laughed and we began to speak.

As it turned out, I maintained my client relationship and made a great new friend, the partner in charge of the Seattle office of the international CPA firm. In addition, the partner in charge of the Houston firm sent me an invitation, all expenses paid, to join him in Houston for a partner meeting. I did not go and thanked him. However, the Seattle partner and I have remained in touch after all of these years. A strange first meeting; however, sometimes good things happen from these types of relationships.

For instance, as our firm grew, we obtained some rather large audit clients and some rather large expert witness engagement opportunities. Our business plan included provisions to try to maximize profits and to only agree to perform services that we could timely and professionally complete. Frankly, we could not perform auditing services and realize the profit margins that we expected. In addition, one certain expert witness engagement opportunity was ongoing and it was in excess of 6 figures (sometimes more than 7) each and every year. Our firm was not large enough to accept this engagement, and accordingly, I referred this engagement together with the other audits to this international CPA partner.

We also obtained business clients from this international firm. Although these clients were generally referred to me, we had tough competition in obtaining these types of clients. One client especially comes to mind. The client was a large mining company with offices in different cities across the United States. They needed income tax planning and assistance with cash flow budgeting. I believe we showed that we were able to better fulfill their needs.

A common occurrence between the predecessor and successor CPA is to meet and for the successor CPA to review the files of the predecessor CPA. This is not only important, but also, there are professional statements as to how and when to actually "pull off a successful meeting". And, like the arrogance displayed towards me by the two international partners, I found that the CPA/accountant in charge of the mining company at the international firm had the same improper conceptions of local CPA firms. In fact, he met me in their lobby and refused to grant me access to any working papers or any other files of the mining company.

At the time, I was a member of the professional standards committee for our state CPA association. Before I could try to persuade the accountant in charge to do "the right thing", the managing partner of the firm walked into the lobby. He said "Chuck, good to see you, what are you doing here?". I said, "I am taking a good client from you". He laughed and said, "Do you have time for coffee?", and he invited me into his private office.

He asked the accountant in charge to carry my briefcase into his office. It appeared that the accountant in charge had never been in this private office of the firm's managing partner before. The partner sat down the accountant in charge in his office with me. He then told the accountant in charge, "Chuck is the best CPA that I have ever met. You are in great company today, you are meeting the finest CPA in the world!". I was not sure if he was trying to make up for what he had said in the night club, but he seemed sincere.

He went on, "Chuck, what do you need?". I asked him that I needed to review the files for the mining client. The partner then asked the accountant in charge, "How many files are there?". The accountant in charge said, "We have three footlockers full of files". The partner in charge then told the accountant in charge to load all of the files into my vehicle. The partner in charge then looked at me and said, "Go ahead and take the files as long as you need them, then return them. If you lose one working paper from our files, I will have you shot!". Then he laughed.

As the accountant in charge loaded my vehicle he was in disbelief. He told me that he was not aware of any other time when his firm allowed their original files to leave the office. By the end of that encounter, he was no longer so arrogant with me. Appearances and prejudices can be worked through given the right circumstances.

Put Your Brain in Gear Before Your Mouth Goes in Motion

One of the clients referred to me by that aforementioned businessman was one of the largest syndicators of this type in the country. This individual owned several businesses and investments himself and also served as the managing partner of dozens of limited partnerships controlled by his wholly owned management company.

The syndicator client was perpetually in litigation because of allegations against one of his businesses, investments or because of his alleged actions in one way or the other. Frankly, I learned more about general business and the legal system from him (and my experiences with him) from many of the legal actions that he was involved than from any other individual.

During this relationship with the syndicator, there seemed to be one other gentleman who had repeatedly invested in several different partnerships, other than the limited partnerships, with this syndicator. The other was a local contractor. Each and every time they had an investment together, it seemed that the court system had to help to resolve a dispute between the two of them. Although their skill sets complimented each other; somehow, the syndicator seemed to consistently behave in a manner to invite a legal action from this gentleman. I do not remember all of the lawsuits concerning this syndicator; however, he always seemed to somehow prevail in the end. Alternatively, he seemed able to frustrate the other side to the extent that the other side was willing to compromise or settle with him on the pertinent legal matters.

In the syndicator's personal life, there could not have been a nicer guy outside of the office than this gentleman. The syndicator was well liked personally by all of the people around him, including his staff. However, as it came to business, it was well known that he could be overly aggressive with his interpretations of all of the agreements he had entered into and/or he had "convenient recollection" as to the original agreements between the parties.

I was able to obtain this syndicator client after two different international firms were concurrently representing his different businesses. And, the prior accounting from one of the national accounting firms that we had received for the then most recent year did not appear to be reconciled. To make matters worse, one of the international CPA firms had issued unqualified (clean) opinions as to the audited financial statements from the books and records for all of the various syndicated partnerships. As I looked through the books of the various companies, I immediately noticed that not one of the dozens of inter-company accounts reconciled to the books of the related companies. None of them! And they all received clean opinions.

In addition, I noted certain income tax errors during my review of the income tax returns. During this part of the discussion, I befriended a tax partner from one of the international accounting firms. He was surprised as to my knowledge and experience with the types of issues that were related to this type of client engagement. And, he was honest and open to the client when the mistakes found were pointed out to him.

Over the next several years, I was able to keep in touch with this international income tax partner. We were able to discuss a wide range of subjects and I believe we interacted very well together. This CPA also donated a substantial amount of his time to helping different not for profit entities in the area. He is a great professional.

As to the syndicator's client's internal staff, I learned that they did not deliberately make these mistakes. Once I showed them the proper procedures on how to maintain inter company accounts for all of these different entities, there was never again an issue with the accounts being out of balance. However, the behavior of not helping the internal staff learn some fairly basic procedures surprised me. There were multiple bookkeeping and accounting issues that we noted upon obtaining this client. And, without exception, the books were consistently given "clean opinions" by the international accounting firm who performed the annual audits.

When we originally took over as the new CPA firm, the prior billings had not been paid in full for these entities to the prior CPA firms. Generally, we would not accept such an engagement if the prior CPA bills had not been paid. However, this time we agreed to accept the client under the condition that the other CPA firms would meet with both the client and me to discuss the billing questions and concerns. I believed this to be a fair manner to help resolve outstanding accounting and income tax questions, and hopefully, allow the other CPA firms to be paid for their prior services. I also wanted to be certain that the client expected to pay reasonable fees for services rendered. This would also be a great forum to learn more about the client.

Fast forward to the end of this meeting --- the international firm realized there were mistakes made, and ultimately, concessions were made to client for the outstanding billings that were then paid. The pending legal actions were then dismissed between the companies as the outstanding professional issues and outstanding fees were thoroughly discussed and agreed upon.

Concurrently, the aforementioned contractor had prior lawsuits with this syndicator concerning other partnerships in which they were partners and investors together. I had met this individual on at least two (2) other disputes between these parties with at least 2 other entities. However, this was another and different entity, and accordingly, there was a separate legal ongoing action between these two guys.

As I recall, the meeting was set up for about 3 PM at the offices of the syndicator. When we arrived, we were taken to a large conference room and served coffee and water. We were told that the syndicator was running late and would be there soon. The contractor, his CPA and I were there at the agreed upon time. As stated, my client was not there on time, and as it turned out no one in his office knew exactly where he was. By this time, based upon our prior experiences with the syndicator, neither the contractor or I truly expected the syndicator to be on time. In fact, by the time we were told he was not there, he had already joked with me that the syndicator may not be at the office until about 8 PM. The CPA for the contractor was not amused. In fact, the CPA was visibly upset about the syndicator being so late for such a meeting. The syndicator finally telephoned his office and asked to speak to me. He then requested that I begin talks with the contractor and his CPA concerning beginning discussion, deliberation and collaboration concerning some kind of settlement between the syndicator and contractor. Then the syndicator told me he had to go and hung up. This was unusual.

As stated above, we never expected the syndicator to be on time. So, the contractor, his CPA and I began to discuss the financial and income tax provisions in the agreement that seemed to be disputed. By the time the syndicator appeared, the significant issues between the 2 of them were able to have been discussed and agreed upon, subject to my client's acquiescence and agreement upon his arrival. My client appeared about 7:30 PM. When he finally appeared, he was carrying a rather large trophy. It seemed he had played in a racquetball tournament that took up most of the day, and he had won the tournament! All the while we had waited for him. Needless to say, the contractor's CPA was still not amused.

All the while, we had patiently waited for him and tried to discuss the issues between them. 2 CPAs and the contractor who was suing the syndicator tried to work out their problems without one of the parties being present. This is unusual, except that it was with "this syndicator". I believe the syndicator's behavior was expected, and also, the behavior was openly rude and it demonstrated a lack of respect and accountability; however, the guy was brilliant. He was also apologetic upon his arrival, or he seemed to be sincere about it. Both his partner and I were aware that this person was habitually late for his scheduled meetings and appointments. Nonetheless, both the contractor and I somehow allowed the behavior to continue.

I believe we also understood that the only manner to try to settle their dispute was to wait until he arrived. I was being paid by the hour and that made it a bit easier to tolerate the behavior.

Upon his arrival, he did not want to discuss the dispute. He said, "Because I am tardy, I want to take all three of you to dinner". The contractor's CPA did not want to go. However, the contractor agreed to go to dinner. During dinner, the syndicator was a complete gentleman. He was apologetic and sympathetic to the issues concerning their dispute. We finally arrived back to the conference room about 10:30 PM. The contractor and the syndicator then began trying to finalize an agreement between them so that the matter did not have to be ultimately litigated. This discussion went on for a few hours. Finally, about 2:30 AM the next morning, the two of them had an agreement "in principle". They shook hands. The contractor's CPA was fast asleep at the conference table.

At that time, I could not help myself. Although the two of them had agreed to substantially every disputed issue, I found myself wanting to help the contractor. This did not mean that I did not want to represent my client. However, a substantial income tax issue was not raised by his CPA, an income tax partner in a large regional CPA firm. And the result to the contractor, if raised and agreed upon, would save him almost seven figures in income taxes without costing my client anything. I could not help myself. I mentioned the strategy to the client and his CPA. The meeting concluded without anymore discussion.

A couple of days went by and I received a telephone call from the regional CPA firm. I expected the call to be from the CPA partner. It was. However, and in addition, eight other CPAs from their income tax department were also a part of the telephone call. Before I could say anything, one of the CPAs on the call began screaming at me "you are recommending income tax fraud!". She went on and on and on. I did not believe it was my place to argue, especially when the other party or parties were yelling. She asked me for an explanation.

Rather than speak to her I was concurrently reaching for the business card of the gentleman contractor. My next move was to make a conference call. I placed the other CPA firm on hold and dialed the telephone number of the contractor. Once the telephone was answered, by his assistant, I merged the two telephone calls. I identified myself and let his assistant know that his then CPAs were on the telephone call with me. I then explained that they wanted me to "train them" and I refused to do that unless the "contractor agrees to pay me for my time".

That same CPA blew up again and yelled at me while the assistant was on the telephone. Rather than address the CPA, I simply pointed out to the assistant that if I was wrong, and if it was really tax fraud as alleged, then I would not expect the contractor to do it, nor would I expect to be paid. However, if I was correct, I would expect payment. I said I believed that was fair and reasonable in the circumstances as it was the contractor who would be saving a substantial amount of income tax. I had nothing to gain or lose if they did not want to pay me.

The assistant put the call through. I reintroduced myself to the contractor and let him know that his existing CPA firm's tax department was on a conference call with him. The loud and boisterous CPA continued to be loud. She told him that my recommendation was tax fraud. I respectfully disagreed and then pointed out to the contractor that I had "no skin in the game; however, if I am right, I expect to get paid". He laughed and said he would be willing to pay me if I was correct.

I then spoke to the loud CPA for the first time, I started by saying, "Young lady, I teach my accountants to put their brain in gear before their mouths go in motion". Well that did not go over very well with her. She said, "I am the senior tax manager here at this "firm"". I then said, "Shame on you, then you should already know this".

I went on to explain how I believed they were interpreting the facts and circumstances. They all agreed. I then began explaining my understanding of the effects of re characterizing the amounts in the settlement agreement. You could hear them all agree once they understood what was going on. I then said to the contractor, "Well sir, I am in another meeting at this moment and have to go, and, I will not charge you for the telephone call if you change your CPA firm to our firm". With that, I hung up on everyone. Well, the other CPA firm completed his income tax returns properly and he was able to save a lot of money in income taxes for him.

And, as expected, he changed his accounting and income tax relationship to our firm and was a great client and continues to be a very good friend for almost 30 years now.

What Would You Do if You Were Advising Your Mother?

Years later our office had grown from a small office in Olympia, Washington to having 3 offices fully staffed. One of these offices was in Bellevue, Washington. As our client base increased, it became more and more prudent for our owners to consider remote offices that made it easier for our clients to meet with us. Our younger CPAs were initially anxious to participate in this growth. They were verbally supportive of this change, at least, initially. However, once opened, the younger CPAs reacted differently than what my original partner and I thought.

The younger CPAs appeared to enjoy sharing the increased profits; however, they demonstrated they had no interest in going to the other offices and/or meeting clients in those remote locations. Instead, we found the younger generation wanted to work fewer hours than my original partner and I believed needed to be worked in order to have a successful CPA practice. My original partner and I spent countless hours on the road and in the remote locations in order to properly support these offices. By the way, we found this was true with other small professional businesses we represented who also opened satellite offices: legal, medical, engineering, architecture, etc.

Ultimately, we sold the remote offices and brought the larger and more loyal clients to the Olympia office. Although this was a bit more inconvenient to the clients, it seemed to make the day to day management of our CPA firm run more efficiently.

However, while we had a remote office in Bellevue we were introduced to many new potential clients. One of those clients was in the franchise business (one that I had a lot of professional experience in). This potential client was one of the highest profile franchisees in the entire franchise system. He was well known in the community and he had had several franchise locations.

This franchisee was special, highly ethical and loyal to the people around him. He was a blessing to get to know. As an example, he assisted one of his former employees to finish college and earn his CPA credential. Upon completion of those studies, this employee returned to work for the franchisee as his "in house" accountant. Working with this CPA was enjoyable. However, at the time we first met with this prospective client, we did not know this CPA.

Another of his former employees was financially assisted all the way through law school. Upon completion of law school, the former employee was hired as the corporate attorney. Not a staff attorney, but an independent attorney who had his own independent law office. In other words, this franchisee demonstrated that he had a big heart and confidence in this attorney.

In addition, this franchisee also spent considerable personal time in different organizations, including a non profit organization. This organization is a significant sponsor to a major charitable organization that is well known around the world. The franchisee sat on the board. Another board member was the tax partner from the aforementioned international CPA firm. This income tax partner is the one whom I respect and had helped work out the differences with the syndicator. We had kept in touch from time to time after that meeting.

I had been referred to the franchisee by several other franchisees whom we represented in the northwest. Although the international tax partner CPA had a broad background in substantial and difficult income tax issues, I sincerely doubted whether or not he had experience in this particular franchisee business.

Nonetheless, this CPA also served on the board with the franchisee of the large charitable organization. As the franchisee was looking for a new CPA firm, I understood that the franchisee had interviewed a few CPA firms and then he narrowed the selection to our 2 CPA firms. The franchisee asked that we both appear together at his corporate offices and we make a proposal in front of the other CPA. The franchisee's hope was that we would both answer questions during this meeting. Although this was unusual, because of my experience in the industry and because of the particular potential client, I agreed to participate.

When we both arrived at the franchisee's office, the franchisee was initially surprised that the other CPA and I knew each other. Regardless, we were invited into his conference room and the franchisee provided us with background information on himself, his company and his goals and expectations for a new CPA firm relationship.

Upon completion of the introduction, he asked the other CPA to present his "sales pitch" first. The tax partner CPA began by giving his background and the background of the international accounting firm. Frankly, the international accounting firm is one of the four largest CPA firms in the world. Its CPAs are some of the most highly trained CPAs in the world. However, this was a sales pitch and I was the only one of us with a sales background. To win this client, I would have to rely on my knowledge of the industry, my experience as a CPA and my sales background. I had to find the client's anxiety at the table, and then, give a reasonable solution.

During his presentation, the other CPA brought out a specially bound notebook concerning the potential client's franchise organization. It must have been two hundred pages long. It was in color. The booklet included references of the international firm with other similar franchise businesses. The booklet contained detailed information about the potential client's business. It had pictures in it. The booklet also included graphs and other pertinent financial information about the client. Frankly, the booklet was incredible.

Our office was much smaller. Our electronic capabilities were much different and not nearly as elaborate as the international CPA firm's electronic capabilities. In fact, we did not even have color capability at that time. There was no way that I could compete with that book. It could have been a client stopper. I had to overcome the great presentation and the booklet that was presented.

When it was my turn to speak, I began by thanking the potential client for inviting me to the meeting and allow me to make a presentation on behalf of our firm. I noted that the other presentation was not less than spectacular. I also said that not only was the international tax partner CPA well known and well respected by me, but also, I had never seen a prospective client booklet put together so well.

I said that the CPA partner and I had crossed paths and we knew each other personally and professionally. I said that I admired the generous contributions of time by the CPA partner and that I was convinced that he had the requisite knowledge to assist this franchisee with all of his accounting and income tax needs.

However, I went on to say that "after today's meeting, the international tax partner CPA will delegate your account to another CPA in his office that did not have his skills or experience". I referred to this CPA as "Yo-man Johnson". I said that the franchisee could not afford to pay the billing rates of the CPA partner. I went on to say that Yo-man Johnson will probably be charging him the same amount that I would be charging.

I tried to close the deal by simply stating to the CPA partner, "You know me and you know my background. You know that if the franchisee chooses to use our firm, that I will be the contact person. You know what your billing rates are and that the franchisee will not be getting your services. Instead, he will be stuck with Yo-man Johnson from your office. Given your knowledge of the business, given your knowledge of the industry, given your knowledge of me, what would you do if you were advising your mother?".

With that I said that I was going to excuse myself and let them have an open and honest conversation as to what would truly be in the franchisee's best interests. When I returned to the conference room, I had a great new client. He also turned out to be a pretty good acquaintance.

What About the Leases?

Many times it is not the other CPA firm that makes a big and substantial mistake. Sometimes it can be someone within your own organization. Although CPA firms should adopt the best internal controls that they can; sometimes, things just can slip through the cracks. Such is what almost happened with this client. It is important to get that "second opinion". In other words, no matter who you are, try to get another professional to review each major planning point. These can be both teaching and learning experiences.

I first met this client when I traveled out of the state to meet another client. The later client was introduced to me by a national franchising organization. The referral came to me because of significant cash flow and financing issues that could result in the closure of that particular franchise. So, I agreed to meet this troubled new businessman in his city. In addition, since the process of identifying the issues and endeavoring to make positive changes was not an immediate process, I understood that I was going to stay in that city for a few days.

When I arrived, and because the businessman could not afford to pay for a hotel, he asked if I would agree to stay in his guest room in his home. This was not only acceptable to me, but also, it proved to be a great way to get to know him and his family much better. After working all day and each day we were together, we would retire and simply keep up the business discussions. Fortunately, we were able to find possible solutions to his financing and cash flow issues.

He was so happy with the professional services that he made it a point to introduce me to other local business owners in that community. By the time I had left the community, he had referred me to at least 5 other small businesses in the area. One of those businesses was a much larger organization, and another, but unrelated, franchise business in a different industry.

At the time, this franchisee had a business that serviced his community in that particular area. I was able to visit his business while visiting the area and learn more about his business, his accounting system and his particular income tax situation. I was able to help him solve certain accounting and income tax issues while there, and accordingly, I ended up with another client, in addition to the 4 other smaller clients referred to me while there. This client was a large client by anyone's standards.

As the years passed, the later client merged his company with even a larger company. During that process, I also met the owner of the other larger company. And ultimately, I ended up representing the newly merged company. And, as those years passed, the company grew into a very strong regional franchise organization for that particular industry. I was able to conduct very thorough retirement planning for these individuals.

Concurrently, and as with most of our business clients, I had assigned the account relationship to another CPA in our office. That CPA became the accountant in charge of the relationship. In other words, the day to day activities of the account relationship would be assumed by this accountant, and, if there were any critical issues that required my care and attention, then the clients were free to contact me directly and/or the accountant in charge was supposed to bring me into the decision making process.

Assigning an accountant in charge of a relationship is not an easy science. The key is assigning someone familiar with the industry and familiar with the client's business. Most important though is the accountant in charge's ability to get along with the client. More often than not this "hand off" goes as planned; sometimes, the transfer of this relationship just does not stick. As was the case with this client.

The particular accountant whom I referred this relationship was very strong in his accounting skills. However, his "bedside manner" left a lot to be desired from time to time. The ultimate result was that I had to refer this relationship to another accountant in the office. This accountant was incredibly book smart and his biggest characteristic flaw in performing professional services was that he seemed to act in a services delivery model as what I refer to "ready, fire, aim". In other words, he might forget there were quality controls in place to help keep our office from overlooking a particular part of a transaction or any other professional engagement. He might skip the review process from time to time.

Both of these CPAs in our office were ultimately owners in our company. Their skills and tenure were assumed to add value to our company at the time. These decisions are not easy and are made after a lot of forethought and contemplation, including planning. The ultimate result was to be able to provide the best possible services to your clients.

As with my own professional services, each and every project that I represented had one of our other professionals involved to review my work and if necessary, make specific suggestions to correct or consider for the client. I believe this is an important quality for all CPA firms as it is part of the quality control process that is integral in operating any CPA firm.

So as I fast forward to the normal sale of a business, there are different steps that a client goes through. In an optimum situation like this, the first step is that the business sale generally occurs after a client has reached certain targeted personal goals that will allow the business to be sold and the client to comfortably retire. Another important step is to value the business with your client to get a general understanding of a range of values for the business. Then the client needs to be confident and comfortable that this range of values is sufficient to meet their needs after consideration for expected income taxes on the sale. There are many other steps that must be followed in order to plan and execute a successful sale of a business and ultimate retirement opportunity for your client.

An important distinction in valuing a company is the difference in value of the company versus the value of the assets of the company. The latter generally presupposes that the seller will pay any and all obligations of the company; whereas, the business value normally is a net value after consideration of the business obligations.

I was initially told that the client was coming into our area to meet with the accountant in charge and me to discuss an offer on the business. After familiarizing myself with the proposed transaction, I agreed to have a conference call with the prospective purchasers to discuss the value and the terms of the sale of the company. The accountant in charge had already met with the client and had indicated that the proposed price was in the range that our client would deem acceptable. I had my doubts after reading all of the preliminary information; hence, I became part of these discussions.

During the conference call to thoroughly discuss the offer, it was my responsibility to help the client understand the offer from this prospective company. Further, I believed it was my responsibility to effectively communicate the financial implications as needed by the client. I found it odd that the accountant in charge of the engagement had moved the process all the way to the final negotiations without involving anyone else from our office in the review process, including me. But now, the final details were going to be discussed so the transaction could move to a timely closing.

When you have a company this size, it is important to note that the business owners not only own the company, but quite often, the business owners also own the real estate premises for the business and lease the real estate to the business. Such was the case with this transaction.

During my discussion on this proposed sale of this business, I became highly skeptical as to the actual verbiage being used by the proposed purchaser. Their attorney had carefully worded certain financial provisions. I needed to understand those provisions. From my initial involvement in listening to them, it appeared to me that the proposed purchaser was going to purchase assets, not the company. In other words, the business owners' corporation was to receive the proceeds from the sale and then pay all of the related obligations of the company. When I discussed this with the proposed sellers, it appeared to me that the sellers were going to sell a very large company for as little as five thousand dollars NET after all the math, payment of all obligations and after reading the provisions carefully. The expectation was for the price to be discussed being the value of the company, not just the assets. In other words, a possible disaster was avoided by simply thoroughly reading the proposed contract.

The client was obviously disappointed with this unfortunate turn of events. However, it is always best to learn these things as soon as possible. And it is imperative to use these experiences as important teaching opportunities. One was for the client and the other was for the accountant in charge of the engagement.

A couple more years passed and another offer came along to purchase the client business. The accountant in charge was able to confirm that the offer was in deed for the business and not just the assets. In other words, the accountant in charge told me that the client was going to receive exactly what the client wanted for the business. Again, I had to review this matter with the client. The client came into the office and we read the proposed purchase and sale agreement. Both the client and the accountant in charge assured me that the proposed purchase and sale agreement met the client's needs. They were so confident that the deal had met the client needs that the attorneys had already drafted the necessary agreements. I was again surprised that our CPA had already substantially led this transaction this far without input from anyone else in our office, including myself.

Nonetheless, I had to read the proposed agreements once again. Admittedly, the value for the company was within the range the client had indicated to me that would result in the net after tax dollars expected by the client. Still, there was something missing I thought. Finally, the missing detail came to me in an instant.

I asked, "What about the leases?". In other words, the purchaser agreed to purchase the company; however, no leases were negotiated between the buyers and the seller. Accordingly, the seller risked having all of his real estate in several different locations all vacated by the purchaser immediately after the transaction closed. I brought this up to the client and the accountant in charge. Their faces flushed when the realization of the magnitude of the downside of this transaction if the real estate lease issue could not be mitigated.

Accordingly, we contacted the proposed buyer and informed them of this unfortunate oversight. Of course, the purchasers appeared to already have thought this through. They knew what they had done. So these negotiations began as to the amount and the length of each lease. Sometimes these types of negotiations can take longer than the overall value of the company. Fortunately, we were in time to include these leases with the purchase and sales transaction. Even his own attorney had completely missed this issue.

The key to this transaction was the implementation and monitoring of our own internal controls. Had the transaction not had a "second opinion", it is more likely than not that our client would have sold his business and would have been left with several empty buildings and warehouses.

This client has also remained as one of my buddies.

I Understand You Are the Best CPA in the World!

First meetings with potential clients are always subject to chance. It is what a CPA does with that first meeting in order to obtain a new client and possible friend. It is best to make a good and positive first impression. You only get one chance. This is in professional demeanor and experience. For the most part, I learned from experience that self made business owners are some of the hardest working people. Admittedly, there are many second generation businesses (and so on). Those are the exception. I was able to write articles and I taught courses on the successful generation planning issues for second generation business. Nonetheless, the vision, work ethic and personality of that self made business owner is always something that I admired.

My wife and I purchased a home in what we believed was a very nice and exclusive area. We understood there were many business owners living in the community. The community had many different amenities for our family. We were very happy that we had worked hard enough to be able to purchase a home in that community.

As an accountant and business owner, I refused to pay someone to do something that I could do with little incremental effort. Such was the case on this particular weekend day. There I was out in our backyard in the fall. I was raking leaves from our maple trees. There were lots of leaves. As I began raking around one side of the home a gentleman, my next door neighbor, was also raking his leaves. We had not met up to that particular moment in time.

"I understand you are the best CPA in the world" was the first thing this neighbor said to me. Not only is it a very nice thing to say, but more important, it is a great ice breaker to say something nice to someone you have not yet met. I said, "Well you must have come from the Harbor (area) and you must know Joe (the name is not important)". He said, "That is exactly where I heard about you".

Well it seems that Joe was the aforementioned hostile investment club member who told me about "this will be the luckiest day in your life". It is remarkable what hard work and loyal clients will do for you and say about you. This was a great way to meet a neighbor, a new friend and a new client.

We must have spoken for a couple of hours by the time we finished our discussion and raking our leaves together. The gentleman was at least thirty years older than I was. He was a first generation business owner who began his business about the time that I was born. One thing led to the other and he followed me into my home. He brought a current financial statement and I brought him a beverage.

His business' financial concerns were very common in my experience. His business had multiple locations and he had his family working in all locations. The business industry was competitive and he originally began the business on a "shoe string". In other words, he never seemed to have enough cash to properly capitalize his company. There was a disproportionate amount of debt within his company as compared to his then existing working capital. Over the years, he and his wife had loaned the business a few hundred thousand dollars. The financial status of his business was suspect; however, it was not for lack of effort on his part up to that time.

He told me he used an accountant familiar with the industry and an accountant who represented many of the top similar businesses in the area. This was probably helpful to his business over the years in some respects. However, having an accountant familiar with the industry does not necessarily mean that the accountant knew how to help the business with difficult cash flow and financing issues.

Regardless, his banks were not going to extend his business any more credit, and if the bank actually followed through with this scenario, the result would negatively impact or even result in a business closure. We spent a few hours talking about his business issues and concerns, especially his concerns about his family, over the next several days. I was able to come up with a possible solution based upon what I had read in his financial statements and what he told me about his business. The next Monday, we both spoke to his bank and we were able to help him obtain reasonable and customary financing for his business. This was something he was never before able to do. That is, borrow conventionally.

He could not be happier after receiving this new financing. The ability to properly leverage his business breathed new life into the company and helped to increase its sales, profits and cash flow. My next door neighbor was happy. And he was also able to sell my wife and I many products. I remember one Thanksgiving when he was in our home dusting some new items that we had purchased from him. He personally delivered those items on Thanksgiving Day as he understood my parents would be there later that day. And he was right. My parents arrived just as he was finishing setting everything up in our home and cleaning them.

My father had no idea who this gentleman was. In fact my father asked him why he had to work on Thanksgiving and asked how long he worked for the company. My father was proud to learn that this was the owner of the company, my next door neighbor and my new friend. The client also told my father what a wonderful solution that I had figured out for his business and he may not be in business had it not been for me. I don't care who you are when you see your father glowing with pride. This was pretty cool.

Over the years, this gentleman became quite close to my family and me. I also was able to get to know his family, including his children and grandchildren. As with other clients, and although this is not necessarily a good trait for a CPA, I felt bad if his business began to suffer. So, as we got to know each other better, I would meet with him in the evenings and weekends without charging his business, in order to help the business succeed. He would gladly have paid me if he had any profits during those times. However, he did not have any profits for long periods of time and could not have afforded to strategize in any other manner in my opinion and experience. Anyway, I believed this was the right thing to do in this circumstance.

Over the time we knew each other, this client and friend introduced me to others in his industry and coincidentally, our firm was able to obtain many new clients as a result of this relationship.

One thing leads to the next and he introduced me to one of his sons who had left the father's business. The son had began a new business in a different industry. The son had no experience with this industry up to that time. The establishment of this business was a bold move for the son. His father was a bit discouraged that the son left the "family business". Nonetheless, the father knew that I had substantial experience in this other industry and he asked if I would help his son.

One thing led to the next and before long I was meeting with his son evenings and weekends for free to help get him started. And as I was able to help the son over the next few years, the son's business grew and prospered. And as the son's business grew, our firm was introduced to more and more clients in the son's business' industry.

I characterize the son as a young professional with certain personal characteristics that I experienced with other young professionals. That is, I experienced that in the earlier years of one's career, a young professional tends to have a higher opinion of themselves. This generally changes as the professional gains more experience and matures into their business' success. Such was the case with this individual. Although he was smart and hard working, he tended to get himself involved in certain transactions that he was unable to manage. In other words, he would get in way over his head. Then, I would get telephone calls asking me to help him through the transaction. He would more than likely be in a frenzy when he would telephone and he would need to meet right away.

Although he was a terrifically bright individual, one of my clients used to use the phrase, "You don't know what you don't know". In other words, if you go to the doctor and find out you need an antibiotic, that does not necessarily mean that each time you go to the doctor you need an antibiotic. However, the only time you ever visited the doctor, you received a prescription for an antibiotic. So you concluded that if you see a doctor, you need a prescription for an antibiotic.

Similarly, an attorney may recommend a Limited Liability Company (LLC) for some business formations but not all. And if this individual sat down with an attorney and the attorney suggested an LLC for a particular client, then the individual would make the leap of faith that all attorneys would recommend an LLC for a transaction this individual would bring to the attorney.

Likewise, I helped the individual with a complicated cash flow model, including significant assumptions that I was asked to employ for a particular client. These assumptions, such as cash flow, financing and income tax would be based upon significant and specific facts and circumstances. The individual would assume that if these assumptions were good for "Peter" they would be good for "Paul". And that was not always the case, in fact, seldom the case. I believe that advice from a professional attorney or accountant would generally depend on the facts and circumstances of the situation, their particular experiences and their combined abilities to employ the professional procedures that they were licenses to practice effectively.

However, this individual would take one model to a group or different groups of other business start ups, mostly doctors, and would endeavor to cut both the attorney and the accountant out of the loop. The result was unfortunately disastrous for all involved from time to time. That is, the business people would independently engage their own attorneys and accountants. The result would be that the new business people would then learn certain industry specific suggestions for their particular facts and circumstances without any binding relationship to this individual.

Like I described about the accountant in our office concerning overlooking the important lease agreements, behaviors of younger professionals is sometimes indicative of their disregard for a checks and balance system. Everyone, regardless of stature, needs to respect and honor the systems in place. This is because qualified professionals were not engaged for each and every project and/or each and every project were not subject to review by another qualified professional. Frankly, it is difficult to speak to some of these younger professionals as they generally demonstrate that they have a higher opinion of their own abilities, knowledge and experiences than they actually have. In other words, they did not know what they did not know.

Regardless, I always tried to do what I could for this individual because his father was a good friend to me and his father asked that I look in on his son from time to time. Even though the son was also older than I am, that did not necessarily mean that he had more experiences with respect to certain transactions. Nor did it mean that he had proper professional training for the same transactions. Because of many difficulties with this individual and lack of respect of learning from his mistakes, over the years I managed to simply forego the evening and weekend meetings with him. Unfortunately and as expected, the son was unable to subject his advice to a checks and balances system within his own organization (similar to what I used and recommended) and he ultimately did not want to pay to have quality professional assistance. Instead, he wanted to capture those other fees, or a major portions of the same, for himself. I finally and rightfully concluded that I did not want to be around him when the newer business transactions imploded because of his own actions.

However, prior to that decision and in the early years, I did travel a bit with the son without charging his business for my time to accompany him and meet with his clients. The son would normally try to consult with prospective business owners to begin another business. During that time period, he requested my presence to help explain certain income and estate planning implications of such a business, the operating entity and its ownership. Sometimes my office would obtain a new client as a result of these meetings; however, more often than not, I did not believe that our office could properly service a remote new business, and accordingly, I would assist the new business to find a qualified local CPA firm.

One of the trips I was involved with for this client was to Cleveland, Ohio. I have a humorous anecdote about this particular trip. As stated above, the individual arrived a couple of days prior to my visit to meet with his clients and for him to get the fundamental questions answered for these clients. Then, I was typically asked to participate to meet with the new client and/or their CPAs and/or attorneys. My air transportation landed about 11 PM and he picked me up at the airport and drove me to our hotel. He had checked us into our rooms at the hotel. We wanted to talk and prepare for the morning meeting so we retired to the hotel's lounge for a beverage. By this time, it was about midnight on a Friday night.

Upon arrival in the lounge, we noted a few well known professional athletes who were in town to play one of the Cleveland franchises. I really like sports and I recognized a few of the professional athletes. Nonetheless, we did not approach them as we had work to prepare. While in the lounge we looked up at the bar and we noticed two nice looking women sitting there and talking: one of the women was wearing a dark business suit and the other was wearing a very nice red dress. We had no idea what these two ladies would be doing in a lounge all alone together at midnight on a Friday in Cleveland. Being unaware of what they were doing, we speculated and began discussing, only between ourselves, what two nice looking women could be doing in a lounge at that time. We concluded with each other that the two women must be hookers!

Our seats from the lounge actually looked out through the bar and into the lobby of the hotel all of the way to the elevators and lobby bathrooms. The 2 women also had the same or similar view from where they were seated. All of a sudden, we noticed that an elevator door opened and we observed a bunch of young men "falling out" drunk from the elevator and into the lobby. They were accompanied by a thinly clad young lady in a skimpy dress. As it turned out, the young men were leaving a bachelor party. They were also accompanied by the young "soon to be" groom. The thinly clad young lady seemed to be hanging on to the groom to be. She was the "dancer".

All of a sudden, the two ladies arose from the bar. The lady in the dark suit approached our table while the lady in the red dress walked up to the group of young men in the lobby. Then the lady in the red dress began beating up the young groom to be. The thinly clad young lady tried to escape to the ladies restroom. However, when the bride to be was done beating up the groom to be, the bride to be followed the thinly clad young lady into the restroom. As it turned out, we learned that the woman in the red dress was supposed to be married to the young man the very next day. The dark suited lady introduced herself to us as the lounge manager. She said that the bride to be was tipped off that there was a bachelor party and the bride to be did not approve.

To this day we do not know if the wedding ever took place! We do know that the young groom's buddies laughed hysterically as the wife to be beat up the groom to be.

Client Relationships

Regardless of the business that you may find yourself in, it is important to have good customers and good relationships with those customers. In the public accounting profession, those customers are generally referred to as clients.

CPAs work on clients in different capacities. When beginning a career, a CPA or young accountant may be working on a client and that CPA will never meet that client. In other words, there is an accountant or partner in charge of that relationship that may be maintaining substantially all or all of the interactions with the specific client. In those particular jobs, a CPA is gaining experience and/or assisting in some other professional capacity for that client. In some cases, those CPAs may be some of the most experienced in the office. Those particular CPAs generally provide a second opinion and/or review a project before it is presented to the client.

Having clients is probably the most important part of any CPA firm. For instance, the education is a given; that is, all CPAs are to meet certain educational requirements. The training and supervision of the accountants should be a given. That is, the more experienced accountants should be helping the younger accountant grow within the profession. The salaries and benefits are generally commensurate to what the professional puts into the profession. However, none of this is possible without a client.

There are certain CPAs who are skilled at meeting new people and helping to convert them to a client of that particular CPA firm. Those CPAs are generally the best and the brightest in the profession. One important reason is that those CPAs can recognize different industries and the related personality(ies) of the prospective client. They are then able to effectively communicate an advantage or a possible solution with their particular CPA firm over another CPA firm.

This does not mean that a CPA says anything wrong or bad about another CPA, including their existing CPA. Whereas, there may be issues that can be improved, I found that a client simply wants to listen to that portion of the presentation. That is, what can the new CPA "bring to the table" to assist the client and help them obtain their objective(s) in the change to a new firm. This may be income tax related, financially related (financial statements, cash flow, financing), consulting, and/or other professional services. I believe saying bad things about another professional is not a good or professional thing to do. Based upon my experience, the new client will say plenty and all you have to do is listen and continue to help them advance their own agenda.

Very important in this process is to recognize and understand that a CPA does not want each and every potential client. That may sound odd at first blush; however, there are certain clients that simply will not work within a firm. The obvious choices are the clients who do not pay their bills, the clients who treat you and/or your staff with disrespect and the clients who demand too much time.

Once the new person becomes a client, the next step is equally difficult. That is, "who will be the contact person for that client?". Many times, that may be the same CPA who introduced the client into the firm. That "finding" CPA generally has a special relationship with the client. A key to maintaining that relationship is to integrate the needs of the client with the best staff available in order to properly represent those needs.

Sometimes, a client will be represented by another member of the CPA firm. This is not unusual. The CPA firm can employ many professionals and others. It is important that the firm tries to match the services to the expertise of the office. Even then, the relationship between the client and the firm may not always "hit it off right" the first time. In those situations, it is then important to help identify both the professional needs and the matching personalities of the client and the CPA.

Most clients, if properly represented, will remain with a CPA firm for a long time. At one time, I was told that clients might only average 5 years with the local CPA firms. My experience was that once our firm obtained a client, the client was with us in perpetuity, unless there was a terrible or unfortunate event. I found that clients do not want to change their CPAs.

There is another wrinkle to this interpretation of why clients do not want to change. From time to time, a CPA may change firms. This may be because the CPA was asked to leave the firm, or alternatively, the CPA chooses to seek other employment. In those circumstances, a client can be naturally confused as to whether or not to remain with the CPA firm, or alternatively, move to the other firm with the CPA whom the client has had ongoing contact. This is difficult on a number of levels.

First, the expertise of the CPA firm that has been professionally representing the client still remains. That is, all of the staff that had been working for that client generally remain, except, one person. I found that the existing CPA firm is generally best able to represent the client. I further believe that it is unethical behavior for any CPA to leave a firm and try to bring clients of the predecessor CPA firm to the new place of employment. I understand that there may be CPAs that may disagree with this belief.

Simply stated, the existing CPA firm is a "professional team". Everyone at the original CPA firm is still working for the same clients and goals, except the CPA who may have left the firm may have a different agenda. Somehow, I believe our profession has avoided setting forth strict rules concerning these types of matters.

A client will sometimes remain with the first person who asks them to use them for professional services. Frankly, this type of an event is difficult on a client. The client does not really understand who is actually performing the professional services for them. Nor do the clients understand the services that are actually performed. That is why they have hired a CPA firm; that is, to help them solve problems and perform services that they themselves cannot solve or perform.

Many CPA firms use employment contracts with their employees to prohibit an employee from taking a client to another CPA firm. In my experience I found that the court system is reluctant to enforce these types of contracts. Frankly, it puzzles me as to why. Here is a written contract between an employer and an employee. Had the terms of the agreement not have been agreed upon, then the employment would never have commenced, and the employee would generally have never have met the client. Nonetheless, I have found that non compete covenants were hard, if not impossible, to enforce.

In growing our own firm, we sometimes lost professionals for different reasons. More often than not, we found that the corporate culture of our office with that professional were not the same. These generally included ethical considerations or even sometimes, dating a subordinate employee or bookkeeper/accountant of one of our clients. In cases where we "parted company"; sometimes, if one or two small clients decided to leave our firm and use our former CPA, it did not make sense to spend a lot of time in trying to maintain that relationship with our client. However, we found there were other CPAs that had left our firm who set their sites a bit higher. In fact, in one such occasion, a former CPA employee tried to take an entire office!

As our firm grew, we recognized that the law was not always about the law. However, the law was about winning, and, winning at any cost. At least that is how many are treating the system. Thus, it is always best to engage the best and the brightest attorneys. These are generally not the cheapest attorneys. They are the best attorneys. And these great attorneys, like great CPAs, have the ability to explain issues in words that could be best understood. We believe we engaged the best attorney in our area to assist us with drafting our employment agreement. This attorney had experience all the way to the state Supreme Court with respect to these exact issues.

We were counseled that some courts simply will not read "the 4 corners of a contract". We were told that many liberal judges simply disregard the contracts. Hence, we asked, why enter into a contract? The attorney told us that without a contract, we would probably be sued. Remarkable.

The attorney then advised us to get rid of our non compete covenant in our contract. This was in our very first few years of operation. Instead, in its place, the attorney advised to use a liquidated damages provision. That is, a former employee could buy a client at a mutually agreed price. If any client left our firm and went to work for a former CPA (within a prescribed time period), then the price would have already been agreed upon. That is, so long as that price agreed upon was not punitive in nature.

As our firm grew, we opened additional offices. Key to the success of the firm's growth was finding and retaining good quality staff. In one of our new offices, we believed we found a good tax person who may be able to help manage the office with our ongoing help. This person had an already existing client base that he would be bringing into our firm. In addition, it was our expectation that the firm would then begin obtaining bigger and bigger clients.

Because of this CPAs experience, he was also familiar with the employment contracts. Although the employment contract was pretty much a standard agreement with most employees, in this particular negotiation, the CPA used his own attorney and our standard employment agreement was changed. Our administrative partner was a fair man and he tried to make each and every agreement as fair as reasonably possible, without exception.

This CPA elected to have our firm purchase his existing client base and all of his equipment, software, supplies and professional subscriptions. In other words, we believe we purchased everything. He had the right to exclude the clients from the purchase and sale agreement. Instead, he opted for the up front money.

Although this person was never the best manager in our company, he remained with us for about 16 1/2 years. During that time, we observed our children growing up together. I believe we got to know each other pretty well. However, the other managers of the firm were critical of the manner in which that particular office was managed. Regardless of what policies and procedures the firm had adopted, this particular manager became "rogue" from time to time. Then one year, this all came to a head, when the annual compensation review team decided to not increase his salary. Granted, each and every year his salary had increased. In addition, each other member of the management team had always received an increase in salary. When I learned of this, I met with the compensation review team and told them that it was my opinion that if this was their final determination, then I would expect that CPA to leave our firm. Their response at the time was "he is making more here than anywhere else, and if he leaves after all he has done, then good riddance!".

Well, he did not get a raise and a few months after income tax season. Concurrently, there seemed to be some changes going on that were heretofore not anticipated. At that time, I was the President and Chair of the Washington Society of Certified Public Accountants (WSCPA). One of my duties while serving as President was as the Board Liaison to the Professional Conduct (Ethics) Committee. I would visit this particular office on the way to the WSCPA office and talk to him. One morning, I met with him about 7 AM. The general conversation was : "how are you doing, how is your family, how is the office going, how are the staff doing, how are the clients doing, and is there anything else we need to discuss?". He was very congenial and did not say anything about leaving the firm.

Later that day, our administrative partner received a letter of resignation in the mail. Our former employee did not give me even the hint that he was leaving the firm. He then told the administrative partner of the firm that he going to work for another CPA firm. Frankly, this seemed to me to be dishonest behavior; however, I was not surprised under the circumstances.

My immediate reaction was to contact our own attorney who was familiar with our employment contracts. We talked about the possible repercussions. It was our attorney's advice for him to begin preparation of a temporary restraining order (TRO) to serve on the employee, the owners of the other CPA firm and the other CPA firm itself. I told him to begin the drafting of the TRO and then we will "wait and see".

Concurrently, I then telephoned the CPA who was leaving, together with the administrative partner, and asked him why he did not tell me he was leaving the firm earlier that day. He told me that there was lots going on at the time and he did not believe the timing was right. This sort of set off a light bulb in my head as to why he could not simply tell me the truth. He mentioned at the time that he had already contacted several clients and they were going to move to the other CPA firm with him. Each and every large client that he was moving was a client that I had generated for the firm. As stated above, I believed this to be unethical behavior. These clients had already been contacted and they were put in a difficult position. This was a position that they did not have to be put in without his leaving our firm.

He then told us that a client attorney of our firm was representing him. He said that the attorney had advised him our contract was unenforceable, and accordingly, he would not be paying us anything. He scheduled his last day for that Friday at the office. This was Monday.

We asked him to meet with us in our executive offices the next morning. Frankly, with or without the unethical behavior, the CPA had worked for us for 16 1/2 years. Maybe, he was entitled to something. However, he chose to try to take the entire firm's client base from that office! Over reaching?

The next morning, we spoke with him concerning why he was leaving. As expected, the "non raise" was a factor. The administrative partner and I had spoken before this CPA's arrival at the office. The administrative partner and myself sort of agreed to allow him to take his original client base that he brought into the practice, even though we had previously purchased it. Then, nothing more.

However, it was obvious that his intentions with the other CPA firm was to "rape and pillage" and take any and every client possible. That is, we believed that it was their intent to close our office. Frankly, I thanked him for his service, we hugged and he left. I telephoned our attorney and told him what happened. He told me to go to the other office the next day and terminate him from our firm.

I had 2 other professionals from the office meet me early the next morning. When the CPA who was changing employment arrived, we invited him into the conference room. We spoke about all the issues and I handed him a termination letter. Rather than wait until Friday, the attorney advised us (and wrote the letter of termination) for that very moment.

He objected and stated, "I have client meetings today that have been scheduled". With that, I reminded him "the firm has client meetings, the clients have been contacted and all the meetings have been "handled" for that day". I walked him to his office and we had boxes there for him to empty his desk. One thing that I found surprising was that he had several computer disks that were going into his box. I was never very "computer literate" so I did not really understand what these disks could have that could be harmful to our firm.

Fast forward to the sheriff serving the TRO's against the CPA, the 3 owners of the other CPA firm and the other firm itself. The next step, according to our attorney, was to try to obtain an injunction. This is a method to permanently (or for a prescribed period of time) prohibit those from receiving the TROs to practice on those clients.

The TRO hearing to move to the injunction went quickly. The former employee alleged we forced him to sign an employment agreement. It did not take the court too long to see that was not true. Our firm had maintained each and every change requested by him and his attorney in their own handwriting (in his employment file). A trial to enforce the injunction was scheduled.

At this time, the partner in charge of the other CPA firm sort of ran up to me and began cursing at me in some incredibly foul language. He told me the employment contract was unenforceable. I said, "I am sorry, we have not met, who are you?". He told me who he was. Rather than argue or speak, I patted him on his behind and said "good luck today".

During discovery for the injunction, we deposed former employees of that CPA firm. In addition, one of the current partners telephoned me and apologized for their firm's behavior. Frankly, the latter meant a lot to me. One of the former employees indicated that she was brought into our office at night to make photocopies of all of our client files and put those files in the office of the partner in charge of the other firm. As stated, she was an employee of the other firm! I could not believe that until we checked the "counter" on our own copying machine. We then learned that we paid for all of their copying charges.

Then, unrelated to the case, I assessed a client income tax return. The return was processed during March of that year; however, it had a July "back up" date. When we checked, we learned that each and every computer file that had been backed up by him had been taken by the CPA. We later learned from the former employee that he had copies of each and every client file on computer. Thus, the aforementioned disks.

We were able to demonstrate that to the court and the judge ruled in our favor. However, by that time, substantial damage had impacted that office. Many of the clients did not like a judge telling them they could not use a particular CPA (hence the original contract). Frankly, I am puzzled why our profession allows this type of behavior by other professionals.

The lesson here was that we had the best attorney who was best prepared to prevail in the matter. We had carefully followed his advice in drafting our contracts and that his advice proved correct.

Incidentally, the Superior Court justice who ruled on this case has now been appointed as a Supreme Court justice for our state. This made me feel a bit better about our State Supreme Court.

CHAPTER TWO – MEETING THE COURT SYSTEM FOR THE FIRST TIME

During college I tried to gain an education, a good resume and have a good time with the experiences of college. With that said, I entered the Presidential Honors Program that allowed me to graduate in only 3 years; however, I had to take or challenge all the requisite classes during that time period. Concurrently, I worked 3 jobs during my entire college career. I sold televisions and stereos at Sears Roebuck, I interned and sold financial products for Northwestern Mutual Life Insurance Company (NML) and I interned in the Volunteer Income Tax Assistance (VITA) department of the Internal Revenue Service (IRS). The advantage to working this hard and at an unbelievable pace was that I was able to interview and receive job offers from all of the international firms at that time (The Big 8).

After graduating from college, I worked at three (3) offices for the international accounting firm that is now known as DeLoitte. The international accounting firms are generally known as the "best of the best" CPA firms. The best and the brightest accounting students generally set their goal to go to work for one of these top firms. I believe the training and experience from these firms is second to none. The mentors in these firms have "walked the same walk" and generally speak at or above most intellectual levels in the accounting profession. I thank my lucky stars that I was able to gain this experience and learn from some of the best in our profession.

Those same international offices generally encourage their young staff to get involved in the local community. Often times, you will find that professionals from these (now) Big 4 firms sit on some of the largest and most important local boards and charities. This kind of public service is not only a benefit to the local service clubs and charities, but more important, a benefit in a young professional's growth.

In the 3rd and final office that I worked at for DeLoitte, I had become active in many activities, service clubs and groups: from a local college, to the local United Way, to a local service club, and more. It was that last service club experience that helped to change my life. And, I was able to become President of a seventy (70) member service club after only being there for a few months (and I helped to grow it to one hundred and two (102) members by the end of my term – 1 year).

One of our members in that service club was an Appellate Court Justice for the State of Idaho. The honorable judge and I got to be "buddies". I was only 22 years old and he was older, well experienced and wiser. I also remember him being shorter than me and he was sort of "pudgy". We both played tennis and our games complemented each other. So, we came together to form our own doubles tennis team. We were not the worst at the club nor were we the best doubles team. But we always had fun.

At the same time as my tennis playing was going on, that Big 4 CPA firm was trying to collect a bill from a former client. This is not unusual for a client not to pay a bill, but it was my first experience with this type of tactic. I immediately learned that in these types of cases that "stories would be told". Specifically, the former client would "say anything" or "make up any story" in order to avoid paying the bill. Even though I worked in the firm, I had no experience with this client. The Partner in Charge of the office (the boss) asked me to review all of the billing records independently. The case did not settle and inevitably and ultimately the matter ended up going to Superior Court (this is generally the local court that initially hears these types of cases).

I was told by the accounting firm's attorney that I would have to testify concerning my knowledge and opinions about the bills concerning the dispute. I had never testified before; although, I had worked on many similar projects that generated similar billings. I was a bit nervous. I told my tennis partner (the judge) about the case and how nervous I was about testifying for the first time. He told me something that I have never forgotten. He said I should be "well prepared" and "simply tell the truth". He said it is "hard to impeach the truth". I never forgot that. He warned me that under cross examination that I simply had to be truthful and try to "go with the flow". He warned me not to volunteer too much information as the opposing counsel can sometimes take advantage of "too much information".

He also said that he knew the local judge that was hearing the case and he believed the judge to be a good and honest man. He promised me that if I was properly prepared, that I would be more relaxed when I testified. He gave me a mischievous smile when he said that. At the time, I had no idea what mischief he had on his mind.

Well, my big day came. And, regardless of the coaching, I was still admittedly nervous. Then my name was called to testify. I made my way to the front of the court room. I immediately noticed that once I got on the witness stand that only 4 people were looking at everyone else in the court room. The judge, the court reporter, the bailiff, and I were all looking back at the folks in attendance for the matter. Everyone else was looking towards us. After I got sworn in and before I testified the back door opened. My tennis partner walked in quietly and just enough to be seen. No one else could see my tennis partner but the 4 of us. My tennis partner waived at me and gave me a "thumbs up". It was apparent that he knew the judge hearing the case as the judge smiled. Then my tennis partner "flipped me off" (gave me the finger), turned and left the court room.

The judge giggled, I smiled and then just as I was promised, I relaxed a bit.

I learned at that moment that everyone in the court room were people. Everyone in the court room should be relaxed and simply tell the truth. The attorneys, the plaintiff, the defendant, the witnesses, the court reporter, the bailiff, and all the other people were just a "part of the process". In the big picture, what I was doing at that time was really no different than the process at a restaurant or at a sports activity. Testifying was just a forum that I was not familiar with at the time.

Over the years I testified dozens of times, if not hundreds of times. I believe I learned a bit more from each experience that benefited me in my growth and knowledge of the legal system from my perspective. Regardless of the case, I refused to compromise the principles of being fair, reasonable and honest. Sometimes the ethics and behaviors of the "other side" tested my character. Nonetheless, I believe I always did the right thing at the right time.

Attorneys speak of "advocacy". I believe in doing the right thing and doing those things right. I believe it is important to prepare and then do the "right things when no one is looking". Then, it is important to be well prepared and testify to the right things. I submit that many times advocacy can cloud the legal system. As an example, is it the truth, is it fair, reasonable, honest, the truth, the right thing to do, or is it shadowed by advocacy? Many attorneys have taken exception to this interpretation of mine. Many more have admired it in my opinion.

Years later, and as a segway to this story, I was blessed to become the President of the WSCPA. In addition, I was on the National Council for the American Institute of Certified Public Accountants (AICPA). Our profession also has checks and balances in place to "police our own profession", such as our accounting and income tax practices. In my opinion, this is tantamount to the perpetuity of our profession. This is what helps to make our profession so great. Good quality internal controls are important to all public accounting firms.

In addition, CPAs are generally thought of as the most "trusted profession". In other words, CPAs are respected more than most people's doctors and all other professionals. This is a trust that should not be taken lightly by any CPA. And therefore, the inherent professionalism that goes with this trust should not be compromised or taken lightly. Not only do we need to do things right, we also have to make sure that we do the right things. This is especially true when we are called to testify.

I was also able to serve on different professional committees for our profession. One of those committees in Washington State was the Professional Standards Committee (Ethics). The members of this committee were some of the best and finest individuals that I had met in our profession. It was an honor to serve on this committee. This committee regularly interacts with the WSCPA members in answering questions from the membership and sometimes private citizens and other businesses.

The committee also works on certain complaints alleged against member CPA's of the WSCPA. In my experience with the Ethics committee, the matters were taken seriously and the members of the committee tried to do the right thing, without exception. I found the committee members honest and sincere. I also believed the members of the committee were sometimes inexperienced at business matters. Nonetheless, the members were insistent on doing the right things. There was lots of deliberation and collaboration on this committee.

On another subject, another important part of the CPA profession is that it now has "credentials". Those credentials are supposed to indicate a "specialty" in some particular field. One of those credentials is in the area of Business Valuations. In my experience, I completed numerous business valuations. Many of these valuations were for actual purchase and sales of businesses (probably the most important valuations) and others for other types matters such as Buy Sell Agreements, Disputes and Divorces, to name a few.

Upon our profession issuing this credential for the first time, I was "grandfathered" (if I wanted the credential). That is, if a CPA in practice wanted that credential, all they had to do was pay the dues and remain professionally current on the particular credential. Today one has to take a test to obtain the credential, but initially all one had to do was pay the annual dues and maintain certain continuing professional education requirements. I did not elect to obtain the credential. I believe this was an important and good decision in my professional career. I did not elect to gain certain credentials "for free" because I do not believe (even today) these credentials are as highly respected as the CPA credential. And there can be professional issues and limitations to these credentials in some circumstances in my opinion.

As stated above, the CPA profession somewhat "polices" the accounting and income tax practices. To my knowledge, the credentials, once issued, are not customarily "policed", certainly not like the CPA credential. Whereas, income tax and accounting services are peer reviewed, the credentials, once obtained, are generally not consistently reviewed by an independent body. In other words, absent a review within our profession, various professionals with a credential can testify to one theory in the morning as true and correct to the best of their knowledge and believe and then testify exactly the opposite in the afternoon. In both of these cases, the "expert" is supposed to be testifying to the truth and nothing but the truth. Advocacy can sometimes cloud this behavior. I believe allowing that type of testimony is wrong and that practice should not be allowed, or the practice should not be implicitly sanctioned by our profession.

I first learned this in the aforementioned fee dispute case. My very first trial. It was obvious to me that the so called "expert" on the other side of the fee dispute was not testifying reasonably or honestly. This added substantial time and costs to the case. However, "the so called expert" was able to confuse the judge. However, I learned in that case that "technically" the expert is still referred to as testifying "under oath".

After the day of this trial wound up, while waiting for the judge's decision, I received a telephone call from the judge presiding over the matter. He asked me to meet with him privately and in his chambers. The judge wanted to ask me a few private questions about the case. We met and spoke about the case. He recognized the unbelievable testimony of the other expert but still wanted to confirm the same. He then rendered his decision.

During my career, this was not the only time I was contacted by a judge in a case prior to the rendering of that judge's decision. Each time a judge contacted me, it was obvious that the judge was trying to get to the truth. By the way, the practice of meeting with a witness for these purposes is not generally allowed. Surprising? I believe in all cases that it helped lead to the truth and the proper decision; regardless of advocacy.

Pizza and Beer

I relocated to Olympia, Washington and began a small CPA firm with another owner about a year after moving to Olympia. At the time, I was still relatively ignorant to the ways of the legal system and I still had the hope that the legal system would result in "the right result". I then experienced mixed reviews from a variety of ridiculous rulings by different judges in different locations.

As an example, our firm was growing quickly during the first few years. And while visiting local restaurants or stores, it is not uncommon for a CPA to run into a client or clients. This was the case one evening while my wife and I were enjoying a pizza at a local pizza place.

Sitting at the next table was what I considered to be a good business client of mine at the time. So, we moved our pizzas together with the client and his spouse and began eating with them --- both the husband and wife. This is a client that I generally met with only once per year. We generally visited and caught up on family and mutual friends as expected in a random meeting such as this. During the dinner conversation, I was told by the husband that his business did not have any cash at the time. This came as a surprise to me. At the time, from what the client had told me at our last meeting, I believed that the client should have been profitable and would have generated some cash. This client was in construction and I understood from casually seeing the client from time to time that the company had sold many homes over the past year. Accordingly, because of my experience and general conversations with him throughout the year, I would have reasonably expected that his business would have had ample cash.

So, a discussion began between us as to "where the cash could have been employed", or where the cash should have gone, assuming the business were successful. Please note that simply because a CPA has a client or simply because there are conversations throughout the year, that does not mean that the CPA has access to the clients books or bank accounts. In fact, a CPA having access to the books would be unusual. Instead, a CPA may only see the year end books one time per year (if at all), and, that would generally be after the close of the client's fiscal year. I had not seen any written financial information on this client in almost a year; however, it appeared evident that there was a potential problem.

So, my inquiries began in order to try to analyze and isolate where the cash may have gone. I then tried to isolate certain issues that were discussed and isolate what could have happened to the cash. I recalled the client telling me about a "Street of Dreams" home that was built during the year. He told me where the funds had come from for the home. So, that home was ruled out as a reason for the lack of cash.

I also recalled the contractor building a warehouse during the year. He also dismissed the warehouse as a use of the cash for other explainable financing reasons. We talked about a number of different items and none of them seemed the source of the loss of cash.

I then asked if there could be any employee theft? He almost went faint. I understood from them at the time that the thought of employee theft was not possible. Since they made the "cash shortage" almost a crisis situation, at the time I simply said that we could go to his office after pizza, about 8 PM on a Sunday evening, and I could look through his files with him. I was concerned about him, and, helping at "odd hours" is what professionals do for their clients in my opinion. He was obviously uncomfortable and I did not know exactly why at the time.

All four (4) of us drove to his office and went into the bookkeeping department. We opened drawers and found the checkbook, bank statements and books of record. It took me no longer than ten (10) minutes to learn that the head bookkeeper had "cooked the books". In less than an hour I discovered that over $100,000 had been creatively taken from the accounts during the year, all of it since the last time our firm had been involved in the books of record of this client (since the client's last income tax return). Our office had not seen the books since before the thefts began. The builder and his wife looked ill. I felt terrible for them.

Together with the client, I telephoned their banker about 10 PM that same evening and discussed this with the banker. The purpose of the call was to stop a few suspicious "outstanding checks" from clearing the bank the next day. The banker was helpful. We then called the police and let them know about the irregularities. We agreed to meet the police at the office at 7 AM the next morning, wait for the bookkeeper at that time, and have her arrested.

We then called the builder's attorney to let him know what was going on. My wife and I went home.

I arrived a bit early the next morning, prior to the police getting there and after the client had already arrived. Upon entering the client's bookkeeping office, I immediately noticed that the file cabinets were missing that we had been using just a few hours before. In fact, the entire bookkeeping department had been "sanitized". All of the bank statements and check books were gone. Invoices were now missing. I was puzzled.

The bookkeeper did not show up.

So, the police went to her home to arrest her.

At the time, it seemed odd, but I did not understand why the records had disappeared in just a few short hours. The only people who were supposed to know about this meeting were the clients, the police, the attorney, and the banker. However, I had to leave as I had to go to work for the already scheduled daily grind. About 4 PM, the builder telephoned me. He asked that we meet "for a drink" at a local popular "watering hole". I agreed.

Upon arriving, he was visibly upset, shaking and sweating. He thanked me for the prompt and efficient services the evening before. He then confessed to me that he was having an affair with the bookkeeper and she had introduced him to illegal drugs. He told me how stupid this was and that he wished he had not had the affair or started using drugs. He then asked what he should do as the company would have trouble paying its bills? A discussion between us occurred as to how to proceed. I told him to make sure his attorney was aware of all of this too. He begged me not to tell his wife. I was unprepared for the subsequent mischief between his attorney and our office.

The next day I met with the other owner at our CPA firm. Professionally and ethically, I had to let him know what had happened and what the client had told me. Our obvious concern was that the client owed us thousands of dollars and that the client was using illegal drugs and having an affair with the bookkeeper. Both the husband and wife were technically clients and we were asked not to tell the wife something that was financially important to her. We decided that prior to doing any more work for the client that he would need to tell her the truth and that our office would need to be paid. We do not take drugs, and now that we understood the issues, we did not want to be "lenders" (creditors) to this business. The client could arrange to pay us from his personal assets for the outstanding charges and then we would continue the relationship.

We asked for payment for prior services prior to performing additional services. He objected and expected us to continue to work even though the company had no money at the time and the company had no ability to pay us for our time to help with this problem. And, incidentally, I did not charge him for the Sunday night work after pizza. An important decision had to be made by our firm that is a critical decision for any CPA firm. We concluded that the drugs and the affair was the primary cause for the alleged embezzlement. And accordingly, the client knew or reasonably should have known there was a problem. We advised him that we would need to disengage if he was unable to pay the bill.

This is when I first "absolutely" learned how unfair and/or corrupt the legal system could be. I believe the legal system has evolved sometimes into something that benefits the wrongdoer. On one hand, as CPA's, we are not allowed to tell people why we resigned. On the other hand, he is able to make up a story to delay our collection of the amounts owed to us. He could also tell local business people in the community that we were bad accountants. The outstanding bill was already almost a year delinquent and there had never been any complaint about services or the amount of the outstanding charges to that time. I learned later from this former client that his attorney advised him that we had "malpractice" insurance. Our office could therefore be a "deep pocket" for the client to recover some of the so called "lost funds". Even though everyone knew this was wrong, the client sued us for malpractice after we resigned and then mad a demand for the outstanding fee!

Yes, we were sued for malpractice because a client had an affair with a dishonest bookkeeper and he was using drugs with her. This was the first time our firm had been sued and we were incensed that a court system would allow this. Because of the way malpractice insurance works, we were not allowed to use our own attorney. Instead, legal counsel would be "appointed" by the insurance carrier.

We could pay our attorney also and separately, but in the circumstances and because our firm was so small at the time, we could not afford to have multiple legal firms represent us. Even our $5,000 deductible was pretty costly to us at the time.

The insurance company sent us their chosen attorney. The attorney had an office in Seattle and Portland. Our office was in Olympia (sort of half way, plus or minus). Frankly, we were not impressed with this attorney. In this particular matter, we did not believe that the insurance company was looking out for our own best interests. We found that the attorney was simply driving from Seattle to Portland, stopping to see us on the way, and we were billed for the entire trip. In addition, we learned that not all attorneys had your best interest in mind. But, we were stuck, we were young and we did not know what to do at the time.

So, we worked through the "system" as best we could with the insurance company attorney. We did not know it at the time, but many of these attorneys have a preconceived method of resolving the case. It includes paying the former client and the result is increased malpractice premiums. We did not like that nor would we agree to it.

At the same time, we began reading our insurance contract concerning legal coverage more closely. We learned that the attorney was supposed to be representing us, not the insurance company. And, we had a meeting with the attorney to discuss how to move the case forward to trial expeditiously. She told us that we would not go to trial, "they (the bad guys) are willing to abandon their law suit if we forgot our fees. We recommend that you accept that settlement". The "we" was the insurance company and the attorney. In other words, we pay the insurance company for the policy, the deductible is paid by our firm, the attorney is paid, and we get nothing. The result was that we did nothing wrong and the insurance company would increase our premium. This is how the legal system works with frivolous lawsuits against professionals of all types.

Unfortunately, I have experienced many professionals who have been forced out of business by this "frivolous" practice. They simply get sued when they have done absolutely nothing wrong. Something that I constantly shared with our Ethics Committee during my tenure as Board Liaison was that there were too many frivolous "complaints filed against CPAs". Many times, it simply appeared to me that those complainants simply did not want to pay their fees either. My first question to the complainant was generally, "Is there an outstanding fee to your CPA?". More often than not, there happened to be an outstanding fee.

A difficult decision had to be made in our case though. Ultimately, our decision at that time was to inform the insurance company that the attorney was not working in our best interest; instead, working only for the insurance company and that was unacceptable. We demanded an attorney to represent our firm as specified in our policy. We wanted an attorney competent in similar matters. We understood the insurance company would be upset with us and may not renew our insurance. However, it was the correct thing to do and it was the right thing to do.

The insurance company finally folded and we were able to find a qualified attorney who was also a litigator highly skilled in the accounting profession. The subsequent legal process took over 4 years but the case finally went to court. We knew we would win. We thought we would simply tell our story and the jury would certainly exonerate us. You know, the truth, the whole truth and nothing but the truth. We liked our attorney. I recall he enjoyed chewing tobacco.

We had our trial date. Then, the day before the trial, we were reminded by the insurance company that the builder's attorney offered us the same settlement once again. That is, if we would forget our fee then they would drop the malpractice action. We had said no and our decision had not changed. Our insurance company then told us that we had to accept this offer. If not, and if we lost, then we would be subject to monetary losses. That is anything and everything if damages were awarded to the other party. Once again, we were shocked. This was the night before the trial and we believed we were being extorted by our own insurance company. Again, this is the way the legal system works to help reward the bad guys.

We then read and re read the insurance contract. We learned we had an "arbitration" provision with the insurance company. That is, if we disagreed with them, that disagreement would go to a completely different arbitration prior to the court case. So, I invoked this provision of our insurance contract. I told them to set up the arbitration. The insurance company complained.

They said to invoke this would require arbitration either that evening or the following morning before the trial started. I reminded them that it was their provision and we were prepared to live with the provision. Did the insurance company want to ignore their own contract or risk they themselves losing the case?

Well, the insurance company then "folded". They agreed that the appropriate thing to do in this case was to go to trial. Since that time, I have had numerous experiences with insurance companies putting pressure on professionals (including many physicians) to settle frivolous claims in this manner. The court system knows it and the court system seems to condone and almost encourage this practice. Speaking from experience, when you are accused of malpractice (and you know there was no malpractice), the result is that a piece of your life has been taken from you and it can never be given back. Later, I learned to not take these matters personally. Instead, I was taught whenever possible to use the emotion of the moment against the other side. When used correctly, it really can drive the other party a bit crazy.

Another client of ours constantly seemed to find himself as a defendant in legal matters. He was a terrific man; however, he tended to leverage too many of his assets. His legal bills were substantial each year in defending himself. One evening, after a lengthy meeting with opposing counsel where such counsel yelled at him and called him terrible names, the client and I were going to dinner. My client caught up to the opposing counsel and asked him to join us. Counsel agreed. I was alarmed. I said "how could you go out to dinner with this attorney who was trying to aggressively represent his clients over you?". He looked at me calmly and said, "Chuck, the meeting is over, that is just "business". It is now time to go eat". With that, the 3 of us went to dinner. This dinner and the surrounding event is something that I will never forget.

So, in our aforementioned case, we showed up for court the next morning expecting a fair tribunal. It continued to get worse.

I then experienced my next lesson in what I considered to be a corrupt legal system. In this particular case, that is, the choosing of the judge to hear the case. We had no idea who the judge would be until the day of the jury selection. When the judge came into the room I was shocked. The builder's wife used to be the legal assistant to the judge. Normally, a judge would refuse to take a case when one of the parties is well known to the judge. Our attorney went ballistic. Our attorney said that "unless we moved quickly" the judge could then "continue the case" for another year or longer and simply step aside from the case. In other words, a well planned delay process choreographed by the other side's attorney with the blessing of the judge to give them more time. However, our attorney wanted the trial to proceed. At that time, we had already waited 4 years. I do not believe the other side was prepared for the trial. They expected the settlement to take place as they had planned. A further delay could hold up the matter another year or longer. The delay would also require an even greater investment in our time.

I have since learned this is a normal and customary ploy that many use in order to frustrate the opposing side. The delays are also costly. It was my experience that most of the participants in legal matters simply could not afford the cost. Once knowing if the other party can afford to continue with a case, it can be used advantageously by the other side. And although we could afford the "financial" cost, we did not want a continued delay to this matter for professional and daily living reasons.

Our attorney immediately stood up, before the judge could speak and continue the case, as it appeared she had planned with the former clients. It was obvious that our attorney was unhappy and at the same time well prepared for this tactic. Our attorney stated (before the judge could speak) that he was "aware she (the judge) used to employ the defendant's wife and that was permissible by us". The judge then wanted to see us in her chambers. She was reluctant to take the case after that. Can you believe it? The judge takes the case all the while knowing that she could give her friends a "continuance". Our attorney did not allow it. Instead, the attorney said that the jury would make the decision and she was simply the trier of fact. The judge did not like it but the trial was allowed to continue. There was an obvious risk of favoritism by the then presiding judge; however, we were confident that the case was frivolous.

In another deceitful act by this judge, prior to her leaving the room, she granted the defendants a "Motion in Limine". Specifically, the judge ruled that we were not allowed to tell the jury about the affair or the drugs. In other words, we were not allowed to tell the jury why we were forced to resign and demand our fee to be paid. So, a very large advantage was given to the defendants by the judge. Maybe a slap in our face as it was apparent the judge did not want the case to proceed. I believe a logical person would want to know why we resigned. However, this is part of the aforementioned favoritism.

We definitely had the better attorney. This attorney has now been a good acquaintance of mine for the past 30 years. He is an attorney that really works for his clients and appears to know the rules and procedures of the trade. Better yet, he prepares and he wins.

He was also in favor of some "gamesmanship". The strategy was after the jury was seated and prior to the judge coming in, to have my wife and our two small children come into the courtroom. I left my place in the courtroom, gave everyone in the family a hug in full view of the jury and then had to give my wife some cash! The attorney said that would make a favorable impression on the jury. It did! The jury laughed. Our attorney said it was important that the "professional be humanized". That was to counter act what our attorney anticipated from the other side. And our attorney was correct. The other attorney attempted to paint us as uncaring people; but alas, they were too late!

Because the builder sued for malpractice (and we had only "demanded our fee" and technically had not sued the builder), the builder was able to present his malpractice case first. Our attorney did a remarkable job. When the builder finally got up to testify, the court room doors opened and several of the local community leaders walked into the court room. I got up and greeted them and the community leaders sat in the court room. Most of the jury were immediately aware of who these people were and they were aware that the community leaders were there in support of our firm.

The judge ordered the jury to leave and wanted "all parties in her chamber". The jury recognized many of the local community leaders as did the judge. Once in her chambers, she asked why the local community leaders were present in the court room. Our attorney responded, "we have been told that the builder told all of these community leaders how our firm had committed malpractice, thus slandering and possibly libeling our firm". The attorney went on to say that he had asked us to "not respond directly to these community leaders about those allegations and only to invite them to watch the builder's testimony. When the testimony of the truth, the whole truth and nothing but the truth was heard, there would be exoneration of our firm".

At that point in the chambers, the builder recognized the seriousness of what he had done. He finally knew his "goose was cooked". The judge told us that hearing the builder's testimony could damage the builder's reputation and possibly result in the closure of his business. Can you believe that? She was not worried about our reputation and the horrible things he had said about us; instead, she was worried about him and his reputation (a drug user and an adulterer). As stated, the legal system is not fair. Here is a guy with a frivolous lawsuit and the judge was more concerned about him than us.

Anyway, the community leaders were allowed to stay in the courtroom. Our attorney artfully dissected the builder's testimony. At the end of his testimony, it was evident the builder had not told the truth in his direct testimony. The builder was sweating, he broke down and he began to cry. It was obvious the builder wanted his testimony to end. The local community leaders initially laughed at his outrageous claims and then everyone began to feel sorry for him, the jury, the leaders and even our firm. Nonetheless, our attorney said it is important that the jury understand the truth. Our attorney was effective. The builder was humiliated because of his prior misrepresentations on the stand. Everyone now knew the truth. Mission accomplished.

At the conclusion of the trial, it only took the jury about 20 minutes to deliberate. We were awarded all of our fees, including interest, and all of the legal fees incurred by the insurance company. This was a financial victory and it felt good to be exonerated after 4 years of horrible things and countless hours to defend a frivolous lawsuit. This also resulted in a new disrespect of our legal system for allowing such a frivolous action to drag on so long.

The morning after the jury verdict, I delivered an entire case of chewing tobacco to our attorney at his office! Over subsequent years, our insurance company came around and understood that if we wanted to fight a particular case that the insurance company would support us. We tried to maintain an open communication process with the insurance company, especially before any lawsuit or collection action was ever initiated by our firm. We were successful in getting attorney fee awards in all cases, no exceptions.

On one hand, our practice of rigorously defending against frivolous lawsuits helps to protect all professionals in all professions. On the other hand, this practice of letting the attorney properly prepare a case, and for the CPA to spend countless hours in preparation, is costly, time consuming and difficult. Nonetheless, if more professionals would "stick this process out", I believe there would be fewer frivolous cases in the legal system.

And by the way, because of this builder's own testimony in this case, his business suffered losses as many of the community leaders would no longer do business with the builder. And finally, our firm would disengage from any client who used the same attorney as the builder. We found it was prudent to let them discuss the case with their attorney (we would not discuss it). We believed that it was easier to lose business than to take a "more than likely risk" that behavior would repeat itself from the same attorney. Each and every client, after discussing the matter with the other attorney, chose to remain as a client and change attorneys. What do you think?

Tigers Will Always Have Spots

One of the local public service activities I participated in over the years was donating my time to helping to instruct various groups certain income tax rules that related to that particular group. While teaching at a client real estate company some tax updates, I was introduced to a young man who was a real estate agent for that company. The young man was confident and arrogant. He lived a bit in the past. He used to play high school football and had a high opinion of his "prior football prowess". We have all met the "former jock". I had never heard of him but his behavior was similar to others that I have known. This particular young man had entered the real estate business and appeared to know many of the same people that I knew. We talked and talked, and, regardless of his lack of maturity, I somehow wanted to help this young man succeed.

An alarm should have gone off in my mind when I accepted him as a client as some of the other Realtors at the same company did not like this individual and told me not to trust him. At the time, I did not know if that was their insecurity or if they had legitimate concerns about the guy. As it turned out, he did not last too long at the real estate company and their warnings to me proved to be correct. Acceptance of a new client is something a CPA should not take lightly. I learned about client acceptance in this case.

When he turned up at our office the next time, he was no longer a Realtor. Instead, he was now a "builder". He had opened a construction company. He told me that he wanted to build commercial office buildings and multi family housing projects. And he requested that our firm prepare his income tax returns. He said he would prepare the company's financial statements himself without our help. He brought in a "partner", another young man. This young man appeared to be honest and sincere. I liked him also.

So, our office prepared income tax returns for the two of them. In addition, I introduced them to different people who I knew in the real estate and construction industry whom I believed could help the two young men. In that process, we went to professional and college sporting events, hosted by my acquaintances, that I had introduced the builders too. Through these referrals, the construction company had gained several construction contracts.

Their company had their own computer and they insisted they did not need CPA prepared financial statements. Instead, they only wanted to pay our firm to prepare their income tax returns. We entered into a standard and customary engagement agreement with them. This is normally referred to as an engagement letter. The engagement letter carefully indicated that we were only preparing income tax returns and no financial statements. Our firm used standard industry engagement letters for these types of letters.

As I was warned, the arrogant partner became more and more arrogant. One day, the "other builder" showed up and needed to discuss some cash flow concerns of the company. We talked briefly. It was apparent that the business was growing too quickly. The company seemed to be trying to do too many things with a limited amount of capital. I told them they seemed to be spending like "drunken sailors"! In addition, I advised them they needed to avoid paying personal type expenses through the company. In fact, I told them they should avoid all unnecessary expenses until the company could afford them. I warned him that if the partners did not take control of their growth and finances that they could lose everything. I was surprised that the arrogant partner was not at this meeting and asked where he was. And the partner just began laughing uncontrollably.

Laughing can be infectious. He was laughing so long that I began laughing and I did not know why. He began choking because he laughed so hard so he had to get a drink of water. He then started, "I am sorry, this is terrible (and it was about the arrogant partner)". He said, "You know how he can be arrogant and he pushes people around. He tried to single-handedly beat up a gang of about 6 guys after a professional football game". This guy could not stop laughing as he described in detail what happened to his business partner.

He said that the arrogant partner told the entire gang to leave another individual alone or he would personally beat up the entire gang. I understand that the gang was having fun after a football game with a street vendor. The head gang leader said, "Do you understand there are several of us and we could hurt you real bad if we wanted to?". And the builder said, "Go ahead, if you think you can, take off my lips!".

--- I understand an ambulance ultimately took the arrogant builder to the hospital after the beating. I understand his face was beaten with pipes and his eyes were knocked out of their sockets. It was a terrible thing; however, according to his own partner, the guy asked for it. And, his business partner was laughing and he could not stop laughing as he explained this to me. Although it is difficult to hear a guy got beat up and laugh, because of the laughter, I began to laugh. I felt terrible about this, but, you have to understand how arrogant this guy is. Someone needed to knock him down a peg or two. It is unfortunate it had to be this way though. Nonetheless, I needed water to stop from laughing too. And thankfully, the hospital was able to put "humpty dumpty back together again".

The above is to set the tone for what was to come.

Not too long after that, I received a telephone call from a banker who wanted to discuss a financial statement that our firm had supposedly prepared for a client. This is not unusual. Probably the number one user of a small company financial statement is the banker. Normal protocol was to get the client's permission. Then I would try to go over the questions with the client in attendance with the banker, or alternatively, having the client join the conference via telephone. So, I asked who the client was to the banker?

The banker told me it was the builder's company and the "financial statement that we prepared did not look right". As stated above, we had never been engaged to prepare a financial statement for this builder. I said I would have to get back to the banker and then I immediately telephoned the builder. I asked the arrogant builder what the banker could be talking about. I was told by the arrogant builder "I will take care of it".

Not too long after that, I was in the bank and the banker came out to greet me. She said that she expected a telephone call from me about our financial statement. I said that I had spoken to the client about it and since it was the client's financial statement, the client wanted to discuss it directly with the banker. The banker left, went into her office and returned with a financial statement "on our company letterhead". That is right, a financial statement on our letterhead for this company. To a third party reader, it appeared that we did indeed prepare a financial statement. However, as you know, we did not.

The builder had somehow created the letterhead and financial statement. Not only that, the financial statement was not prepared properly or even close to our firm policies. Our letterhead was used without our permission and without our knowledge. The client's actions were impermissible and wrong. In addition, the manner in which the letterhead was used was not in accordance with our company's financial presentation of a financial statement.

I could not comment to the banker other than to say that I was unfamiliar with the financial statement. I excused myself and telephoned the builder. He brushed it off, laughed and said "I did what I had to do". In other words, the arrogant builder had phonied up a financial statement and passed it on as something from our office.

After returning to the accounting practice, we had a professional meeting among our owners. The decision was made to contact the American Institute of Certified Public Accountants (AICPA) professional conduct committee as to how to proceed. We were told to "terminate the client and demand that the client withdraws the financial statement from the bank". We also demanded our outstanding accounting fees to be paid immediately. We did as we were advised to do.

Once again, we then got sued for malpractice from the arrogant builder because the financial statements he phonied up were not done in accordance with professional standards! The financial statements they gave to the bank was a fraud. The builder admitted this to me. Regardless, some attorneys will do anything. And we got served with a lawsuit. Now, protocol was that we had to report this to our insurance carrier. The insurance company appointed us legal counsel once again. We used the same attorney who successfully helped with the first case (above).

The arrogant builder had hired an attorney well known to our firm. In fact, we represented the legal firm as its CPA firm. This really made me upset. So we asked that the legal firm resign from the lawsuit because of its relationship to our firm. I then received a telephone call from the partner in charge of the legal firm. This was an older gentleman who was truly trying to give me good advice (that I did not want to hear at the time). However, I could not see it at the time as I was mad about the fraudulent financial statement, the builder, the action, etc. Seems the arrogant builder had "married well" and the builder's father in law was a successful local politician; thus, the connection to this successful attorney.

The attorney asked me, "Who would you rather have representing a matter like this, us, or a contentious legal firm?". It is hard to explain the emotions of getting sued when you know that the whole matter is frivolous. And when you know the legal firm who wanted to represent the "other guy" (like we did) only compounded the emotion. I thought the courts would immediately see this case for what it was. I wanted to make it as hard on the builder as possible for his dishonesty. I became a bit emotionally involved in the case at the time. We asked the legal firm (a client of our firm) to resign from the builder. This legal firm is a reputable firm. They resigned. The builder then hired a really irritable and frivolous attorney. In retrospect, I should have listened to the advice from the old and wise attorney. The emotional part is really hard to explain though.

When there is a totally frivolous suit, it is possible to get the frivolous lawsuit dismissed through what I understand is generally referred to as a summary judgment action. Our attorney simply goes into court, explains what happened and then the court rules to make the case go away. The result is that we get exonerated with the bank and we also get paid if we prevail. And in a case this egregious, it seemed logical that this would be taken care of immediately.

This is generally true, "except when the father in law is politically connected". The judge initially ruled that she believed the builder had a good case and denied the summary judgment action! Can you believe that? We later learn that the initial judge ruling on the initial summary judgment action was also a close personal friend of the "father in law". Again, another judge and more judicial misconduct. I do not believe in these circumstances that this judge should have heard this case.

So, after another 3 years for this case, and as we went into court, we were offered a stipulated judgment. In other words, they would pay both our prior accounting fees plus our attorney's fees. We just had to wait until the builder sold something. We took this offer; rather than proceeding. There seemed to be no downside. A few years passed, interest accrued on the outstanding obligation and I received a telephone call from the arrogant builder. He had not changed.

The former client told me he had a real estate transaction closing and he needed us to release the judgment so he could close a particular property. He then said he would pay off the judgment but in order to do so, he needed a "slight discount". He told me how "bad it was for his wife and family" and apologized for his prior behavior. I felt sorry for him and said we would discount the amount he owed by $5,000, subject to one condition. That condition was he never spoke to anyone at our firm or he never spoke to anyone in the families of my partner and I again. Frankly, I would have paid a lot more than that to get away from the "stench" that this guy had all over him. He agreed. This was one of the best decisions I ever made.

And by the way, his business partner also left the builder due to trust reasons. And when I think back about the builder I remember the gang members beating him to near death. I still laugh when I think about it. By the way, I read that the legal firm that represented the matter against our firm did not get paid. Ultimately, that attorney also sued the arrogant builder for non payment of fees in the case with our firm. Surprising?

Do Not Landscape With Mud

The best referrals to a CPA generally come from happy clients. High quality professional service is a CPA's best marketing tool. If a CPA has a happy client, that client will introduce a CPA to other business people who also need a good CPA. Over the years, I received many good referrals from happy clients. And occasionally an unanticipated terrible referral comes along from one of those good clients. I am confident this was not done purposely by this client in referring this "dirt bag" to our firm.

One of my favorite clients owned a company that sold landscaping products to landscape companies. I can not explain just how great a person this individual is; that is, the already existing client. While the existing client was in my office one day, he mentioned that one of his landscape installation customers was going through a messy divorce. He told me that his customer was having serious cash flow problems and needed to consult with me. He told me that he understood the "estranged wife" emptied the company bank account. He then asked me if I would meet with his customer/individual. I agreed.

During the first meeting with a client, I try to keep good notes as to what the client's expectation is for the CPA, what they believe the problems are, what I believe we can do for them, including whether or not we want to represent the client. Over the years, I gained valuable experience in learning which clients we could not only help, but in addition, which clients we could establish a good relationship with. During this time period I was right more often than I was wrong. But occasionally, as in this case, I was wrong.

The client told me that his estranged spouse had stolen money from his business. He showed me where the funds had left the business account. As a result, he told me that he was unable to pay his bills as they became due. He said he had made arrangements with his suppliers to defer payment until he could work himself out of the problem. He told me that his wife had kept all of the company books and that he was shocked that she would take the money without his knowledge and without his permission. I kept good notes of this initial meeting.

We met several times to help him with the overall accounting of the business. This included introducing his new bookkeeper to one of our accountants, helping the client write letters to his bank and other vendors and generally try to help bring his accounting current. When everything was progressing as expected based upon my experience with these types of matters, I assigned the account to one of our other CPA offices and to another owner in the firm. Whereas, I would still be available, the services that were then needed were reasonably able to be provided by others within our firm.

About a year later, I noticed that there was a large outstanding bill from this client. I recalled that his business was doing better and he had been current on the bill while I was involved in the client work. However, the bill seemed to be increasing and payments had not been received in quite a while. The general office policy would be to have a primary responsible billing person review each client's bill each month. If something appeared unusual with the account, the matter should be resolved immediately. The next month, if the matter had not been resolved, then I would get involved with contacting the client.

The reason I was initially told the bill had not paid was that the client "reconciled with his wife" and the wife "was doing the books again". This reconciliation was one that I did not anticipate. The immediate concern was that she may have been up to her old tricks again. And, that was not paying vendor bills and taking money from the company accounts.

We also learned that other vendors were not being paid again. My concern was absolutely right.

So, as was normal and customary, I telephoned the client. Although I was assured "payment was coming", it did not show up. It was then my standard practice to schedule a meeting with the client, together with the accountant in charge of the engagement and another owner of our firm. The client came in for the meeting with his spouse. And, the meeting did not go well.

The spouse was not a good bookkeeper. But saying this was very touchy, especially because of their fragile marital history and what the client had told us about her taking money from the accounts. I found over the years that when a business is not keeping regular and continuous "proper books" that there is more often than not a reason. And that is, if you are taking money from the company improperly, the last thing you want someone to find out is that you are manipulating the books. Thus, the books fall behind, the books become sloppy and the financial statements simply are wrong. She was trying desperately to get her husband to change back to the original accounting firm. It seemed that the other firm was not as "hands on" and she was able to get away with doing her books however she wanted. We had higher expectations for our clients and certain behaviors would lead to termination by our firm if the client refused to properly maintain their books.

While the husband wanted to believe things were different, in his heart I believe he knew what the problems were once again. I gave him credit for being loyal to his spouse. Our firm demanded payment for the bill.

At that point in the meeting, the wife became "hostile" ranting and raving and yelling and screaming using horrible language. That type of behavior is never good. My normal response was, "I understand you believe you do not have the money at this time; however, I do not like the tone of how you are expressing yourself". I asked her to bring the language down and not to swear at anyone from our firm.

They left and the bill did not get paid. We suspended services and demanded the bill. We were sued for malpractice.

Concurrently, they told many of our clients that we were incompetent, including my aforementioned friend and client. That bothered me; however, we are not allowed to give confidential information concerning a client account. Instead, we could only say how sorry we were that our other clients were getting into the middle of something, but hopefully, at the end of the matter, they would be more fully informed.

At this point in time, because of all the hullabaloo that the former client had made, we had to make a decision to either walk away, or alternatively, pursue the matter through the legal system. Frankly, because of all of the feedback from our client base, we concluded that we would let this issue go through the normal legal process, if for no other reason, than to simply clear our name and maintain our reputation.

Of course the former client found the "type of attorney" who has to represent these types of matters. As the matter got closer to a court date, the accusations and allegations against our firm escalated. Then, the local court, together with agreement by the parties via our engagement letter, moved the matter to a binding arbitration forum. Sometimes, this is better for a professional. Sometimes, a professional does not want a jury to listen to a case as the "other side" simply tries to profile a professional prejudice in order to win. And I have found the allegations do not have to be true before a jury, the allegations simply need to be "convincing". Advocacy?

With an arbitrator or mediator, the "innocent" party simply hopes for a well qualified arbitrator or mediator with experience in similar matters. This is important because some arbitrators and mediators who I have known are not either qualified or experienced in all matters. Sometimes, they are "failing attorneys" simply trying to supplement their own personal income. Sometimes these arbitrators have their own personal agenda. Many times the arbitrators can be even worse. The hope is that on your "day in court" that you get a good, honest, qualified, and experienced individual to arbitrate or mediate your case. By and large there are many great arbitrators and mediators. However, if you go to arbitration/mediation, once again, you take your chances.

I had not met the arbitrator for our case that was assigned by the court. However, I knew the arbitrator by reputation and also was aware of the legal firm by reputation. Both were favorable. Accordingly, I felt "better" about the process concerning this particular matter. Nonetheless, it is always possible to get a poor ruling even from a good arbitrator. Those are in the minority though.

Prior to the arbitration, we were offered "you forget your fee and we will drop our charges" by the other side. What a surprise! They literally make up charges and make up an entire case and then do what all the frivolous attorneys try to do. And that is, they do not want to really have to go to work.

On the other hand, we were required to prepare for the case. That is, we needed to have support for all of the items in our complaint against them, but also, support to impugn anything that the other side may allege. And, we were prepared. The accountant in charge, the other owner and I were all in attendance. So the net result is that our CPA firm lost a lost of money because of a loss of productivity to have all of these professionals in attendance. We otherwise would have made that money if we had not prepared for this case and had we simply been working on anything else in our office.

By the way, when a frivolous complaint is filed, regardless of what your contract with the client states, courts have been unwilling to reimburse the CPA for the time they have to put into a case to simply defend themselves from frivolous charges. I believe this is well known to the court system and legal community and that this unfair practice is allowed to simply go on and perpetuate itself within the legal system.

The other side counts on the fact that we might want to simply settle the case. What they underestimated was the nature and hostile comments that had been made about our firm to many of our clients. We had to pursue this matter to the bitter end.

As another segway, I recall a private dinner that my wife and I attended with a few elected officials and their spouses. At the time, I was President of the WSCPA. I was asked a question about "tort reform". It seems one of the elected officials had written a bill concerning a "3 strikes and your out" rule for the medical profession. In other words, if a doctor commits malpractice 3 times in 10 years, then the doctor should lose his license. He asked me what I thought about his bill?

I told him that his bill "did not include CPAs so I did not need to worry about it". He then pressed me if I knew about the bill. My response was backhanded. I said, "Yes, I believe any attorney who files 3 frivolous lawsuits in 10 years should be disbarred". He said that was not how his bill was written. I told him that I understood that and asked why he wouldn't write the bill that way too. I told him of the numerous frivolous lawsuits that I had seen, just in our own doctor client base.

He told me that the frivolous lawsuit issue is not a concern. "It really does not happen", according to the politician. I said, "You are living in denial if you believe it does not happen". I then told him of at least seven (7) medical clients that I had who had all left the State of Washington over frivolous lawsuits (that they had all won). I summarized some important details about each case. Then, when each of those doctors received their malpractice renewal costs, the premiums were unaffordable. Ultimately, each doctor had to move to another state that allowed them to work at a reasonable insurance cost. I explained to the politician that I met with these individuals, some of whom were crying in my office, they were literally crying. They had done nothing wrong, but they were getting sued. The court system allows it, the insurance companies profit by it and the doctors can not afford it. One way to bring the health care costs down would be to eliminate frivolous lawsuits. He apologized and told me that he just did not know. I told him, "You were not listening to the folks who told you otherwise". Since then, that politician and I have become pretty good acquaintances --- not friends though.

Another quick segway concerning our legal system --- I was fortunate to be in another country and meeting with a communist party leader in that part of the country (sort of like a governor of a state if here in the US). While in that country I noticed garbage on the sides of the road, air pollution and the fact that you could not drink groundwater in that country (due to the garbage and pollution). As a guest in his county, I was surprised to learn how disrespected our country's legal system is compared to their own. His wife was initially afraid to touch me as I was seen as American and uncivilized. Because of his position in government, there were uniformed people in the room with us with semi automatic rifles the first night we had dinner (remember our country allows guns and we are the only country to launch a nuclear attack).

He said at the time that we have the most corrupt legal system in the world. We are the only country to allow people to kill people, rape women, molest children, sell drugs --- and --- we give our criminals free legal help, free room and board, free health care, and free legal help --- and we give our victims nothing! Quite an observation from clear across the world.

So, back to our case. The arbitrator did not really want to arbitrate. He wanted us to settle and to walk away. We refused. And the other party was in the room. The arbitrator asked why we would want to arbitrate such a small amount? Our attorneys told him (the collection attorney and the malpractice defense attorney) that we had no choice. That the other party had said some horrific things about us to many of our clients. And many of those clients who have told us of the libelous statements we had referred to the person whom we are now suing to collect our accounting fee (initially we tried to help his business). Upon completion of this case, we would simply let the clients who had contacted us know of the result from the arbitration. Then we would disengage from any client who wanted to continue to use the defendant in this matter.

Ultimately, the case went on. Once again, we had to listen to some ridiculous and untrue allegations. Nothing the other side alleged had any support. The stories went on and on and on and on and on and on --- get the point. Sometimes if you keep saying the same thing over and over again, the mediator will begin to believe it. Although this sounds crazy, it can be absolutely true.

The former client then made a serious allegation about me. He said that our original contract called for a payment of $5,000. He testified, under oath, under the penalty of perjury, that he had given me $5,000 all in cash. And, he testified that I personally kept the money and did not give it to our accounting firm. He also testified that he could prove that I took the $5,000. He testified that he always carried large sums of cash in his wallet. He was making stuff up on the spot.

I noticed a little "body language" from the arbitrator. It was clear that the arbitrator did not believe the guy. However, the testimony was "under oath and under the penalty of perjury".

Upon cross examination, we simply took the high road and asked him many questions. First of all, and to deflect the actual "tough testimony", we asked him questions about our initial meeting. We went through my copious notes. It was funny that he was denying everything. He denied seeing it and denied saying any of it. And, the information that he was reading was coming from an email that he ultimately learned that he had sent to me.

We were also able to show "balanced books" from our accounting department that did not agree to his wife's books. We asked him how he could explain her changes. Although she was there, they could not answer the questions concerning the changes.

However, once you get a guy that is willing to misrepresent anything, you can "lead them to slaughter". We then got back to the $5,000 cash questions and he must have believed those allegations against me to be an "after thought" and we would let that statement "go". We asked if he remembered that he testified that he could prove that I took $5,000. He said "absolutely". We asked him how long it would take. He said he could do it almost immediately.

The arbitrator had heard enough. The arbitrator asked "How long do you need to take to prove it?". Well, a few days went to a week, then to a few weeks, and finally to 2 months. We agreed. We could wait 2 months. The arbitrator looked at me and asked if he could prove it. I said that "It never happened, and if he can prove it to anyone, I will give everyone in the room $5,000 each. That was, the former client, his wife, his attorney, our attorneys, the other two from our firm and the arbitrator!". The arbitrator then told him that if he could not prove it, he would lose the entire case.

Then to mess with him a bit we asked a closing question, "Please open your wallet and show the arbitrator how much cash you are carrying with you today". Is it any surprise that he had $3 in his wallet!

We all walked out to the parking lot together. By now, the former client and his wife were well aware that they were going to lose this case. More important though is that they figured out that they were also going to lose all of our mutual clients. As the realization of what was going to happen sunk in to those people, they tried to apologize for all the lies, the inconvenience and trouble that he had caused our firm and to me for the past 3 years. He begged our forgiveness.

As expected, in the end, they lost the case and they also lost substantially all of the mutual clients. The original client who had referred this person to me was very apologetic for involving our office with such a schmuck! He also terminated his relationship with that deadbeat.

Time to Fight Back

In 33 years, I was only told 3 times that we "did not charge enough"! Normally, the telephone calls would go the "other way". Sometimes I could get 3 calls in a day questioning our billings. Although that was unusual, I want to show that it is not unusual to get telephone calls from clients who are trying to figure out why the bill is what the bill is.

A majority of the time, the client simply needs to be listened to, then I simply explained what we did, how much time it took to do it and I always closed by saying I was sorry about the bill. In other words, empathize with the client. And, if your clients are good business people, you would expect them to call you from time to time.

There are generally 3 types of "billing" telephone calls that you get:

1   Provide the client with the correct information as efficiently as possible and the bill would generally be resolved during the telephone call,

2   Provide the same information and make a concession on the bill, and,

3   Sometimes you "can not deal with stupid".

As to #2, if there is a good client and they still question the bill, even if the bill is justified, then the CPA firm has a problem, even if the bill is correct. So, a decision has to be made. And that is, how to adjust the bill. A majority of these calls are taken care of with only one telephone call. Frankly, the clients sometime "want a break" but sometimes the client is "absolutely right". Regardless, if it is a good client that does not complain "a lot" then I found the concession was a great way to go. You do it, they like it and long term everyone wins.

As to #3, "sometimes you can not deal with stupid", this goes without saying. Regardless of what you may say, the client has either an ulterior motive for the call or they just do not want to pay. Sometimes, they do want a concession because you already gave them one in #2 above. So a decision has to be made. Generally, this includes resigning from the account. But what is the best way to resign?

I found that with many clients in #3, they are not going to pay anything regardless. So, it was not uncommon to send these clients to collection and simply move on. Many times it could take months or years to get paid. Sometimes, the client would act surprised by a collection notice and simply try to pay you directly. But even before that, I found there was something else that I could do. That was to simply tell the client to "Pay what you believe is fair for our services". Once we received that amount, we would wait for their check to clear, then resign. We found it was the easiest way to collect a compromised amount and simply move on.

Out of 100 telephone calls, probably 67% were #1, 30% were #2 and the balance #3. No one likes to resign from a client, but it is sometimes the best thing to do.

In this particular case that I am now going to summarize, I had been practicing over 20 years. I had not met this client. He was a client of a CPA working in another office of our firm. The background of the client was that we performed services for 3 years worth of accounting and income tax services. Upon inception of this engagement, the client had not filed business forms, payroll taxes or forms, or income tax returns in 3 years. The other office of ours caught everything up with them and they did not pay us anything. We turned them over to collection.

3 years later, we got paid through the collection company. Then, the client wanted us to perform more services for them. Our firm policy is NO. Prior behavior by these types of clients is an indication of their future behavior. However, I had not met this client as this client's services were performed in another office. Although our firm policies were clear concerning disengaging from a former client such as this, at least we thought so, the manager of our office agreed to perform more services for this client once again.

And guess what? The client had not filed business forms, payroll taxes or forms, or income tax returns in the 3 years since we suspended services the last time! So, our professional staff had to gather information for 3 more years --- accounting, business and payroll taxes, income taxes, and other records. The professional staff were able to catch everything up for this client and assist in getting all tax returns filed to the proper authorities. And guess what? After our office caught up all of the work the client did not pay us once again! Is it any surprise?

The fee for the professional services provided totaled about $17,000. As a result of our services, the client had received more than $100,000 in refunds. Nonetheless, the client initially refused to pay for these services once again. Then the client alleged that he never received the income tax refunds. Prior to forwarding this delinquent bill to collection, I was asked to step in by our management team and try to help resolve the unpaid bill directly with the client. So, I researched the matter prior to telephoning the owner of the client company. I also wanted to familiarize myself with the history of the account relationship and the specific services that were provided by our firm.

I then telephoned the client to discuss the unpaid bill. He told me at the time that he did not get the refunds and he was waiting for those refunds in order to pay his bill. I explained to him that our engagement letter (agreement) was clear. That we expected to be paid monthly regardless of whether or not he would receive any refunds. A CPA cannot promise a refund and generally cannot work on a contingency anyway. Based upon my experience in similar types of telephone calls I came to the conclusion that he was simply trying to stall me.

Frankly, we did not know if he got refunds or not, we only knew he was entitled to the refunds and that the requisite forms were filed with the proper taxing authorities. I then asked him again why he had not paid the bill. He explained to me that his business had "cash flow issues". Frankly, it all began to sound reasonable to me. So, my compromise proposal with him was that if he paid his bill by the end of the calendar year that we would simply write off all of our finance charges. I also told him that I would personally have the files transferred to me so I could personally review them. He said thank you and assured me the bill would be fully paid by the end of the month, which was our year end.

We only received a token $2,000 payment on the account. So, once again we sent his delinquent bill to our collection agency. That is, another one of his accounts to collection. And this time he counter sued us for malpractice in order to try to avoid paying his bill to our firm.

Unfortunately for him, this was poor timing on his part. At the same time, one of our partners was retiring and we were concurrently bringing in 3 new partners to our firm. One of those 3 new partners was seriously ill at the time. In other words, there was a lot going on at the time and I finally had enough of the frivolous lawsuits. So, it was time for me to have fun with a "complete dirt bag"!

I had the files all moved to the local office that I worked out of, our "home office". It turned out this was a good thing. And, in those days while in good health, I could commit a file to almost absolute memory. That was a good thing too! And I believed the work that the firm did was very good, certainly at or above industry and professional standards. In other words, he did not have a case. I was not surprised as my suspicions came true; that is, this was a frivolous lawsuit.

To help protect our firm, our CPA firm generally entered contracts for professional services with all of our business clients. Generally, a CPA obtains an "engagement letter" (contract) with a client. Even though we had 3 offices, venue for any disputes would always be nearest to our executive office (my office). So, I knew that a key in this case to accomplishing what I wanted was to fight to keep venue in our "home town". We put a lot of time into just that. There was quite a bit of discovery on the issue. And of course, his legal counsel was complaining and objecting to this venue. Although it initially cost us a lot to insure that venue would be near our home office, we prevailed on that issue.

And, an engagement letter generally provides for interest to be paid on the delinquent bill at the maximum rate allowed by law. In addition, in the case of a dispute, assuming we prevailed in the collection and the defense of the frivolous lawsuit, an additional award of attorney and related fees was included in our standard engagement letter. So, in the big picture, the spirit and intent of the engagement letter was that if the CPA prevails in the case, the CPA should be made monetarily whole by being paid the bill, plus interest plus the costs of the matter. This does not include the CPA's time to collect the bill or the time of the administrative and other people in the CPA firm. But, it did include reimbursement for attorney fees and other legal costs.

During the time this matter was ongoing, I found that it was more fun to sit back and observe as his attorney endeavored to craftfully manipulate the case. Our strategy was more simple with the frivolous allegations against our firm. We simply waited and waited and allowed the case to be dragged on and on and on. And guess what? If the former client did not pay us, he did not pay his attorney either! Hence, different legal firms on their side seemed to come and go over this time period. I recall about 6 different legal firms were used over the course of our dispute. I understand that he did not pay his legal firms either. There seems to be a pattern of poor behavior with professionals. "Go figure".

As a segway here, we represented many legal firms. I found that many of their clients did not pay their legal bills. A prudent person might think that a legal firm would simply sue a client or former client for their fees. However, I found most legal firms to be terrible "collectors" and simply would not rigorously pursue their unpaid legal fees. Maybe the attorneys were smarter than me. Maybe they were not as good of business people. Maybe they should understand that if another professional is not being paid that they may not be paid either.

Such was the case with the first 5 different legal firms over the first 10 years of this case! Yes, 6 different legal firms represented our former client against us in a frivolous case. All of which ultimately resigned for non payment of their fees too! As this matter progressed, rather than identify the attorney by name, I simply identified the attorney by number! By the way, the attorneys did not like that.

And, it took almost 10 years for the former client's attorneys to depose me. I understood they had been trying to get me in the same room with the former client for not paying his bill and to try to intimidate me somehow. Prior to my deposition with the former client and his attorney, we deposed his successor CPA. Among other issues, they were trying to learn who our expert witness(es) was/were. For your information, at one time I was President of the WSCPA and had been a liaison to our professional conduct committee. Our expert in the case was the then chair of the professional conduct and ethics committee. Our questions for him were "was the work good, and, was the fee reasonable?". For both questions, his answer was a simple "yes".

Accordingly, the former client's successor CPA would not testify to malpractice on the part of our office. In fact, during a break in his deposition, he introduced himself to me and said he knew of me by my "stellar reputation", to use his words. And, as it turned out, at no time could the former client's attorneys find an expert to testify against our firm in this matter. I had also done our homework and sort of "covered all the bases of all the leading experts", in order to make it difficult for them to find one of the top notch experts. So these experts became aware of this case and these experts refused to testify against us also. The experts I had missed or did not know obviously passed on this case too. Sometimes the experts are smarter than the attorneys. They expect to be paid!

So, we deposed the then (successor) CPA of our former client. The CPA could not find any fault with our services, so his concern became about the amount of the fees that we charged for the 3 years of services. Remember, by this time we had the client's sworn testimony that "the refunds were never received". And, by the way, the former client was unable to attend this deposition. The former client told us through his attorney that he was "in hospital for a much needed surgery".

When we asked the new CPA about the whereabouts of his client, he told us that the guy was "in Hawaii on vacation!". Contradicting testimony? Of course the other attorney said that was "not relevant to the case". When we asked the new CPA if he knew about the status of the refunds, the CPA did something that I did not expect. And, I thought that I had seen just about everything in this type of testimony over the years. I learned to expect the worst. As it turned out, the new CPA had ordered a "transcript" from the Internal Revenue Service (IRS) in anticipation of the deposition.

A transcript is normally a "year by year" document that summarizes all of the income taxes assessed and when they were paid. And, if any refunds were issued, when those refunds were issued. The CPA voluntarily brought the transcript to his deposition and began reading from the transcript like it was a "revelation". He was certainly proud that he had requested this document. He told us that the former client received all of the refunds, plus interest, from the IRS. He then gave the date of the refunds. As it turned out, the actual date that the taxpayer received all of the refunds was MONTHS BEFORE I SPOKE TO THE FORMER CLIENT THE FIRST TIME. In other words, when the client originally told me he did not get the refunds, he already had them! I was not surprised that he had the refunds. I was surprised that his new CPA told us about that.

Requests for production of the documents are a common occurrence in these types of matters. Frankly, we wanted a copy of the transcripts from the IRS. We were not allowed to ask for these ourselves from the IRS as we were no longer the CPA for that client. But now we received testimony form his CPA that the transcripts were in this CPA's possession. Generally, there is a procedure to go through the courts to obtain a copy of the documents in the other party to the matter's possession. First, we tried to get the transcript attached to the new CPA's deposition in order to obtain such transcript the same day. Then, we had to go through the court system to obtain the transcripts. So, a couple of perjuries were noted by the former client's sworn testimony under oath in sworn statements to the court. First, he was not getting a surgery (and was instead vacationing in Hawaii) and second he had received the IRS refunds that he testified that he never had received. I had learned over and over that the court system is reluctant to hold people like this liable for such perjurious statements. That is an ongoing disappointment for me. And the court system did nothing in this case either.

Rather than move for summary judgment in this matter and accelerate the case with this new information, we became even more patient. And upon the "return from Hawaii/so called surgery", we finally subpoenaed the former client to his first deposition (after more than 9 years). By this time, he was invested in 5 legal firms and hundreds of thousands of dollars in legal fees and his new CPA fees (to get out of paying us $15,000). I assumed by this time he was into his defense a couple or a few hundred thousand dollars. I learned he was a very proud and arrogant man and he was trying to win this frivolous case and was surprised that we would not walk away from such a bill.

Prior to his deposition though, he wanted to have a prior and retired owner of our firm deposed. At the time, it seemed the client was alleging that I had said bad things about him to this former owner of our firm. The schmuck (former client) learned through another affidavit from this prior owner, that the prior owner had spoken to me about this case. So, naturally, his attorney wanted to "try to sue me!" personally. Remarkable. The dirt-bag refused to pay his bill and his attorney wanted to make me somehow liable.

During the the retired partner's testimony, I was pleasantly surprised that when he was asked what kind of accountant I am, his response was, "the absolute very best CPA I had ever met". He then asked about if he spoke to me about this case outside of the office. The prior partner said "yes". He then asked "where did this discussion take place?". As it turned out, the discussion was brief, it was on the green of a golf course, and the prior partner had indicated that he "needed access to the client files to answer questions from our attorney" about this case. His testimony was that my involvement was making a cell phone call to our file clerk and directing her to "allow access" to these records. The former partner was asked again and again, "what else did you talk about?". He kept telling the truth, that is, that was the only discussion we had about this case prior to the date of my former partner's deposition.

So, during the former client's deposition, I finally got to meet the dirt-bag face to face for the first time; almost 10 years after the former client created the mess. And, he was not a "happy guy about this". He did not like having to pay what he had paid already to our firm, the new CPA firm and to all of the attorneys, not to mention what he did not pay to this group of professionals. I tried to be as professional and cordial as I could be, under the circumstances. I referred to the delinquent client as "Sir" and "Mister "name"". He was not so gracious. And at normal and customary breaks during the deposition, I was even nice to his current attorney. During his verbal testimony he bragged, "you will never get paid anyway, I transferred all of the assets from the old company to a new company!".

What a stupid thing to testify to. I began writing down questions while our attorney plugged on with the original questioning.

The new questions included:

"1   What is the name of the new company?

2   What is the physical address of the new company?

3   What is the telephone number of the new company?

4   Who are the owners of the new company?

5   What are their addresses?

6   What are their telephone numbers?

7   How do we get a hold of these people?

8   Were they aware of this lawsuit?"

It turned out the address of the new business was the same, the telephone numbers were the same and the spouse and child of the guy were also owners in the new company. He bragged that they knew about this lawsuit and his attorney told him we would not get paid --- EVER. We took great notes and his deposition testimony was being recorded. Upon completion of these questions, we took a short break. The break was needed to bring the legal assistant into the mix. We decided that it was timely to prepare all the documents while the other parties were in our attorney's office to sue the new company and the other owners. In other words, they wrongfully received assets from the original company that could be construed to be a "fraudulent conveyance" based upon his own testimony under oath and under the penalty of perjury. It was my goal to have the wife and son served with the new lawsuit prior to the former client finishing the deposition that same day! And, of course we insisted that they get their own independent attorneys. That was the "proper" thing to do.

In other words, the goal was to allow them to pay hundreds of thousands of dollars for their frivolous claim in order for them to try to get out of paying the $15,000 (plus interest and attorney fees) that they owed our firm. I believed this would be a great lesson for this guy.

At the end of the deposition day, I thanked both the former client and the then attorney for their time and said "I wished that the lawsuit had not been filed as he seemed like a nice guy". This was word for word what our attorney had told me to say. Almost simultaneously, I remember the former client receiving a telephone call from his wife. She was not pleased she was now getting sued too! I could hear her screaming at him to settle this case. He was not happy. Our attorney said, "All we want is to get paid". He refused. We left.

The next week the former client showed up at my office without an appointment and without any notice whatsoever. He demanded to see me to try to "settle the case". I agreed and invited another owner into the office to "witness" the discussion that would occur. The former client refused to come in because another owner would be present and he demanded that I "meet with him alone". I then explained to him that "you lied to me 10 years ago when you told me you would pay the bill by the end of the month, so you will never get to speak to me alone, ever again. If you do not like that, then you are free to leave". He stayed.

He began talking about the so called "merits of his case". I told him that he had no case. I reminded him who our expert was and pointed out that we understood he did not have one. I said that all we need to wait for is the court date and we would receive what he owed us. I told him I was surprised that he would do this over $15,000. He then asked "if I pay you the $15,000 then you will walk away from the case?". I said it was not "our intent to make more than the contract allowed" and I paged our billing clerk to bring in the current statement on his account. The total had grown to about "$126,000, plus or minus, with finance charges at 18% and with our attorney fees".

He said he was "shocked". He refused to pay that amount. I explained to him that "all we wanted was what he owed us". He said we "would never get that #**#** amount". I mentioned that if he did not want to pay it that we would begin preparing for the court case and I would try to finally obtain a court date (that had been so elusive to him up to that time). He did not leave very happy.

Later, he had another attorney. At the time, we were preparing for trial and I wanted to end the case for other personal reasons. So, we engaged another attorney to assist our primary attorney for settlement purposes only. The attorney I had selected had a reputation of being the best litigator in these types of cases. I wanted "the appearance" of him in order for the "other side" to know I was serious. When it was evident that there was an imminent court date, we once again allowed the other side to settle.

They settled with us. We got paid! In the process, I believe the other side incurred hundreds of thousands of dollars litigating a frivolous lawsuit over what initially began as only $15,000. A lawsuit that he started and later learned that he could not get out of the litigation until it ran its course. Lesson learned? By this time, I had substantial experience with this and other frivolous lawsuits against our firm and others, and, as bad as it was to allow this to happen, I believe it "screamed loudly that our legal system does not work when the system openly allows frivolous lawsuits against professionals". Of course justice was served with this case, and it took over 10 years to do this. I am confident most people would not have done what I did to "educate" this person. The moral of the story was that I can be a bit sneaky with the legal system too.

Give Me Your Best Shot

A prominent young local real estate businessman was introduced to me. At the time we met, he seemed to say all of the right things to me. He had acquired different real estate holdings, all in different entities. In addition, he also owned a local restaurant. Plus, he had his own development company.

I was able to consult with him and to "add value" to his companies. He paid for the consultations as the consultations and subsequent followup saved him hundreds of thousands of dollars. When it was income tax time, I introduced his bookkeeper to another one of our firm CPAs who was competent to prepare all of the various income tax returns.

As stated, there were several entities and it took months to complete all of the income tax returns. The client's bookkeeper did not prioritize the income tax returns, there were several delays by the client and ultimately the services for the income tax returns were not paid. Months and months of services were provided. Frankly, the accountant whom I had assigned the relationship to should have called my attention to the delinquent billings immediately. I believe it becomes partly the fault of the CPA if the CPA allows that type of behavior by the client. Any disagreement or difference with a bill should be addressed at the end of the first month of nonpayment by a client.

Nonetheless, because of the "local reputation" of the businessman, he was able to get away with a few additional months of non payment. When it came to my attention, it was concurrent with an income tax return that I was asked to "sign off" on. In other words, one of the latter income tax returns required some of my services and I was unwilling to perform any services until the client and I had an "opportunity" to discuss the outstanding balances. I therefore asked our CPA and the client bookkeeper to arrange a meeting with the client and asked the bookkeeper to make sure he brought a checkbook to pay for our services.

When he came in, it was obvious that he was not happy. I asked him how he was, how is businesses were doing, etc.? Then, I asked him why we had not received any payment for several months on any of his different companies for our services. He leaned back in his chair and said "I haven't seen any of your bills". By that time, I had experience with these types of clients and came prepared to this meeting. I immediately put a stack of bills for each company in front of him. He was startled and surprised the bills were already prepared and neatly organized for him. And these were just copies of the bills he had already received each month. He then said, "I have not been given anything to review the time spent by your firm on any of these bills". I then handed him a file for each one of the stacks of billing files, one for each entity, showing the charges, by tenth of an hour for each and every billing. In other words, every charge for several months was already summarized for him.

It was obvious that he still wanted to delay payment. He looked at me and said, "I do not believe you trust me". I simply said, "You have not paid your bill in months, our owners are coming to our own conclusions about you". He then said that he "felt he shouldn't pay anything in these circumstances". I said "OK and asked him to leave the office". Because he was a popular businessman in town, I simply wanted him to leave.

He then asked about the income tax return that I was asked to review and sign. I explained to him that we would not be issuing a return and I would not be performing any more services unless all the bills were agreed upon and paid. He then said he "refused to pay us anything then". I told him that I didn't believe he was going to pay the bills anyway and asked him to leave. Good riddance!

Later that day, two of his attorneys showed up in our lobby and began loudly threatening our receptionist. They demanded the incomplete income tax return. They demanded that I review the income tax return immediately and issue the return with our receptionist! Our receptionist was visibly shaken. I was listening to the exchange from my office and did not tolerate that type of behavior towards our staff.

I dialed "911" and I then walked into our lobby to speak to the attorneys while the police were in route to our office. Not long into the conversation the local police showed up. I explained the threats that I had witnessed and before long, one of the attorneys was handcuffed. I said that we had never before met these individuals (attorneys), we did not even know who they said they were, we did not tolerate threats, and our intent was to press charges.

As an aside, in those days, I volunteered my time for all 3 of the local police departments, plus the sheriff's office. The local police were simply returning a favor by showing up so quickly.

Once the loud attorney was handcuffed, he did not seem to yell as loud anymore. Go figure. I then asked him who he was and what he wanted? I asked him if anyone from our office had done anything to him that resulted in his poor behavior? He became apologetic. With the police there, I asked if he could think of a reasonable solution to the problem that he had caused.

After searching his conscience, he proposed that if I finished the last return that day, he would personally see that all of our bills were paid from all of the entities. That seemed fair. So I stayed late, finished everything and the attorney came in the next day with several checks, one from each of the entities. Prior to delivering the income tax return, our office obtained current and signed engagement letters and representation letters. Each representation letter indicated that our work was proper and the fee for the work was reasonable. We had both the client and one of the attorneys sign each letter.

The checks did not clear. We later found out that we were given checks from accounts that were closed and the former client had stopped payment on all of the other checks. I subsequently learned that knowingly issuing a check form a closed account can be a crime. So, we decided to engage the sheriff's office to have this man served with several subpoenas around town, only, one at a time in a very public place: as examples, Master Builders, Economic Development Council, Chamber of Commerce, Rotary, Church, etc. Seemed if he wanted to play the multiple entity game, that we should play too.

It did not take long for him to call me to "chat" about what he had done. He said that he was embarrassed to have been served in front of people who respected him. I told him it was my goal to explore all legal channels against him for what he had done, regardless of the money. I went on to tell him that he still had our money (as he owed the amounts billed) and we would allow him to go to court to learn who would ultimately prevail. Nonetheless, we were able to come to an agreement and get paid for our services.

We did not press charges against the attorney for the threats nor against him for issuing checks on closed accounts.

Be Careful When You Donate Time

I donated professional services to a local fraternal organization. This is not uncommon for a professional to assist these types of organizations. One of my duties was to attend the monthly board meeting after the regular weekly fraternal organizational meeting. I also belonged to this organization.

I found that the bookkeeping for this organization was well organized. The club manager had been there for years and he insisted that each and every aspect of the organization had a budget and operated within or above that budget.

However, one of the "side things" the fraternal organization did was to sell raffle tickets each week for the weekly meeting. Local businesses would donate some small items and gifts and sometimes there would be bigger items that were raffled off at the meeting. Each raffle ticket cost $1. The tickets were pre numbered. And, each week this fund would bring in roughly $100 in ticket sales.

At one of the monthly board meetings, I was asked in front of the board by the then board chairman, "if you believed you could steal money from this organization, how would you try to do it?". I said, the raffle seemed to be the only program with "no accountability" whatsoever. I said it appeared to me that there were over 100 people at the meeting so it seemed odd that there would only be $100 per week as everyone seemed to have multiple tickets. The chairman was originally "shocked" and reminded me the same member of the organization (not the manager) had donated his time for years for these raffles and that he had never missed a meeting. In addition, he had a team of volunteers (3 of them) who helped to sell those tickets.

Nonetheless, I agreed there may not be a problem but said there did not seem to be a "check and balance" to the system. They asked if I could "audit" the program. I said probably not as to the sales that had already occurred. However, I was confident that I could audit the fund prospectively. This assumed the board members did not mention the forensic work "outside of the room". And I was allowed into the raffle room before and after each weekly meeting for the next few weeks.

My procedure was easy. All the tickets were prenumbered. All I had to do was write down the beginning and the ending numbers. Then, take the difference times $1 and the result would be total ticket sales. Over the first 3 weeks, the same $100, plus or minus was turned into the organization. Over that same time period, the shortage was $190 to $315 each week. There was a problem.

We simply observed what was going on. The member who had been there for years was "stuffing his pockets" with the cash sales. He was "buying drinks" and carrying on with the members. In other words, he was playing a "big shot" and was stealing money each and every week.

The key was in proving who was stealing and how many were involved. I came up with a plan. This would take about 4 weeks. I rotated the first 3 guys out of the program the 1st - 3 weeks. Each week there was a shortage in cash. I believed I needed one more week to be able to properly testify that if he rotated off, and if there was no resultant shortage after the 1st 3 weeks, that he was acting alone.

After these 3 weeks, the directors were becoming madder and madder. Our "mini board" meeting occurred after the membership meeting, and accordingly, the timing of the meeting was poor as alcohol had "hit the board of directors" by then. They did not want to wait another week. Instead, they wanted to lynch the guy! Probably rightfully so but the wrong thing to do in the circumstances. The board invited him into the board meeting and told him that there was a shortage of cash in his raffle program. The board asked me to tell him what I had found.

I then explained what I had done the past 3 weeks and that he would be rotated off the following week. I told him the exact shortages that I had found for the prior 3 weeks and asked if there was any explanation that he could think of for the shortage (I remember even his shirt pocket had cash in it at the time). He said no and became very hostile. He then "quit the organization" there on the spot and stormed out of the room.

Beginning the next week, all the raffle sales were properly deposited and the organization almost tripled what they historically had earned from this program. They did not prosecute their friend and did not allow him back into the organization. Now each and every week, there is a double check to the number of tickets sold that is observed within the organization.

Grand Jury 1

This sounds sort of foreboding. That is, I was obviously a bit afraid when I first learned of a client of ours being investigated by a Federal grand jury. Even the sound of "grand jury" is quite intimidating to me. At the time, I believed that if someone was being investigated by a grand jury, that someone must have done something pretty bad. After all, why else would a grand jury convene? Could there be political motives or other business motives for a grand jury? I found that doing something bad is not always prerequisite to a grand jury (as I learned with this client).

Anyway, my involvement all started when a U.S. Marshall appeared in our lobby without an appointment and demanded to see me in speaking with our receptionist. He would not tell our receptionist why he was insisting on seeing me. I therefore did not come out of my office as I had other things to do. As an aside, I generally found a "double standard" during my experience with most governmental authorities. That is, when you need something from the government, it can take months, years, etc. However, when someone from the government wants something, they generally expect that you drop everything and attend to them at that moment.

I am not sure how this was allowed to happen. At what point did we begin working for the government? I was taught the government was there for the people and that the government worked for us. Regardless, if I was always scheduled, I found it difficult to explain to a client already sitting in my office that I had to leave to meet anyone else. I could not rationally explain that the government somehow held some trump card to get me to drop everything for them at anytime. Many times, the client maybe had scheduled this time with me weeks in advance and that the client also had to make a special trip to our office to see me and/or make special plans for either having someone watch their business while with me, or even plan for day care for their children, etc..

So, I continued on my regularly scheduled daily grind. Finally, after the U.S. Marshall waited a couple of hours in our lobby, he finally understood my schedule as he witnessed a few clients coming in and out of my office. He therefore told the receptionist that he was investigating a particular client and told her which client it was.

Upon my first break, I then was able to take action. I was always careful not to talk about a client without their permission or without the client being present. So, prior to meeting with the U.S. Marshall, I telephoned the client and asked "why would a U.S. Marshall be in our lobby asking questions about him?". The client told me that he understood that a Federal Grand Jury Investigation had started against him. He explained to me that he understood that Native American Indians were trying to shut down his entire industry and he believed they were behind these frivolous allegations. Nonetheless, he asked me to talk to the U.S. Marshall. The client was going to remain on the line on "speaker phone".

I therefore invited the U.S. Marshall into my private office. As he walked through my office door, I introduced myself and before I could tell him that he was on speaker phone, the officer almost shoved me back into my chair and started reading from a Grand Jury Subpoena. I was unable interrupt him and he simply read the entire subpoena to me. He seemed to be proud of himself that he finally got into my office, and without any provocation, seemed to exert a lot of testosterone. Nonetheless, it confirmed who the client was and exactly what he was looking for from our office.

I explained to him when he finally finished that I was trying to interrupt him. He said he knew that but he was going to be sure to say everything before I had a chance to speak to him. I then told him he was on speaker phone with the client listening to everything he said.

In case you do not know this already, one of the unusual things about a grand jury subpoena is that you are not allowed to tell the defendant what was in the subpoena. Here, the U.S. Marshall had just read the whole thing to him. So, I told the client I would call him back and then called the U.S. Attorney's office to report the incident while the U.S. Marshall was still in my office.

I remember this U.S. attorney being very understanding about the whole thing. I explained our office policy, that I would not see anyone without knowing what it was about. He said he understood. I told him the U.S. Marshall came in and almost shoved me into my chair and simply read the subpoena out loud and I could not stop him. The U.S. Marshall agreed that it happened exactly how I explained it. The U.S. Attorney could only say, "Well, I guess the cat is out of the bag". He did not seem concerned.

To this day, I do not know if the client did anything illegal. I do know that if we knew about it, we would not have worked for the client. However, this client seemed like a good guy and seemed like he was sharing everything he knew about the investigation with us after that time.

So, we received a subpoena to turn over all of our records to the U.S. Attorney's office concerning this client. Being a bit unsophisticated at the time, I allowed the U.S. Marshalls to take our original files. This was under the understanding that we would be able to access these files if and when we needed them for ongoing client work, income tax returns, financial statements, etc.. I did not know at the time, we could have requested the files to be copied so the U.S. Attorney's office would have a complete set of files.

Because the industry this client dominated was being operated pretty much only by his corporation and the Native Americans, there seemed to be a lot to be gained if the Native Americans could shut him down, regardless if the allegations were right or wrong. At least that was the client's perspective when he was talking to me.

At the center of the investigation concerned volumes of a particular type of seafood. And the number of pounds of that particular seafood that was being harvested. This was a cutting edge industry and many of the regulations were not clear. As an example, the seafood was required to be weighed. The regulations did not state "where".

So, did you weigh the seafood on the fishing boat?

Or, would you wait until you got the fishing boat to the dock (and water weight would evaporate)?

Or, would you wait until you got the seafood to the truck and more water weight would evaporate and jiggle loose?

Or, would you wait until the seafood got to the plant and then weigh it after all evaporation and jiggling took place?

Absent an absolute rule, it was obviously to the taxpayer's advantage to weigh the seafood at the last available opportunity. In this case, at the plant. Then, the taxpayer would clean the seafood. Afterward and before packaging, water was then re injected back into the seafood. The result of doing this is that the weight would then increase. I walked through this methodology and explained this with the U.S. attorney's office forensic people and they seemed to "get it" almost immediately.

Concurrently, there was an ongoing IRS criminal fraud audit. IRS audits are never good and "criminal" IRS audits are even worse. These audits are administered by special auditors with special training and these auditors carry guns. By the time these auditors get involved, the IRS tends to believe that something is seriously wrong.

A CPA generally has dozens, if not hundreds, of clients. Therefore, it is not possible for a CPA to generally "know all of their clients"; although, I believe a CPA "gets a good or bad feeling" about some or all of their clients. This was the case with this client. I liked the primary owner of the company and I believed that he was innocent.

The criminal audits are generally managed by a qualified income tax attorney. Sometimes, a CPA, such as myself, could assist or take over the audit. However, in this case, the taxpayer's regular business attorney was managing the criminal audit. It seemed to me that the audit was going "on and on and on, etc.". Thus, curiosity got the best of me and I finally had to ask the client, "Why do you believe the criminal IRS guys are here in addition to the Federal Grand Jury people?". Frankly, I was a bit afraid of the answer.

Originally, I was told that the "travel and entertainment" were a bit excessive by the attorney. This is not unusual for a small business that has customers internationally, such as this one. However, in this case, I was told the "documentation was not very good", which is bad.

I had not worked many other other criminal IRS audits, maybe one other, up to this point. So I telephoned an old acquaintance of mine from when I was with an international accounting firm. This acquaintance was himself a criminal IRS auditor.

I mentioned to him that I was asked to help in a criminal IRS audit and told him about the "travel and entertainment". He was amused. He told me "Our criminal IRS auditors are not concerned about poor books, we are concerned about lots of unreported income!". I said that I understood this client had reported all of its sales. He told me to not worry about the audit; instead, try to cooperate and get the IRS matters resolved.

I explained this to the client the next day. The client seemed to be forthright with me when he told me that the company had reported all of its income, except a small portion of "cash" sales. I assumed he was then taking the money. He said he did not take the money. He told me the company had to "pay under the table" a local utility company and directly to the truck drivers.

He said that in the vicinity where his plant was located, the company could only get garbage pick up two days per week, and they had the largest trash bins allowed by the utility company. He said the company sets aside cash sales to pay these truck drivers "under the table" to come each and every day to pick up the garbage. He told me the truck drivers had told him that the utility company was not to know about this or his production would go down dramatically.

This did not sound too bad to me. On one hand, the drivers were certainly at risk, especially if the drivers did not report this cash as income. However, my client seemed to then report the proper taxable income, assuming garbage hauling is normal, customary and reasonable in this industry. The key was in how to communicate this to the criminal IRS auditor.

After explanation with the client attorney, the client's attorney asked me to try to intervene with this auditor. Frankly, the audit had been ongoing for about 2 1/2 years when I got involved and the auditor was a bit "ticked off" that he was not provided requested information up to that date.

I simply explained to him that I understood the client was originally concerned about travel and entertainment type expenses. He confirmed he was not looking for those. I then invited him in to "see the books". Frankly, I believed the client books to be in pretty good shape, except for the cash sales.

So, I told the auditor what was going on. That the utility drivers were being paid under the table to haul away debris. I said the net taxable income would be about the same. He agreed. I thought it was funny at the time that the IRS did not pursue the utility truck drivers. I was able to put this issue to rest though, almost immediately.

Another area of concern by the U.S. Attorney's was one of the other owners of the company. It seemed that she was using two different names simultaneously and there was no evidence of one of the names in the United States. I found this kind of strange myself. Why would a U.S. Japanese woman have two names? So, I asked my client and I asked her.

Her explanation was that she was born in Japan and raised in the United States. Her birth name and the name she used in the United States was her Japanese name. She was bilingual and one of her responsibilities was being in charge of company sales to Japan.

They told me that traditional Japanese customers generally only do business with Japanese "men". Thus, the problem. So, our client had adopted a generic U.S. name, a pretty "plain Jane" type of name. As a result of having this name (which looked like she may have been born and raised in the U.S.) she had tremendous personal sales to Japan. Once this was properly communicated to the U.S. Attorney's office, it was easier for them to understand the confusion surrounding the duplicate names.

Nonetheless, there was a prosecuting attorney who seemed to be willing to do anything to prove these individuals were criminals, even if it was not true. It seemed to me that she was trying to assist the Native Americans in drastically changing the industry. Ultimately, the prosecutor was threatening to me during a deposition. Her boss was present at the time and seemed to understand that my involvement was only because I was the CPA for the company. However, the prosecutor's questions became very personal and not relevant to the case in my opinion. Ultimately, I simply refused to answer any more of her questions. Her boss apologized to me about her demeanor and he finished the deposition. In the big picture, "why would a CPA know about crime in a small business client". Simply stated, the CPA should not know anything about it in my opinion. Regardless, the "evil" prosecutor would not let this go.

As with all court room matters, this matter seemed to take years to get it to trial. As stated above, all of the files that we had concerning the individuals and the related businesses were subpoenaed. These files all went into a vault in the jurisdictions Prosecuting Attorney's office. We continued to need access to these files though. So, each year, as we completed the income tax returns and performed other services, we would simply log out our files, then send the files back by way of our file clerk when we were done. This went on for a couple or few years prior to trial. It was a bit frustrating, but we liked the client at the time and believed this was the best for all parties, given the circumstances.

During the trial, the mean prosecutor was once again examining me, this time by cross examination. To my surprise, she asked me where certain client files of ours were that were supposed to already have been in her possession. She implied to the court that some of our files had been purposely lost and/or destroyed, probably by me. She then accused me of destroying them. As I was on the witness stand, both the judge and the grand jury heard these serious accusations.

By the way, I understood that when a witness was on the stand, that the attorney simply asked questions. I learned this is not always the case. She went somewhat ballistic in the courtroom and was taking out some "anger issues" with me. Simply stated with respect to this matter, I assumed that all of the client files were back in her office. We had a file clerk and the files were to go to her office when we were not using them. The prosecuting attorney said these files were not returned. Then I did something she did not expect. While on the stand, I simply telephoned our office and asked our file clerk where the "alleged missing files" were. I left the conversation on speaker phone so the judge and the rest of the people in attendance could hear the answer.

The judge said my behavior of telephoning my office during my testimony was somewhat out of order, but the judge seemed to understand that I was trying to help. Our file clerk explained on the speaker phone that she had personally returned all of the files, including the alleged missing files, back to the prosecuting attorney's office.

This did not appease this particular prosecutor. The prosecutor then told the judge that I must have purposely lost or destroyed the client files in question. She went on to say that I should be held in contempt of court, that I should be prosecuted and that I should lose my license to practice as a CPA. Frankly, I found her demeanor to be "remarkable". And frankly, I became concerned for myself because of her frivolous and outrageous accusations.

Well, court finally broke for lunch. During this matter I had met the boss of this prosecutor. As I was leaving for lunch, the prosecutor's boss had two agents present from the FBI and one criminal auditor from the IRS. The boss wanted me to explain the inventory system of the company under investigation to these three gentlemen over a working lunch. They all seemed like reasonable people. I agreed.

We then went into the "bowels of the prosecutor's office" during the lunch break. As I recall, these three were actually pretty good guys. I explained my understanding of the inventory system, how we accounted for it, and then I shared our working papers with them and generally helped them to better understand the industry, especially from an accounting perspective. They were thankful.

Then, I could not help being mischievous and I was trying to think of a tricky way to get into their vault to see if our files were in fact "missing". I therefore had some papers to file into our files. I then told them I had papers to put in our files "for their boss" and asked them to take me to the vault where all of our files were. They did. There were numerous "footlockers" of our files. I inspected all of them under the auspices of filing the other papers and noted the files the mean prosecutor was referring to were not in the vault. I was puzzled. As these three guys were not in the court room while the mean prosecutor was threatening me, they did not understand the significance of my surprised look. I mentioned that it did not appear that all of our files were in these foot lockers.

I was told by one of these gentlemen that it was possible that our files were in the lead prosecutor's office. They then walked me down the hall to the boss' office. The files were not there. Then one of the guys mentioned that our files could be in "Dragon Lady's office" (the mean prosecutor). And guess what? All three files were stacked neatly ON TOP OF HER DESK when we walked into the prosecutor's office. In other words, she was hiding them all the time while concurrently accusing me of destroying them.

Since the three gentlemen I was with were not in the morning session courtroom, they did not understand my smile when the files were located. Without then saying anything to these three guys, I picked up one of the files and put the loose papers that I had in the files. Then, I wanted to make certain the files were not "lost again" by the prosecutor. So, I then asked them to log in my files and we took the files into the vault and put them all in their respective foot lockers.

Frankly, I was a bit upset of the under handedness of the mean prosecutor. After all, "shouldn't they want to get the truth?". I then asked the 3 guys I worked with over lunch to accompany me into the courtroom for what was about to happen. They asked about why, but I said they had to "trust me" as the next part of the trial was going to be fun for me. Anyway, I told them it would not take long, they owed me a favor for helping them and they all complied. We all went back into the courtroom after lunch.

As I was still on the witness stand after the break for lunch, it is customary for everyone to stand when the judge enters the courtroom, then sit down. When everyone else sat down, I continued to stand. The judge looked at me a bit bewildered and asked if everything was OK. I told him that I had great news and that I was able to "find the missing files" over the lunch hour.

The judge was impressed. He asked where I found them? The mean prosecutor immediately stood up and began to object. I asked the judge to have her quiet down so I could explain how the files were found and where they were found. The judge complied. The mean prosecutor had to sit down. She was fuming.

I explained that I did not believe that the files would have been found if not for the help of the two guys from the FBI and the guy from the IRS. I asked the three of them to stand and then to identify themselves. They complied. I then told the judge where the files were. As I was explaining where we found the missing files I was looking at all of the prosecuting attorneys for the case, both the local prosecutors and the one from the U.S. Attorney's office. Frankly, by the time I was done testifying, I was convinced that the only prosecutor who knew about her impropriety was the mean prosecutor. The other two prosecutors did not seem or appear to know anything about the "so called" missing files.

I was a bit upset over her misleading the court and being mean to me. I therefore asked the judge to do to her what she wanted the judge to do to me. That is: to prosecute her and to take away her ability to practice as an attorney. Well, it was clear the judge did not want to do that. I explained that I expected the trial to get to the truth --- that a man's life and reputation was at stake. And dishonest behavior by one of the prosecutors was simply not right. I said it appeared that the only people allowed to openly lie in court were the attorneys. I said that I did not want to answer any more of her questions. The judge agreed and I did not have to answer any more of her questions. To my surprise, the judge did not sanction the prosecutor either.

After conclusion of my testimony, the head prosecutor apologized to me and assured me he had no knowledge of the poor behavior of the mean prosecutor. Over the years I have kept in touch with the head prosecutor and he has always seemed to treat me with mutual respect and common courtesy.

Nonetheless, if I ever get a speeding ticket in that area of the country, I will probably get a life sentence if the mean prosecutor has anything to say about it.

Grand Jury 2

Not too long after the first grand jury investigation concluded against one of our clients, another one was just getting started. As I understood this particular investigation, the investigation concerned alleged illegal dumping by one of our clients.

Frankly, I did not know the "founder" of this client very well. I had met the President of the company at a seminar that I was teaching. One of the topics that I was leading concerned generational planning of small businesses. I guess my talk sort of hit home with the President as the company he worked for was owned by a family in town. So, the President telephoned me to discuss the company and introduced me to the then Chairman of the Board, the founder's son. The President was not part of the family that owned the company. We were unaware of any investigation when we initially met with this client.

I found that both the President and the founder's son were hard working. They extended a tremendous amount of effort to run the company. There were other siblings that would be equally included in the generational planning.

Parents are interesting individuals. They unite, have children, raise those children, and then they get to observe the fruits of all of their work with the children. Regardless of the success of one child over the other, I have found that most parents still want to divide their assets equally among their family members. And, it is always up to the parents. Whereas, I could counsel them about alternatives, I generally found that most parents have their own belief systems of what is fair and equitable for their own family. That was one of the joys of public accounting. And that was to observe how some of these successful families thought of generational planning.

Upon getting introduced to this client, I generally asked to see a general ledger and I simply asked questions after making specific observations in the books and records. Many times I could immediately pinpoint questions and possible errors in their bookkeeping system. This was the case with this client.

At the time and prior to engaging our firm, the client had been represented by a large national CPA firm. And although the larger firms generally have broader and exceptional experience, many times I found that little things may have been overlooked. This was the case with this client.

As an example, our firm required copies of bank reconciliations each year that balanced to the general ledger amounts. If the amounts agreed, more often than not the balance was correct. If the balances did not agree, this would be an indication of a bookkeeping or accounting problem and then we would try to help solve that problem. I not only found that certain bank accounts for this client had not been balanced in years, I also found that one bank account was not even included in the general ledger system.

In addition, the company had changed to a new computer general ledger system a couple of years before I met them. The national CPA firm appeared unable to help the client set up the system properly so that the system provided the needed information to the company. We were able to solve both issues. That is, our firm was able to help the client learn how to balance each and every check book, and, we were able to get the computer system working at maximum efficiency. In other words, the information from the computer system was able to enhance future business decisions.

The generational planning issues were the most important to this family. This was something that the national CPA firm either could not provide or did not provide. Regardless, the planning issues were complex. The net result was a recommendation of a series of family trust and limited liability company combinations. The client was thankful that the estate planning was completed when the grand jury investigation started.

In performing family planning, I believe 3 issues are important to clearly understand: 1) How each family member relates to the issues, 2) That the "parents" were the actual estate planning clients regardless of pressure from their children, and 3) That the advice given was in the client's best interests in the circumstances and using the assumptions employed at the time. I believe I did this with this client.

Well, a group of 3 U.S. Marshalls showed up in our lobby demanding to see another owner of our firm and myself. As I recall, this was a Thursday. Both of us were busy at the time (again the government expected us to be available for them at anytime). Anyway, there was quite a commotion in our lobby. So, I invited the Marshalls into my private office as I was available at that time.

Upon arriving in my office, the U.S. Marshalls served me with a subpoena to our records with respect to this client. In addition, the subpoena "requested my presence" the following Monday in court, the day the trial was scheduled.

Frankly, I may have heard some "rumblings" about this case; however, I was not privy to either the trial date nor the fact that the our records and owners' time would be needed. Imagine, this was an alleged illegal dumping case! What would a CPA bring to this trial? What could a CPA bring to this trial? And what would our files provide as good an valuable information related to this grand jury investigation?

The bad news was that I had been busily involved in "building our company". I had gone 11 years without a vacation with my wife. We had taken a few "3 day week end" trips during that time period, but never a whole week off at one time. So, I explained to the Marshalls that I was unavailable the next week. That did not seem to "impress" them. And, for one of the Marshalls, testosterone appeared to take over once again.

I therefore invited them to sit with me around my interview table. They also told me at the time that they expected to take our files with them that afternoon. I tried to explain to them that I was scheduled to be on vacation the week the trial began. Frankly, I did not understand what "value" either the other owner or I could bring to the trial. I then explained that they could not take our files. Instead, and because of the actions of the prosecutor's office in the prior grand jury investigation, that they would only be able to look through our files, if they needed access to them right away. Then, if they found working papers or other documents that they could simply mark those and have someone then copy those pages.

Mr. "Testosterone" Marshall was not impressed. He took his gun out of his holster and placed it on my interview table. He then told me in a threatening voice that "he" had the power to use any force necessary to get our files and to get me into the court room. I guess the intimidation had worked in the past for this guy. Nonetheless, I have never believed that force or coercion is any excuse for a CPA to act improperly in the circumstances.

I immediately got up from my chair and opened the door to my office. I told them that I needed coffee and asked them if they wanted coffee. They all declined coffee. I then asked the receptionist to bring me a cup of coffee and I asked her to make sure that "John Smith" came in to meet these individuals. I told her it was fairly urgent.

About the same time the coffee was brought into my office, local police officer "John Smith" showed up (I have changed the name). He entered my office with another police officer. He asked me what I needed. I told him that "Marshall Testosterone" had a gun, he threatened me with it and the other two guys were my witnesses.

This is where the fun started. The local police officer asked if the U.S. Marshall had a gun. The U.S. Marshall said yes and identified himself. All three indicated they were U.S. Marshalls. The police officer then asked if he threatened me with it. Officer Testosterone indicated he did and then asked "what are you going to do about it"? The local officer said he was placing him under arrest and asked him to get up. Before you knew it, the Marshall was in handcuffs. The other police officer walked him out of our office.

As stated earlier, I volunteered my time to 4 of the local police guilds. The local guilds were appreciative of this and I believe this was sort of a quid pro quo. I would hope that all local police would protect the citizens in a similar manner.

Nonetheless, I was served a subpoena and believed that I should telephone the U.S. Attorney General's office while the rest of the Marshalls and the local police officer were still in my office. I was transferred during the call from the Washington DC office to the actual jurisdiction office where I spoke to a U.S. Attorney (I will call her Ann). I told Ann what had happened with the U.S. Marshall and that he was in handcuffs. She immediately said, "I am not sure the local police has jurisdiction to do that". I told her she was on speaker phone and the other two Marshalls were still there and one of the local police officers. I said that the local police were unsure if they had jurisdiction to arrest a U.S. Marshall.

I went on to say that there was no way that I would release our client files to a U.S. Marshall again, after the last experience. She seemed to know what I was referring to. And, I said that I would not be in court on Monday or there would be additional trouble. She said, "Oh, will you have your attorney contact me?". I told her I was leaving to go to Mexico. She said that I could be "arrested". I acknowledged that and told her that they could not arrest me until I got back (and explained my vacation with my wife). I explained to her that "piss poor planning" on their part to barge into my office in the last minute on some kind of a "witch hunt" was not going to change my life.

She paused and said, "I guess there is middle ground here". She then asked the Marshalls if there was any reason they needed my presence the first week of the trial. They said they did not know of one and the other CPA would be available as he was also to be served a subpoena. She then told me that she would appreciate it if I did not press charges against one of her Marshalls. I agreed. She said I could go to Mexico then.

We then spoke about the files. I told her the files would be made available to them then next day and they could mark whatever pages they wanted and the pages would be copied. She agreed.

The following day the U.S. Attorney representatives showed up. I was not present. They were led into our conference room and proceeded to mark a few hundred pages. My instructions were to have 3 copies made of the requested information. As to those 3 copies, it was my expectation to give 1 copy to the U.S. Attorney's office, 1 copy to remain with me and another copy to go to our attorney's office to provide to our client's attorney if allowed by the court. In the big picture, I thought of this as nothing more than "discovery" and all parties should have a chance to know what was going on. Regardless, nothing copied had anything to do with the alleged illegal dumping.

Concurrently, the U.S. Marshalls asked me to walk through the "series of entities" that we helped set up for the family. They did not know about the estate planning at that time. I did not believe it was appropriate to explain this to them. I simply invited them to have me deposed so all parties would be present if they had questions of me. They never did that; however, it was apparent that they did not understand why these entities were established.

Well, the trial went on as scheduled and guess what? None of the CPA files were used in the trial. And neither the other CPA or myself were ever called to testify before the grand jury.

By the way, the founder of this company ended up having to serve time as a result of this investigation. I was told that had it not been for the estate planning entities and transfers that were made through my estate planning advice that the family would probably have lost all of their assets. However, since the gifting occurred before knowledge of the investigation began, then the estate plan was left intact.

During the time of our representation this client was able to grow to add offices in other states and the company was able to expand internationally. The profits of the company increased substantially during this time. We believe we were able to add value above and beyond our fees to this company and to the family.

Concurrently, the non working family members were receiving more and more cash flow from the operations and related investments of the estate plan. And, as they received more they seemed to demand even more. This also frustrated the Chairman of the Board from time to time and he shared his thoughts about this with me on numerous occasions. Frankly, I did not like working with the rest of the family, what I call the non working members or the "hanger-onners".

A few years later, after the prison time was over, there was a request by the then board of directors to meet with the other CPA from our office to discuss the amount of the fees that our firm was charging this client. As stated, I believed that the President and the Chair of the company were both hard working. As to the rest of the board, I was personally not impressed. They demanded a meeting with the CPA "before the board". Our specific accountant in charge CPA's "nature" would not allow him to go to the meeting. He was uncomfortable. He asked me if I would attend in his place.

I agreed. I showed up at the "family" meeting (board meeting). As I recall, they were all sitting in nice chairs behind a large table and "put me in a metal chair" in front of the table. Frankly, I did not believe that was a manner to treat anyone. Even the appearance of this manner of treating a professional was rude to me.

I was told by one of the non working family members that they had "put the accounting to bid" and found a national accounting firm that would do what we were doing for about 20% of our cost to them. In other words, they tried to convince me that a national accounting firm, with typically higher billing rates than our firm, could perform all of the services that our firm provided for an 80% discount. I believe that to be totally absurd. They asked me to respond. I explained to them what we found when we began representing the company, what we were able to help accomplish and the fact that they were able to engage with "owners" of our firm who were skilled and experienced in matters that I believed were important to their company. I reminded them how their firm had been able to grow domestically and internationally with our help. I also told them that we had a "no return" policy. That is, if they leave, we will not take them back. It would be my job to simply replace their revenues with equally or more profitable ones so our staff gets fairly rewarded for their efforts.

They were not impressed. They continued to demand a substantial fee decrease and the same level of service. Frankly, one of my sayings is that you cannot negotiate with "stupid". I then stood up and thanked them for their business in the past. I said, "under the circumstances, you should take the deal from the national CPA firm". I then left the building.

The Chairman of the Board followed me to my car and apologized to me. He asked me to come back in as they were "merely trying to negotiate". I said that we had a no return policy policy, shook his hand and wished him well.

Each and every year for the next 4 years, this gentleman would telephone me and ask me to reconsider. Frankly, if it were just him, I explained that I would consider doing it; however, we simply did not want the relationship with the rest of the family. He understands our position. Even recently, a few years after my retirement, this gentleman showed up at my residence "just to talk". I enjoy talking with him; however, I will never again discuss business with him. I learned that they have changed CPA firms 4 times since we resigned. And they are still not happy.

Recently, I was at dinner with another friend. We also assisted his business to go international. The above former client joined our table and told my friend that "I was the smartest guy he ever met" and told him what a mistake their company had made in the manner that they treated me. The former client had assumed that I had already told my friend and current client of the story. My friend shook his hand and wished him well also. My friend and I have never again spoken of this meeting nor did my friend know of why the former client had joined us. I keep these things confidential and professional.

Bottom line, the lesson to this story is to treat everyone fair. If only one party to a transaction prospers, then there is no reason for the other party(ies) to want to participate. I found that a good CPA should disengage at their first opportunity from a relationship such as this; that is, if they are smart and can find more business. The problem with many people are that they are too afraid to let bad business go. This is a hard lesson to learn.

Gotcha

In divorce situations, it is not unusual for a dominant spouse to try to use that former role in the marital relationship to try to leverage a better than 50% settlement in a marital community. Sometimes, and unfortunately, the professionals who have represented the business of the couple tend to favor that dominant spouse over the other spouse. Hence, in this case the "other spouse" was referred to me.

As a segway, I found that the CPA can be fair and impartial if they agree to be fair and impartial. After all, the CPA normally knows more about the financial affairs of the couple. I found that family practice attorneys were very good at the procedural issues related to a dissolution. However, I found that many times simple things were not recognized or overlooked. As one example that I found happening from time to time, a simple reading of the couple's income tax return could have gone a long way to facilitate the dissolution proceedings. This reading exercise should include the past 3 to 5 years, so as not to overlook an asset that may have been improperly converted into another undisclosed asset by one of the spouses.

For example, the income tax return, if prepared properly, will normally list any and all bank and investment accounts that report income to the IRS. Accordingly, it is important to read that portion of the income tax return carefully and note the number of accounts. And, a simple math estimate will provide an estimate of the balance in each account.

There are other items that can also be traced to an income tax return. Those include, but are not limited to: real estate, raw land, businesses, contracts/notes receivable, rentals, trusts, partnerships and similar investments.

There are many ways to value a family business. And, in a dissolution, it is important to value the business over a period of years, and sometimes, especially if the business operations suddenly decrease, for a valuation expert to look at the value immediately before the suspected marital issues began. Such was the case in this particular dissolution.

The couple had been married almost 40 years. Their children were all grown, married with grandchildren. The children were actively involved in helping to run the family business. And the children seemed a bit afraid of the controlling spouse. I found that was not unusual. And the children obviously wanted to maintain their livelihoods.

The other spouse scheduled an appointment with me to look over the proposed asset division. And it is important to note that both spouses were actively involved in running the family business. The children were managing most of the day to day operations of the business. During our initial interview, it appeared that some of the investment accounts reported in prior years on the income tax return has somehow "disappeared". Therefore, the first matter to was try to learn what happened to those particular assets.

The bigger issue though was the value established for the family business. The family business had been very profitable. Accordingly, the two of them had enjoyed a very high standard of living. I was surprised by the valuation of the company. My initial input was that I would read the valuation over and over; however, it appeared that the family business was worth much more than proposed by the so called valuation expert.

This is a good time to say that regardless of which side I represented in a divorce, I always tried to be fair in the valuation range of the family business. With that said, please note that the family business is generally not for sale. Accordingly, absent a sale to an unrelated party, it is difficult to come to an "absolute" value. Ranges of values can be identified though.

In this case, the actual valuation seemed to be about a fourth of the expected value as I read through the prior income tax returns and financial information that was provided to me. And as expected, the controlling spouse wanted this particular asset at the much lesser valuation (if he could pull it off). Needless to say, there was substantial disagreement as to what the actual value of the family business was.

My recommendation to my client was that she should simply ask for a division of that asset to her; rather than, to her estranged spouse. If the value was the value, and she did not mind continuing in the family business, then it was my conclusion that "apples to apples" would allow him to have the assets he was proposing that she would receive in the dissolution. That is, after the assets that were "missing" for a short time (as discussed above) were brought back into the settlement.

Accordingly, we tried to do our "homework". We went through each and every asset, one at a time, line by line. The key to a fair settlement is adequate preparation and a thorough understanding of all of the assets in the marital community.

As expected, the couple was required to enter into a settlement conference in order to solve their disputes relative to the division of assets. Upon arrival to the meeting, I was surprised as to the condescending and patronizing attitude from the controlling spouse. It appeared to me that he truly believed that the asset division was already a sure thing.

His wife was a bit nervous, maybe a bit scared because of all of the antics that the controlling spouse had shown. Nonetheless, she was strong enough to be there and be ready with her plan to be able to have a fair an equitable asset division. We prepared for the meeting and by the time we were there, I believe it is safe to say that she was ready for whatever "curves" her estranged husband could throw.

The settlement judge was well experienced. He introduced himself, went over the rules and swore us all in "under oath". He was careful to point out that he wanted to try to work through all of the questions and disagreements and try to come to a fair and equitable division of assets.

The discussions began that day about a fair and equitable settlement. It was my job, as her representative to ask questions. His "expert" was seemingly talking down to us. In other words, it appeared that he also was of the understanding that the business would be simply awarded to the husband.

I began to try to be the "bad guy". In other words, I could ask all of the questions. She could participate somewhat passively as was her nature. Nonetheless, she was prepared to be patient and ultimately receive what was already hers.

I questioned the other expert. I pressed at the key factors that was used by that expert in arriving at the value that was proposed to my client. I stated that I believed the value purported was far less than what the actual value of the business was. The "expert" could not defend himself. The estranged husband could only raise his voice and argue.

As stated, there were other assets in the marital community. There were sufficient other assets to make an equal division and allow the other spouse to also be awarded other assets.

The husband was then allowed to rant and rave about why the value of the business was the value. I pressed him with numerous questions. He became impatient. He became mad. He became desperate.

He then went on to say one thing that I truly believed. That was, that he had spoken to his bank and was able to refinance all of the company debt. This would remove my client as guarantor of any of the debt of the business. He spoke of this as an absolute gain for my client.

I then continued to question the value of the business while the settlement judge was listening and learning. The husband became indignant. He became quite mad. He then made one last convincing pledge to his former spouse, and that was, "If you do not want to do what is proposed, I will be happy to swap positions with you and take the proposed assets to you and you can take the proposed assets to me".

Actually, that was my cue. In other words, we put certain loan papers on the table and indicated that we had also met with bankers and that those bankers had already agreed to loan her the money to remove him as an owner of the business. We told the settlement judge that she was ready, willing and able to run the business together with her children.

The settlement judge indicated that under the circumstances, he was inclined to award her the assets that she wanted. The husband became irate. As we left the meeting, she looked over at him and said with a smile, "Gotcha!".

Psychic Energy

As I look back at my career, there are some things that I believe should never have been allowed to have happened. Hence, I would not have had to get involved. Such was the case with this matter concerning a specific land syndicator. The background that lead up to the litigation was that there were many limited partnerships that had been set up by this syndicator. In addition, his company acted as the "general partner" (management) for the various partnerships. Those partnerships reimbursed certain management expenses of the general partner. The general partner used these reimbursements to operate his office, pay his staff and himself.

The original attorney for the various limited partnerships had been terminated and other attorneys had been engaged. However, the original attorney somehow was in touch with all of the limited partners from the limited partnerships. That attorney wanted to lead a lawsuit against the general partner. The lawsuit was to try to eliminate or substantially reduce the amount of management fees that the general partner was receiving.

This was odd to me as the attorney who wrote the agreements that allowed the management fees was now representing the partnerships to eliminate or reduce those expenses. Advocacy?

Each partnership had received an annual audit from an international accounting firm each year. The audit reports were of the highest and best nature (unqualified). Nonetheless, the partnerships agreed to the lawsuit. The general partner then had to engage independent counsel in order to defend and help substantiate the amounts of the general partner's management fees.

This is where I entered. Each partnership agreement generally stated that each partnership will reimburse their share of the general partner's management expenses. Unfortunately, there was no specific formula for that. Up to that time, the general partner's staff had tried to fairly allocate these expenses. However, that was not good enough according to the lawsuit. Instead, it was important for the general partner to "prove" a fair allocation formula that was not subject to speculation. I understand this sounds confusing; however, it is true.

I was asked to help with a reasonable formula that the general partner could compel the court system to sustain. On the other hand, the limited partnerships were asking for refunds of prior management fees and suspension of future management fees.

Incidentally, each and every limited partnership that had ultimately been sold had resulted in an average rate of return, after all expenses, of at least 38%. In my experience, this was well above average, almost spectacular.

I recognized that whatever formula that could be ultimately used could be construed to include some sort of speculation. Hence, my "thinking cap" had to go on.

The limited partnerships engaged 3 different CPA firms in order to assist them with their plaintiff case. These included 2 international firms and 1 large local CPA firm. They were all aggressively representing the limited partners.

Then here was little old me, trying to assist the general partner. In the big picture, it seems that common sense would rule. That is, there certainly were expenses of managing these partnerships.

I finished my expert report and also printed out about three hundred (300) pages of formulas using the old fashioned dot matrix printers. Once finished, the reports were issued and I was immediately deposed by opposing counsel.

Opposing counsel asked me how I thought the expenses should be allocated. Although the attorney had my report (as did the CPAs), I chose to testify without my report. I believed I would accomplish the "result intended" without the report.

I told him that I thought the expenses should be allocated using 4 different measurements and then average those over all the partnerships using all general partner expenses.

Those 4 measurements were:

     1   The total number of partners in all of the partnerships,

     2   The original capitalization of all of the partnerships,

     3   The current assessed values of all of the partnership real property, and,

     4   Psychic Energy.

The attorney appeared to understand #'s 1, 2 and 3 above. However, he did not understand the concept of psychic energy. Nor did his CPAs. So he asked me to explain. I referred to the explanation in my report.

That was, in the day to day management of these limited partnerships, certain partnerships created more time and/or certain limited partners of those partnerships, including their professional help, would require more time of the general partner and/or his staff. Hence, I indicated that I thought a weighted average system should be employed. That is, a limited partnership should be weighted from 1 to 10, with 1 being the least amount of psychic energy and 10 being the highest amount of psychic energy. Then, the general partner's staff should weight these partnerships accordingly. Later, I thought all 4 methods could be averaged to assign specific costs to each partnership.

The attorney was almost laughing when he confronted me on this testimony. He admitted he understood the first 3; however, he was hung up on #4. He kept questioning me and I kept telling him what I thought.

This continued until the matter got to court. At this time, another attorney was engaged. This attorney specialized in securities litigation. In court, during cross examination, this attorney intended to impugn my testimony and show it as worthless. Accordingly, I had to be "on my toes". I sort of expected him and his experts to do likewise.

Frankly, he admitted to the court that the first 3 were probably permissible in the allocation of management fees; however, #4 was subject to too much speculation; hence, the general partner should get nothing. He then questioned me before the court and I once again told him what I thought.

The judge also agreed with the attorney for the plaintiffs. He was so confused by my testimony that the judge questioned me from the bench, "Mr. Hallett, if you used psychic energy in your report, I am not accepting your report. Is it your testimony that psychic energy is a determinant for the general partner's compensation?".

I answered, "No your honor. The plaintiffs have had my expert witness report for over 2 years now, in addition to the actual computer formula. You will note that although psychic energy is referred to in my report, I also dismiss it in my report and just use the first 3 that the plaintiffs' attorneys and CPAs agree to with respect to the calculation".

Well, you could have heard a pin drop. The attorneys and the CPAs immediately began reading the report "carefully". They were all shocked and surprised to learn that the psychic energy portion was not used. Instead it was dismissed in the report as being subject to too much speculation.

Opposing counsel reminded me that I had testified under oath. I reminded him that my testimony was what I "thought should be fair"; however, since it was subject to too much speculation that it could not be used. I suggested he check all of my testimony. I then looked at the judge and reminded him that the experts and opposing counsel had already agreed with the other 3 allocation methodologies in a weighted average approach.

The judge simply smiled. The ruling from the court supported my client's belief that the general partner management fees should be billed and paid by the limited partnerships.

After the ruling, I was in the hall outside of the court room. The securities attorney sort of pushed me up against a wall and put a hand around my throat. He told me that I would never pull that kind of trick against him ever again. I smiled and said, "You understand that I will have to try". The case was appealed to the State of Washington Supreme Court. And the allocation methodology that I used was upheld at each level.

The lesson here is to try to "anchor" someone in the tiny steps and building blocks of a difficult case. Once done, those experts and professional people will use their own imagination. Sometimes they think they are smarter than their opponent. I do not believe that at that level anyone is really any smarter than the opposition.

CHAPTER THREE - A TEST OF CHARACTER

Forming a CPA firm along with another individual was probably the most challenging and rewarding experience that I ever had. The other individual and I who began the company had the same or similar work ethic and moral behavior. I believe this is important to have a successful company. That is, corporate culture must be set and the owners have to then set the example and tone for all of the other employees. Although, that does not mean the other employees will follow suit, I found that you can "only lead a horse to water". After that, it is the employee's own upbringing and a sense of personal pride.

In the CPA world, one of the important considerations is "who the client belongs to"?. That is, does the client belong to the firm or to the accountant in charge of the account? The latter has the constant contact. However, the latter only has the contact because of the former. Many times, the employer/employee relationship is reduced to writing and the new employee is required to execute a contract acknowledging the same when they are hired. That is, the client belongs to the firm.

Then, if for any reason that the employee leaves, the ownership of the client has already been established. Specifically, the contract has already set forth that the client relationship belongs to the firm. Sometimes there are carve outs. That means that one or more clients may be specifically excluded from the contract in writing. Sometimes, there is a buy/sell feature (or liquidated damages clause) in the contract. In other words, the CPA can leave and then if the client decides to use the former "accountant in charge", then the "price" is already set.

I understand the legal profession does not like to allow this per se. Whereas, a CPAs can sell his or her clients, I understand that attorney's are not allowed to sell their clients. Regardless, attorneys do buy into legal firms with the understanding that the clients will be there. After all, you can be the best CPA or the best attorney; but, without a client you will not make any money. Protection of the greatest firm asset, the clients, is important to any professional firm.

Of course, many professional firms do not have employee contracts that spell this out. This was the case when I began working for an international CPA firm. I had the fortune of working in 3 of their offices (more if you count visiting other offices to temporarily help). One of my favorite bosses at the time, a great mentor and a partner in that CPA firm somehow liked me and spent considerable time with me. He was the working mentor that made public accounting interesting and challenging to me. He was the mentor that helped me see the benefits of what public accounting could do to help the client and to add value to my personal character and financial worth.

Simply stated, he explained to me how the client/firm relationship should be. That is, the client "belongs" to the firm. Everyone works for the firm. Everyone is paid by the firm to bring in clients. Everyone if paid by the firm to work on the account. And, everyone is paid by the firm to be nice and attentive to each and every client. There was no question in my mind that this mentor truly "walked the walk" that he was talking. A team concept.

One of the client relationships that I was able to build concerned a national franchising organization. The local franchisee and myself became very good friends (and still are to this day). I was able to help him with the CPA work. He was also able to help mentor me in other areas. It was a win win situation for both of us. I spent considerable time "learning the ropes" in that franchisee world.

Well, 2 of the 3 international offices that I was with actually "demerged" from the international firm (and became local firms) and the other sold to another national CPA firm. As I recall, I was the only CPA with experience in all 3 of those offices. And, the last office that I was with is where the "mentor" was. It was somewhat easy for me to stay with the local firm that he began with 2 other former partners of the same international CPA firm.

Well, things did not work out in the successor firm and I moved from Idaho to the State of Washington. Slightly more than a year after moving to Washington, I met my first "partner" in the CPA world and we formed a new CPA firm. I only looked to begin a CPA firm as I had found that my boss in the firm I moved to Washington to work for was doing things that I did not agree with. So, I became an owner in a small CPA firm.

Months later, I was introduced to a new client. His business happened to be in the same franchise organization that I was already familiar with. Well, he introduced me to more and more franchisees in the area. They introduced to me to more franchisees and our business rapidly grew in this market segment.

During this time period, I stayed in touch with my friend, the original franchisee. We continued to vacation together and play golf together. On one trip while he was visiting in our office and dining with my partner, he asked me to represent his business once again. Simply stated, he said the "replacement CPA" at my old office did not give him the same professional attention that I provided and he needed to find someone like myself who would do that for him once again. He heard I was doing the accounting for several of his business associates and asked if I would represent him.

I respectfully declined. My partner and he were visibly taken back. My partner reminded me that I did not have an employment contract with the prior firm and that I could legally do anything I wanted. The friend and franchisee agreed.

However, the self belief system would not allow me to do this. My mentor had taught me well in my opinion. The right thing has to be done in these circumstances.

As a compromise, I said that I would telephone my former boss and ask him if he would mind if I did the accounting and income tax work for my friend. Accordingly, we went back to the office and I telephoned him. We caught up with each other pretty quickly and then I asked him if I could put him on speaker phone. He agreed.

I told him my partner was there (introduced them) and that my friend (his client) was there too. My former boss was aware that my friend and I got together from time to time. And, I told him what was going on, that I had been asked to represent him as his CPA. Before my former boss could answer, my partner chirped in, "technically, Chuck does not have a contract, so he can do whatever he wants to do with this friend".

This is where ethics is very important to me. My former boss said, "I understand your position with respect to Chuck not having an employment contract and now recognize why you are telephoning me. I believe that Chuck has refused to represent his friend at this time, regardless of whether or not that he has a contract. I know Chuck and can tell you that Chuck does not need a contract to do the right thing. Thus, your telephone call to me this evening". Well, he was dead on.

As it turned out, my former boss said he was OK with me representing this friend. He thanked me for helping him transition many of my former clients (while I was with him) and then helping him from time to time as they needed help with one or more of those clients. The key was that he had given permission for me to be able to work on the client relationship. That meant a lot to me and I would not have done that, except for my former boss' approval.

I still think fondly of this mentor and my former boss!

Another example concerns the sale of some former clients. During the time that I was with our firm, we sold 2 groups of clients as we left the general geographical area. Rather than sell selective clients, we moved many clients into our main office, but some were sold. And in the sale, there was generally about a 3 year provision whereby we could not represent the same client.

The odd ball thing was that in both instances we had issues with different CPAs who formerly worked for us. In the first, we had complaints against one of the managers, both with our State Board of Accountancy and Sexual Harassment claims. Although he seemed like a pretty good guy we found that he certainly had limitations. Ultimately, we made the decision to leave that market place. This individual had an employment contract with us. I found at that time that many Superior Courts in the State of Washington do not tend to uphold written employment contracts.

As an aside, I have professionally testified from Alaska to Florida. In all other Superior Courts, except in the State of Washington, I found the courts to generally respect the written contract. After all, that is all business people have to document their understanding prior to getting into business together. And this is not to say that all Superior Courts in the State of Washington did not respect the contracts. However, in my experience I found that many Superior Courts in Washington did not respect the written contract.

So, when we decided to leave a market that we had an office, we decided we were going to sell the practice. The former employee did not want to buy what he thought he could "get" for free. Frankly, after a few years, regardless of the contract, this behavior no longer surprised me. Hence, it did not bother me too much. That CPA's particular ethics were not in line with my partner and myself anyway, thus, I did not want to work with him any longer. Nonetheless, he was not entitled to access to these clients without a fair, reasonable and honest payment in my opinion. As stated, that was my opinion. In this case, both our State Board of Accountancy and the local Superior Court did not seem interested in a written contract in my opinion.

The bottom line was that we were able to maintain some of the larger clients in our main office and sell the rest of the business clients to another local CPA firm. The local CPA firm was charged only based on the clients that it actually received client fees (its new business). I believe we received these payments over 3 to 5 years. The owner of this firm appeared to be honest and sincere to us, certainly a CPA with high ethical conduct.

One of the clients that he paid us for was a fairly large client by any small CPA firm standard. Although, the President of that company enjoyed working with me, he also liked having the services of a local CPA firm in his own community. In the end, he selected the local CPA and that local CPA paid us as agreed upon for the servicing of the client.

After the agreement ran out, our agreement with the local CPA firm provided that we could come in and audit the CPA's books to be "certain" that we were paid in accordance with the agreement. Well, anytime an audit takes place, some sort of mistake will be found. And, I would not like it if he underpaid us, and, I would totally not like it if he overpaid us and we would have to pay him back. Because we believed that the local CPA acted in good faith and had high moral character and ethics, we simply told him that there was no need to audit.

And, after the agreement ran out, we were approached by this former client to begin providing consulting services for his business again. He said he recognized that the local CPA firm was not able to provide the same level of consulting that his business needed. I explained to him that we were not able to perform any accounting or income tax services for him. Although, the agreement had lapsed, it was not the right thing to do. He then told me he would change to a regional accounting firm for all of his accounting needs.

I therefore telephoned the local CPA firm and explained this to the partner in charge. We came to a solution. That was, we would provide the consulting services and his firm could continue to perform the accounting and income tax services. It was a "win win" if the client agreed. The client agreed. We also recognized that our firm could have provided all of the accounting and income tax services because the contract had "run its term". However, that was not the right thing to do.

And by the way, the client continues to like doing his business locally. So, everyone won!

A final example that I will give that every CPA in practice will be challenged. Every CPA will be challenged with concerns of doing the right thing, especially when put under pressure by a large client of your firm to do something that you do not believe is correct.

Say Good Bye to a Great Client

This is what happened with a large professional organization that we represented. Actually, as background, in the beginning of our relationship with these individuals, they were a group of different proprietors and partnerships in the area. We were able to help them to "come together" as a larger organization and to build what I referred to as ancillary income. A common type of ancillary income is rental income from the building that the organization is operating within. And there are other types of ancillary income, depending upon the industry.

The economies of scale can prove beneficial to these groups if merged successfully, as was the case with this group. And, over a period of many years, this organization became successful and the owners of the organization were doing well financially and had developed several different types of ancillary income. And, as some organizations do when they get successful, they tend to make unnecessary changes in my opinion. Thus was the case in this example.

A controversial business manager was engaged upon inception of the "initial merger". This business manager "grew apart" from the organization and the organization decided to make a change to find a business manager that was not so expensive and/or controversial. One of the opportunities was to merge with a larger group of professionals. These upstream mergers are done from time to time and many of them work out if done properly. And some can be done income tax free.

Attorneys were brought on board to discuss the merger. In addition, the attorneys then brought "tax attorneys" from their offices to some of the meetings. And, what I learned was that our clients were not going to do the right thing. As an example, if done wrong, in an outright "merger" there was the potential for millions of dollars of income tax because of the capital structures of the various organizations involved. Our office carefully calculated this income tax estimate and provided it to our clients while with the income tax attorneys and other attorneys. The amount of the income tax was quite frankly unaffordable by the group of professionals that we represented.

So, the advice that I heard from the attorneys was not to report the transaction to the IRS in that manner. Rather, I heard from the tax attorneys that the likelihood of the IRS finding this problem was low, and to "go ahead and ignore the proper reporting" when we prepared the year end income tax returns. The "anchor" that the attorneys thought they had with me was that this client was paying me about $130k per year, plus or minus. And, after the merger, our company would continue to receive about the same amount of fees from this group.

The decision was easy from a professional and ethical standpoint. That was, simply to inform the client that we could no longer represent them. We discussed our termination with the client in front of the tax attorneys. We wanted them to understand that we had a strong disagreement with the "income tax attorneys". We said this while the income tax attorneys were also present. At the end of the day, the professional believed that "they would get something for free" and elected to go with the income tax attorneys' advice.

I was contacted by this professional group each and every year thereafter to consider helping them with their accounting and income tax services. My fear was that I believed there was a 6 year statute of limitations that I believed the IRS had to open up the "mess" and I did not believe it to be appropriate that our firm could be involved with the client, at least for that period, maybe longer. I never had to consider what happened after the 6 year statute period was over as I retired at about the same time.

The new CPA firm that was selected to replace our firm was much smaller than our firm. A couple of the CPAs came to visit our firm to look through our working papers and other client files to help them transition with this new business. We were not allowed to share with the new CPA Firm our concerns as to the income tax exposure, nor did we deem it requisite in the circumstances (advice from our insurance carrier and attorney). However, it was apparent to me that the new CPA firm did not possess the level of knowledge and experience necessary to represent a professional group of this size and with the related income tax considerations of their organization.

To this day, I believe the client knew they did the wrong thing for Federal income tax purposes. I also believe that the income tax attorneys are aware of my concerns and observations concerning the merger. Regardless, I believe that I knew the right thing to do and I tried to do it at the time.

CHAPTER FOUR - IRS AUDITS ARE CHALLENGING

Over the years, I represented dozens, if not hundreds of IRS audits of one kind or another. Some audits were simply through the mail (correspondence audits), some required my presence at the IRS (office audits) and some were in my office (field audits). Sometimes I would have to meet an auditor outside of both of our offices, such as at the client's place of business. In addition, from time to time other professionals (attorneys and CPAs) asked for my assistance in helping to represent an existing audit or examination that they were trying to complete. In my experience, I generally found the IRS audit process to be extremely slow and frustrating. However, I believe that in my experience about 80% of the auditors were truly trying to do the right thing. And, in the other audits, the auditors could be challenging under any set of circumstances. However, that is probably true in just about any walk of life. There are a certain few people that no matter what, they do not seem to be trying to do the right thing.

However, if the client is fundamentally doing things right, and concurrently trying to do the right things, then I found that most audits went through without a hitch. Sometimes I had to find "a hook" or a manner to "break the ice" with an auditor I had not previously met in order to help facilitate the audit process. Once that was done, I found it was easier to openly discuss and deliberate relevant issues with the auditor. Frankly, the auditors are "people" and they should be respected as that. However, an auditor has a professional "boundary" and one should not try to invade that space. Instead, I found that one should try to work with the auditor, if and when the auditor was in the "frame of mind" to also do the right thing.

O.J. Simpson

The first audit that comes to mind concerns a referral from another CPA that I formerly worked with at another CPA office. In addition I had to also work with that client's attorney. It seemed that the taxpayer was importing products and reselling those products both here in the U.S. and internationally. And, the taxpayer was doing quite well for financial purposes. The owner of the corporation was a former attorney. And the former attorney seemed to like to banter with the auditor. This is not always good. Many auditors simply want to do their job and go home without getting personally involved in the audit. In addition, in my opinion the initial CPA in this matter did not possess the experience necessary to resolve the audit issues; thus, he contacted me and asked me to help. In the circumstances, this was the right thing to do.

By the time I met with the auditor, the auditor was a bit frustrated with all of the issues. The client, his CPA and his attorney had frustrated the auditor for several months. Although, I tried to come into the audit process without any "baggage", I sort of inherited the baggage from the prior CPA, attorney, and client/former attorney. Nonetheless, the auditor was not immediately impressed with my introduction to this audit.

As I recall, the computer general ledger did not balance and inventories were not properly accounted for, at least, according to the auditor. It did not take me too long to resolve the computer issues and then the remaining issue was the "inventory issue". Some professionals may refer to this as a "timing" issue. That is, when is a business allowed to expense its costs related to the inventory? And this was before a law that helps clarify this was passed, Internal Revenue Code Section (IRC Sec) (§) 263(A).

And, during the audit process, for whatever reason, the auditor can request to be "toured" throughout the company's primary place of business. Although I found this request was generally made when the auditor was a bit frustrated with the information presented, I understood that I was going to help the auditor tour this business. In all the audits that I represented and all the tours that I gave to different auditors, I do not believe there was ever any meaningful contribution to the audit simply because of a tour of the business. Instead, I tried to use this time to get to know the auditor a little better.

There are sometimes very good reasons for an auditor to tour a business. Some very easy issues to identify include: making sure that personal assets are not being stored at the business, making sure that the business appears to be a business and the auditor is able to see where and how the original books of record are maintained.

As I stated above, there was no way up to this time for me to find a "hook" or a way to amicably discuss anything, including this audit with the taxpayer. We drove together to the taxpayer's place of business from my office. This drive was about 40 minutes each way. On the way to the taxpayer's place of business, I tried to ask general questions to the auditor. These are generally pretty basic, such as: where did you go to college?, do you have a CPA license?, how long have you worked for the IRS?, etc. Still, the auditor would not "warm up" and talk in a casual conversation. It was apparent that the auditor was a bit frustrated by this taxpayer and his original professional representation prior to my involvement. Further, I had never before met this particular auditor.

Well, the tour of the business went fine, the taxpayer was on his best behavior and we were able to answer all of the questions except the inventory capitalization question. So, we returned to my vehicle and began the 40 minute drive back to my office where the inventory discussion was to occur.

To put the time period in perspective, this was right at the end of the O.J. Simpson trial. For months, most of the public had followed about each and every step and piece of evidence in the trial. The trial was polarizing. And, at about the time we drove into my parking lot, we both had heard over my radio that the jury verdict was going to be announced after months and months of waiting, almost at any moment. I simply parked and looked over at the auditor and said, "Well, we can go inside and argue about the inventory, or, we can wait here, listen to the verdict and then go inside". I did not know it until I said that, but, I found the "hook". Not only did the auditor want to hear the verdict too, but the auditor then began to open up a bit, like a normal person.

We heard the verdict, we both discussed being surprised by the verdict and then we went inside to discuss the inventory issue. After the verdict, the capitalization formula did not take long to resolve once we got inside. It seemed all we needed to do was to begin a reconciliation process to open communication between us to lead to a fair and reasonable resolution of all remaining audit issues.

By the way, that client has become a very good friend of mine over the years.

Was I Being Extorted?

Another audit that I was referred into concerned many different issues. This audit had been ongoing at least two years when I was asked to assist. Frankly, the auditor had a quick temper and the professional representation up to that time had admittedly frustrated the auditor. In other words, the CPA and the auditor did not get along. The result was that the auditor was going to take it out on the client. The auditor was taking a very aggressive approach that I believed would penalize the taxpayers. The taxpayers were "right in the middle" of the audit, as it was their business. As the auditor and prior representation "fought", the professional fees escalated and the proposed additional income taxes and penalties escalated. The taxpayer was frustrated. They came to me.

I met with the taxpayers and I came to the conclusion that they were generally an example of typical small business people. And, it appeared to me that the prior representatives were not sharing the requested audit documents for whatever reason. This could have been because of the auditor's demeanor; however, it could have been a stall by the prior representation and escalate their fees. Nonetheless, I prepared for each and every issue and was prepared to share the documentation with the auditor in our first meeting. My goal was to try to resolve all outstanding issues at that time. This would also require that the IRS auditor would also be receptive to settling the issues.

Another request an auditor can make is to "interview the taxpayer". That is a physical meeting with the taxpayers. Generally, I do not want a client to have to talk to an auditor. The bottom line is that if I am doing my job properly, the auditor should not have to meet the taxpayer. Instead, the CPA and auditor should be able to amicably resolve all of the issues if the CPA is properly prepared and if the auditor is ready, willing and able to come to a fair and reasonable conclusion for the audit. A client may say something that could result in either extending the audit or simply opening up other issues that were not already open in the examination.

In this case, after I was prepared, I was ready to go over the information that I had summarized with the auditor. Rather than reviewing the information that I had organized, the auditor requested a meeting "with the taxpayers". The auditor indicated she wanted to go over all of the information. In addition, the auditor said she wanted to ask specific questions that she would not disclose in advance (to each taxpayer). Based upon the issues, I endeavored to prepare the taxpayers for the "expected" questions that I anticipated would be asked by the auditor. We then prepared proper responses and the proper manner to answer the question without volunteering additional unrelated information. If the question asked by the auditor was unclear in my opinion, then I advised them that I would interrupt them and ask the question another way before the question was answered. This can anger an auditor; however, as in this case, the auditor can ask unfair and or misleading questions.

As an example, I use the question "Do you still beat your spouse?". If the answer is "yes" you are perceived as a terrible person. If the answer is "no", the response is "when did you stop?" and you are a terrible person once again. In other words, you lose either way you answer the question. And taxpayers generally want to be too helpful in my opinion. They may try to answer a question that was not asked directly, and by their own statements, additional issues are identified by the auditor. Thus, it is generally never good to have a taxpayer meet with an auditor, even if everything is perfectly OK. There may be no ultimate income tax, but the fee for services rendered can go up exponentially if the taxpayer says something that the taxpayer should not say. If they do, the professional's time is then increased to clear up the situation.

Well, this particular IRS interview was not going very well. It was evident to me that the auditor had been frustrated by the audit representation prior to my involvement. Up to this time, as I recall, the audit had been ongoing for over 2 years. Statute of limitation extensions had been executed and the delay was not totally attributable to the auditor. The auditor had somehow (and probably a normal reaction) internalized that it was "these nasty taxpayers" who have caused this audit to be open for so long. And, based upon my limited experience with these taxpayers up to that time, I was confident that was not the case. Nonetheless, it appeared to me that the auditor was going to try to be "extra" mean in proportion to the "extra" time that the prior representation had caused the auditor to spend on this matter up to that time.

As expected, the auditor asked many of the questions that were generally anticipated and the taxpayers answered the questions. Then the auditor began going a bit "sideways" with her questions. In other words, the auditor began asking the types of questions that could not be easily or rightfully answered. I believe it was purposely done this way by the auditor. I had to take action. In other words, the interview became a "fishing" expedition. I believed it was my responsibility to interrupt and to rephrase the question with the auditor until the question could be answered properly.

The auditor objected to my trying to clarify the questions. In fact the auditor looked at me and yelled, "I will ask they questions and the taxpayers will answer them or I will assert tax, penalties and interest to the maximum amount that I can!".

At that time, I just stood up and said the interview was over. I explained that the auditor's statement sounded like extortion to me and I simply did not know the legal consequences of continuing the audit at that time without a resolution to my question. I told her that we would consult an attorney as to the "next proper response" and we would get back to the auditor.
The auditor was visibly angry and I asked the auditor to go back to the IRS office and have the audit supervisor (her boss) telephone me along with the auditor. In other words, this was my "out" for the taxpayer if the strategy worked. I needed to speak to the supervisor. I found that most of the supervisors were pretty good to work with, and, I knew most of them, including this one.

As stated, it was my understanding that the auditor was simply frustrated with the entire audit process to date with this audit and particularly with the prior representatives of the taxpayer. Nonetheless, it was my responsibility to come to a fair and equitable resolution to the audit process void of personalities and void of prior problems. And to be fair, once a party believes they have been violated, right or wrong, they can be difficult to deal with in a fair manner. This was true for both the client and the auditor.

And, I knew this particular auditor's boss pretty well.

I received a telephone call from the boss the next day. He asked me, and as I expected he asked, "What in the Hell are you doing?" but in an expected polite and humorous tone. I explained my understanding of what happened with the audit to date, the prior representation, my involvement, the auditor's response (natural or otherwise) and then asked the boss to simply review the file and telephone me and give me an "amount" of what he believed the taxpayer owed, given these circumstances and the books of record that the auditor had well documented. He said he would and would telephone me when he had an estimate.

I had already given the taxpayers an estimate of what I believed they would owe based upon my understanding of the "global audit issues". Or said another way, because of the mistakes in the original income tax return, I had calculated an estimate based upon what I believed the correct income tax should be. My estimate was about 15% of the proposal "on the table" from the auditor who had been working the case.

Well, the boss telephoned me back later that day. He had discussed the audit issues with the auditor and gave me an estimate of about $2k less than the 15% that I had estimated. I simply said to write it up, no penalties, no interest. He reminded me that the interest was statutory (I always had the IRS remind me) and he said there would be no penalties if I accepted the audit report which I immediately did.

The hook in this audit was to find a manner to efficiently manage the audit process at a reasonable fee to come to a reasonable solution for the taxpayer. I believe "mission accomplished".

By the way, I worked with this auditor on other audits after this audit was resolved without any acrimony or unfairness with any other taxpayer.

Big Toy

Sometimes audits can have a fun side to them. This generally requires an auditor who has a good understanding of their role and a good sense of humor. And, I have told many people, "the perfect income tax return has never been done". So, I am not surprised if there are errors in a client's set of books. Generally, the auditors are not surprised either. And, depending upon the nature and extent of the error, the auditor will react differently.

In this case, the taxpayers owned a corporation. It was a successful corporation and the corporation had purchased lots of business "equipment". As a CPA, we generally believe our clients when they make entries in their books for different equipment purchases. For that matter, we believe our clients if they tell us that the disbursement was for materials, supplies, entertainment, travel, etc., unless we lose confidence in them. If that occurred, we generally would disengage from the client.

This particular taxpayer was located about 2 hours from our office.

The auditor was well known to me and one whom I had worked with for many years (the O.J. auditor). By this time, the auditor and I sort of knew each other personally and we also knew the various members of each other's families and our hobbies, etc. These were the best audits to work on. Not only was the dialogue open and friendly, but we both worked with the understanding that the result would be fair and reasonable. And, from my standpoint, it was always more fun to explain to the taxpayer client that the auditor was a "fair and reasonable" auditor. Many clients did not want to hear that; however, it was absolutely true. Regardless of the press, at least 80% of the auditors I met with were great people.

It took the auditor about 3 days to summarize all of the questions. We were able to answer all of the questions except 1 of the questions. It seemed that these taxpayers had small children, all under the age of 8 at the time. And one of the invoices that was provided to the auditor to support an "equipment" purchase turned out to be an invoice for a "Big Toy". And in those days, a Big Toy cost about $12k as I recall.

Well, the auditor looked at the invoice and then looked at me. Then the auditor asked, "Are you trying to tell me that if I drove to their office there would be a Big Toy either at the business or in their parking lot?". I responded, "Please note that it is a 2 hour drive and I can assure you that by the time you are there, a Big Toy will be in the parking lot". She laughed and the audit was closed without an adjustment.

I found that many times auditors are looking for big ticket items and they generally do not "sweat the small stuff". However, it seemed to me that the auditor could have made an adjustment with respect to this audit if there was not a Big Toy in the parking lot if she chose to drive there! To this day, I do not know if there was a Big Toy there.

Pray for Better Business

Some of the audits that our firm represented were managed by another CPA professional or owner within our firm. Then, if the issues became "insurmountable" I would be asked to step in. As was the case with this particular audit that involve one of our longest term clients, one that had been with us since we opened our firm.

It seemed the auditor was conducting her very first IRS examination. And the auditor formerly worked for another client of our firm as the controller. Simply stated, we helped to educate the controller as to the industry. Accordingly, the auditor was well known to our firm. She was also known as being a bit "hot headed". Whereas, the auditor was technically very good, the auditor was unable to compromise or be fair. This was the case with this particular auditor's very first audit.

And, as stated above, the industry of the examination was an industry that the auditor worked in while the auditor was a controller for our client. The auditor knew exactly what our advice was to other clients in this same industry. That is not a bad thing as I do not believe we assisted any client in evading any income tax.

This client had a clean set of books and some of the normal and customary questions were raised during the course of the examination.

When the audit was over, the original report summarized that our small business client (emphasis on small) was to owe about $600k, plus or minus, plus interest. My CPA junior partner at the time was a bit frustrated with the preliminary audit report and he asked me to meet with the auditor to review the preliminary audit report. I agreed, but, under the condition the auditor's supervisor was in attendance at that meeting also. The auditor did not like that. She confronted me about my wanting her supervisor to be in attendance. I simply pointed out that I was our office supervisor when it came to IRS audits. Therefore, if I was being called in for her first audit with our firm, then I believed that it would be appropriate to have her supervisor there also.

The IRS audit supervisor at the time was well known to me. She had worked many audits with me previously and we tended to get along pretty well. That did not mean she would give us a "pass" but I believed that the resolution of the audit would be more fair and attainable if she were present as I reviewed the audit report with the new auditor.

The meeting convened in our conference room. My CPA partner was present in addition to both the auditor and her supervisor. The auditor seemed very proud that the audit report showed such a high proposed amount of additional tax. And this was on her very first audit with our firm! The auditor placed a preliminary audit report in front of both my partner and myself. I looked at it, looked up at the supervisor and then said, "This report is simply wrong".

With that, the young auditor reached into her audit bag, took out 5 different 3-ring binders of audit detail and stated firmly that "a lot of work went into this audit and there is support of each and every issue in the audit report". I then stated that I was confident that she had support for all of her proposed adjustments as I had known her a long time.

I said, "let me make this easy for you. If your audit report is right and this guy owes $600k, he will kill me. I do not want to die, so your audit report must be wrong." The supervisor smiled and the auditor was not amused, --- "yet".

Then I was prepared to speak about the "big picture issues" to her supervisor. Therefore, I went to our white board and explained the taxpayer's policy concerning each and every adjustment proposal, except one, to the audit supervisor. The audit supervisor had been "around the block" and was very much aware that if properly challenged, we would generally prevail with these issues. Thus, the audit supervisor immediately conceded those issues to me.

Then the auditor asked me a question about the taxpayer's general ledger. She pointed to an expense of about $29k that was coded to "materials" in the taxpayer's books of record. Because the taxpayer was "unable" to provide the receipt, the auditor had summoned the bank records to learn who the payee was for that expense. Then the auditor summoned the related receipt from the payee company to learn exactly what the so called material expense was for. The auditor asked me, "Do you know what it was for?". I said no. I said that I was unable to look through the taxpayer records and that I was only interested in the issues.

The auditor told me, "The $29k was written to a travel company. When I summoned the records from the travel company I learned that the $29k was for an all expense trip for 4 people to go to Israel". The people who went to Israel was the taxpayer, his spouse, his daughter (bookkeeper) and her husband.

I thought about how to proceed. Obviously, this should not have been deducted in the books. However, I wanted to resolve the audit as quickly as possible. So I asked the auditor in front of her supervisor, "What is the problem then?". The auditor pretty much leaped out of the chair and said, "Do you mean that you believe this is deductible?". I then explained that the auditor had learned that the taxpayer had a very religious family. The auditor agreed. I said, "I understand that business was slow so they went to Israel to pray for better business!". The auditor jumped out of her chair again.

Before the auditor could challenge me, her supervisor said, "Sit down, I believe Chuck is going to give you this "one"". Then the supervisor turned to me and said, "Did you know about that receipt?". I said, "No". The supervisor then said, "That was impressive to think of that explanation on the spur of the moment. Of course, your client is not going to be able to deduct that, but, nonetheless, I continue to be impressed with your ability to think fast!".

Bottom line, about $11k, plus interest was the final adjustment. No penalties, no $600k.

No Fishing in Alaska

I love visiting Alaska. Over the years, I have met some pretty neat people in Alaska. The "longest day" I ever spent was in Anchorage during June (it never got dark). And the coldest I ever remember being was in Ketchikan in January. However, I love to fish and have been to Alaska fishing for the past 30 years or so. I believe it is the best salmon fishing in the world.

On the other hand, it is sometimes fun to meet a new auditor. Sometimes, it can be difficult to meet a "brand new" auditor. Frankly, auditors may be no different than other professionals. Like doctors they have to give bad news from time to time. And, like many professionals, when they enter the job market, they have a bit of a "chip on their shoulders". This is not unusual. However, dealing with a new auditor can be troubling.

As an example, a client of mine in Alaska received an audit notice. This was a normal "field audit". In this type of audit, we would normally have the audit moved to the closest IRS office to our office. This is the most efficient manner to help with an audit as we generally controlled the books and records from our office for these types of clients. And, the cost benefit to the taxpayer of having the audit transferred locally is not having to pay for our travel, meals, lodging, and incidental expenses to "wherever". This savings in fees would be substantial to simply have the audit reassigned to something close to our office. And, I could never rationalize any benefit to the IRS or to the taxpayer of me having to "leave town for a few days" to meet at an obscure location if the same result would happen locally and close to our office.

This particular audit notice was from the Anchorage office of the IRS. I am not sure if there are other IRS offices in Alaska; however, this auditor demanded to meet me at the client's place of business in Alaska, another Burrough though in Alaska rather than Anchorage (similar to a county). In other words, the auditor would get to fly in to another city for a few days and I would have to "travel there" for a few days at great expense to our client.

The audit issues were all routine. As background, the IRS seldom audits each and every expense and/or line item in an income tax return. Although, many of those types of audits are also conducted by the IRS. Instead, the IRS has learned that "statistically" and based upon the nature of the taxpayer's business that certain expenses are more likely to lead to an audit adjustment than other expenses will lead to an audit adjustment. So, the IRS tends to go for these items to quickly adjust, get as much money as they can as fast as they can and then get out of the audit. This can result in a faster and more efficient tax adjustment, also known as the "low hanging fruit".

Well, in my experience in dealing with the IRS, for about 38 or so years, I never had a theory issue go against a client of mine. Sometimes the taxpayer may not have maintained a receipt or two, but the overall tax theory was intact. My reputation was a good asset in dealing with auditors who I did not immediately know. I understand the IRS keeps an unpublished "scorecard" on different income tax preparers. A relatively new auditor, such as this one, has little to no experience with taxpayer representatives, as was the case with this auditor.

And, as stated above, some have chips on their shoulders. This auditor seemed to have an entire tree on his shoulders when we first met.

And, I underestimated the auditor at the inception of our initial conversation. After providing the Power of Attorney to represent the taxpayer, I simply asked that the audit be moved to a nearby office where the taxpayer could be represented at a much reduced cost by our firm. Well, this did not impress the auditor. The auditor insisted that the audit be conducted in Alaska. I tried to be as polite as I could and tried to explain that this was a small business and that the taxpayer could not afford to fly me and pay for all of my time and expenses in Alaska. I said that it appeared this audit was so routine that it could simply be transferred close to our office in Washington.

The auditor was still not impressed or convinced to allow the office to be reassigned to the Olympia office. Instead, the auditor exclaimed, "Well, I can still require you to come up to Alaska and let me tour the business facilities and interview the taxpayer". Technically, that is true; although, it is somewhat financially punitive to the taxpayer in these cases, not to mention unusual.

I simply asked the auditor to reconsider and again reminded the auditor of the additional costs involved. I asked the auditor to "think about it and to call me back the next day to make a final decision". The auditor agreed.

Well, I hung up and made a telephone call to someone I knew quite well at the IRS. Not too long afterward, the auditor called me back. He was a bit upset with me. The auditor told me, "I understand that you called my boss about this audit. Why did you do that? Why did you not just try to work it out with me?".

And, it was true I knew the boss quite well after about 25 years. And, I was not trying to get acrimonious with the auditor. So I explained to the auditor I simply had to ask the supervisor one question before I agreed to come to Alaska. The auditor said, "What was that?". I said, "I asked your boss if you were an asshole or not?". The auditor seemed perplexed and said, "Well, what did he tell you?". I only said, "He suggested I have the taxpayer buy me a ticket and let you tour the business". Implicitly we both knew what that meant.

So, up to Alaska I went to meet with the auditor and allow the auditor to tour the business. This business had two locations and I was there for the day and leaving that evening, if I could "pull everything off OK". However, the auditor knew my schedule and if there was additional time after the tour, I recognized that the auditor would try to open the audit issues while I was there. If I allowed that to happen, then the audit may become more like a correspondence audit. In other words, the rest of the audit would take place through the postal system at an additional expense to my client. These types of audits to me were the worst kinds of an audit. The correspondence audit can be void of personality and tend to drag on in perpetuity. If there is no "personality" involved, I found the IRS personnel could simply write up some unreasonable and unfair questions, and then the resultant audit reports. This is never in the taxpayer's best interests.

So, I had 8 hours with the auditor to tour just 2 local facilities. In the process, I knew I had to take all of the 8 hours, plus lunch, in touring the auditor and making sure the auditor knew "where everything was" at the taxpayer's facilities. I was nothing but polite and cordial the entire time with the auditor. And, I made it a very long long day for the auditor. The auditor was able to tour the business and confirm related issues at the taxpayer's business locations to the audit questions for 8 horribly long and painful hours. And, as I left to go to the airport, the auditor apologized for having me come to Alaska. He told me that the audit would be closed, with no changes. At that time, the auditor had not seen any information other than an 8 hour tour of the facility.

And I did not get to go fishing.

Bad Clients Yield Bad Results

A bad client is not necessarily one that does not pay its bills. Although, a CPA should generally not represent a client if it/they will not pay their bills timely. I generally found these to be the most difficult clients. After all, they generally expect their customers to pay them timely.

The most rude clients are the ones who yell at your receptionist or junior accountants and/or make unreasonable demands of you or the firm. I found that if I let a client be rude to one of the staff members without some sort of corrective retribution in front of that staff member (while the client was there) that I would lose some respect of the staff member. So, there is this fine line to walk, that of keeping a good client relationship and making it clear to a client that an "abusive relationship" was not tolerated. Of course, this conversation can be very difficult.

Some clients have lots of money and some clients are used to "getting their own way". Granted, this behavior is not the norm. Regardless, there is no excuse (or very seldom a reasonable excuse) for exceptionally poor behavior. And, with each client/taxpayer being represented before the IRS, you are not only representing that particular taxpayer, but, you are also representing your entire client base whether directly or indirectly. For instance, if one taxpayer is allowed to treat the IRS poorly or try to take questionable deductions, then the IRS auditor may imply that we allowed all of our taxpayers to exercise the same poor behaviors with the IRS. Sometimes this practice can be found in the client demeanor, and other times, it is in the manner that the clients prepare their own books.

Accordingly, the CPA becomes the gatekeeper, so to speak, for a potentially huge base of clients. This is true each and every time a CPA is before the IRS. This is something that never should be forgotten by a CPA.

In this case, a major contractor in the area was being audited. He was a long time client and one who was always on the verge of losing his temper with anyone around him. I did not believe there would be any audit adjustments based upon the IRS requests for documents; however, sometimes there can be errors in the client bookkeeping. Thus, we never know for sure.

In this audit, an IRS supervisor was conducting the examination. Frankly, I believed that particular IRS office was assigned too many audits and the supervisor had to "take one for the team" so to speak. Nonetheless, this supervisor was well experienced and well qualified to know "where the land mines could be" with a contractor's set of books. And, this IRS auditor was also "old school"; that is, the auditor brought his own coffee, wore gloves into the office and worked with the door closed. This auditor was thorough.

Regardless of the documentation you provide to the auditor, it is normal and customary for the auditor to still have questions. And, after a few days, I met with the auditor and received a follow up request for documentation. This is normal and customary. However, in my experience this document request was quite small, especially for this size of a business and this taxpayer industry.

So frankly, I was relieved. All I had to do was to get a few items from the taxpayer for the auditor and the audit would be completed. And none of the items on the request seemed to be insurmountable nor did any of the items on the request appeared to be items that I believed would lead to an audit adjustment.

Accordingly, our office policy was to simply have the "accountant in charge" contact the client bookkeeper and request the information. My goal was, because of the limited and type of requests, to have the bookkeeper immediately respond and provide the information while the auditor was still present in our office. If this happened, I was confident that the audit would then have the best chance to finalize or "close" with no adjustments and that our fee for services would cease and be minimized. It was my experience that our clients understood we had to charge for these things, but none of them ever thanked me for charging them for IRS audit representation! This particular client always paid their bill on time. This client also could be extremely rude from time to time.

The accountant in charge returned to my office and said, "There is a problem with the client". I asked, "What is the problem?". The accountant told me the bookkeeper told the accountant that they "refused to provide any more documentation to the IRS". If this were true, the result could be disastrous to the client. The trickle down of this to other clients of our firm could also be unfavorable.

I simply picked up the telephone to call the bookkeeper. I asked the bookkeeper about this as I wanted to be "clear" about what they believed was going on. I explained the request was not only routine, but also explained the importance of the client complying with the request as soon as possible for all the reasons stated above. I took very good notes of this conversation.

At the time, I did not know that the owner of the company was out of town. I also did not know that the owner's son was participating in the telephone call via a speaker phone at the time. The son, using some rather foul and disgusting language told me, "When my father is out of town, I run the company. So you need to know that I refuse to provide any additional information". I cleaned up the actual language that he used and his tone was rude, disgusting and threatening.

I always tried to keep good and contemporaneous notes with my client conversations, such as this one. I simply told the son, "Well, please pass a message along to your father for me when he returns. Please explain to him that while you were running the company, we resigned and you will be receiving our letter of resignation later today". I then hung up the telephone without any further conversation.

Needless to say, the son immediately called our office back. He demanded to immediately speak to me. As stated, I have found that "you can not deal with stupid", thus, I refused to take the telephone call. I understand he swore and threatened our receptionist on numerous occasions with repeated telephone calls that day. Finally, I received a telephone call from "dad" while dad was out of town. When I answered his call, he immediately began to also yell and swear at me. I simply hung up the telephone.

He returned the call and I answered the call again. He began to yell and swear. I again hung up.

He then called another time and immediately asked me not to hang up. I said that if he raised his voice or used foul language that I would hang up. I explained to him the entire situation, and that I would be able to end the audit that day if the requested information was provided. I told him we would then resign after the audit as the "behavior and the language" to both our firm and myself was unacceptable and this was the "last straw". He thanked me and then told me the information would be delivered to me immediately.

This took a bit of time and by the time I got back to the auditor, he was all packed and ready to go. I explained there had been a bit of a problem in obtaining the information. He asked "how so?". I showed him my copious notes of the telephone conversations, including bad language. With that, the supervisor carefully reviewed my notes and learned exactly what had transpired. He "apologized" to me for me having to listen to that kind of language from a client. He said, I will simply close this audit as a "no change" and he apologized to me for the inconvenience and my loss of a client. Frankly, I told the auditor it was not his fault and he just sort of helped us make the right decision with respect to this client.

Upon returning from his vacation, the former client asked me to lunch. I took along another partner of the firm. The client apologized for his behavior and the behavior of his son. Over the prior years, these behavior patterns simply got worse and worse. I thanked him for the apology and told him that I appreciated him saying that. He then asked to come meet with me again at our office. I reminded him that we had resigned and explained to him that decision was final. I explained that if he were allowed to remain as a client, I would expect the same behavior once again if any situation became stressful to him. I told him that I did not want our staff to be abused anymore under any set of circumstances. He was not pleased. My decision was final.

And, this client always paid his bills for our services.

As expected, I closed the audit with no changes to income tax and never regretted sending this client down the road.

Doing Laundry in Mexico

At one time, I was introduced to what I considered to be a very interesting individual who subsequently became a client. We were able to immediately "add value" to the client relationship by assisting with some income tax planning opportunities and refinancing suggestions. These suggestions immediately resulted in enhancing the client's cash flow and substantial income tax savings. Again, the income tax savings were substantial. As a result, the client was able to go onto a real estate "buying spree" at the right time in the local economy. He was able to obtain several income producing properties. Things were going very well for the client and our relationship began to grow.

As the client received more and more money from his businesses, the client looked for different ways to save income taxes. We did all that we could to help optimize the income tax situation. As the client made more and more money and built his personal net worth, he began to become a bit distant to our office. In other words, sometimes he was not responsive to our inquiries for information and to answer routine questions. Something about this relationship did not "feel good".

Not too long afterward, the client was selected for examination by the IRS.

Frankly, the audit requests were once again fairly routine. And, I personally knew the auditor. As stated above, when we represent one client before the IRS, we are indirectly representing all of our clients. If one of our clients becomes unreasonable, unresponsive or if the client does things that are not legal, then the IRS could construe that all of our clients were behaving the same way. Hence, a result of a bad client can be additional unnecessary audits of other clients in our client base. I can assure you that clients never liked to be audited. Accordingly, I believe it was in their best interests that we did everything possible to avoid audit confrontations whenever possible.

So, in this case, the client had many business interests. Thus, there were multiple businesses being audited. And, we were able to "wade through" all of the client documentation with the auditor. The audit requests were summarized to the best of our ability and the audit then came down to a final audit documentation request from the auditor. Requests from an auditor is normal and customary and should be considered as just that, part of the audit process. And, it is normal and customary to respond respectfully to the auditor and to do that as soon as possible.

We therefore contacted the client to obtain the remaining information. For whatever reason, the client simply did not take our telephone calls or return them. So, we wrote emails. And our emails were not responded to either. Then we wrote registered letters to the client. And those were not responded to either. In other words, we tried as best we could to communicate with our client. We had no idea at the time why the client would be unresponsive to our requests. During this process, there were other ongoing audits with this same auditor on other clients that we represented. And, in the circumstances, I found that it was simply normal for the auditor to continue to ask, "where is the information on the other audit and when can I expect it?".

Well, it is sort of embarrassing to tell an auditor that the client refuses to respond to us. As time went by, we became suspicious as to why the client would do this to us. So, I looked at the information request more closely and with more of a skeptical position. I still could not figure it out. However, I concluded that "there must be something to the request". Ultimately, I had to explain to the auditor that I had been unable to contact the taxpayer. The IRS then summoned the taxpayer directly to produce the requested information.

The auditor explained to me that the IRS believed that the taxpayer had leveraged corporate assets to purchase personal assets outside of the United States. This was certainly news to me.

Upon receiving the summons, the taxpayer finally returned our telephone calls. He asked to meet with me. And during this time, there had been a few months when our outstanding billings for services rendered were not paid. I explained to the client that I would be pleased to meet with him and expected a check for our services prior to providing any more services. The client said he understood our position.

I then directed our accountant in charge to "try to take a closer look" at the books to see if there could be any credence to the auditors suspicions. The accountant in charge found some troubling information and this specific information was not being questioned by the auditor. However, we became aware of it and it seemed to confirm the auditor's suspicions.

So a preponderance of what had happened: the client's intransigence, the failure to respond to our requests, the lack of payment on our billings for services rendered, and the questionable information in the client's books resulted in a partner meeting of our firm. During this meeting, our firm concluded that we would simply resign when the client showed up to discuss the IRS summons.

Prior to meeting with the client, and after the client entered our lobby, I telephoned his attorney who was someone that I knew pretty well at the time. I told him that I figured I should telephone him as a common courtesy. I told him that I believed after our meeting with this mutual client, the attorney would not be able to speak to us about the mutual client. I explained to the attorney that I fully expected the client to go ballistic when I explained to him that we felt we had to resign. During that conversation, the attorney admitted to me that he understood our position.

I then went into the meeting with the client and the accountant in charge of the engagement. The client admitted to me that he had borrowed on the company assets to buy real estate (held personally) in Mexico without telling us. And, because of the amounts involved, the disclosures on the income tax returns were not correct. However, based upon his initial representations to our firm, we had signed those income tax returns for him. And because of how he "paid for those properties", the income tax returns were wrong, thus his prior representation letters to us were knowingly incorrect by him when he signed them. A representation letter is generally a standard CPA/client letter that the client signs indicating that everything on the income tax return(s) is(are) true and correct. I therefore suggested that the client engage a qualified income tax attorney to complete the audit, provided him a letter of resignation and explained that we were resigning for this and the other reasons as stated above.

He then did something that I did not expect. He reached over and grabbed the check that he had written to our firm. He then ripped the check up and through it up in the air. Pieces of the check landed all over our conference table, chairs, files and carpeting. I then told him that his attorney already had a copy of our resignation and I had already spoken with his attorney about our resignation earlier that same day. I stood up, thanked him for his business and asked him to leave. He was not happy as we escorted him out of our office.

Like I said, some "rich" people believe that they own you. This was the case with this former client. I expected something was going to happen and tried to "help bridge the acrimony". I explained to both the attorney and the former client that I would be pleased to meet with any successor accountant and discuss the account, the IRS or audit or whatever I could do to help facilitate the transition with the successor.

Well, the "blindside" arrived. The former client had another (unrelated) attorney "draft" a complaint for malpractice against our firm. Although the complaint was not filed as of that time, it was a fairly comprehensive complaint and it was drafted by a local attorney who had absolutely no knowledge as to what we had done on the account to date. And the complaint was drafted by an attorney that I knew of; although, I had not physically met the attorney. And, there was absolutely no basis for the allegations in the draft. I believed this would be another frivolous lawsuit if filed, or we were being black mailed to complete the audit for a client who had not been honest with us. We refused to bend.

I therefore we contacted that former client's attorney and I discussed my concerns with him. He "tried to make me initially believe that he had no idea of what was going on" with a proposed lawsuit against our firm by an unrelated attorney. He told me that his client had engaged another attorney for these allegations against our firm and he did not have any idea what they were working on together. I told him that I was "born during the day, but not yesterday". We then commenced a "chat" whereby my position was that the former client issue our office a formal written apology and a check for our services rendered within 24 hours. I further indicated that if this request was not met, that I would be uncomfortable representing any mutual clients with his law firm at any time in the future. I said I was prepared to contact each client, and he was welcome to help write the letter. That the letter would state that we would no longer represent any client that his firm was involved in. We would be happy to refer them a new accountant if they liked and we would not discuss the issues with them; although, the attorney was welcome to tell them anything he believed relevant to our position.

I believe the attorney understood that it was in his client's best interests to pay the outstanding bill and write us an apology. The bad news is that this took more than 24 hours. So, by the time the check came in and the letter of apology arrived, we had already issued our letter to our other clients. We were able to maintain each and every relationship with our clients. I learned that clients are more loyal to CPAs than their attorneys as a result of this exchange. As a result of these threats of the legal system against our client, this particular attorney lost several business clients. I stand firm that we did the right thing.

Ultimately, I understood that the former client hired a new CPA and tax attorney to complete the examination with the IRS. I understand the former client was criminally prosecuted for his actions with respect to his record keeping and failure to disclose the appropriate information on his personal and business income tax returns.

As to the local attorney who drafted the complaint that never got filed, I am confident that he does not know to this day what actually happened concerning why a complaint was never filed against our firm. I believe attorneys should have a basic responsibility to understand the issues prior to filing any complaint, including their frivolous complaints. Advocacy? After that time, I also refused to represent any client who used that particular local attorney. I told each and every one of them that I would not comment on the particulars as to why we would not represent them; however, they were free to discuss our position with that particular attorney.

From this CPAs perspective, frivolous legal matters simply take quality time away from other small business clients that really need your professional services. I am not apologetic to the frivolous attorneys. There are too many in my opinion, the judges know it and to date they have not done enough to keep these attorneys from harming well qualified professionals. I believe this is true for many professions whose practitioners are truly trying to help their clients and patients.

My concern about frivolous litigation is sort of interesting. For instance, I was at a local dinner that was attended by my wife, myself and various elected officials and their spouses. One lobbyist was present. During the dinner, one of the elected politicians had written a proposed law concerning "tort reform". Specifically, he asked me how I felt about the bill. The major provision in the bill was that any doctor with 3 malpractice claims in 10 years should lose their license to practice medicine. I referred to this earlier in this summary.

My initial response was, "your legislative bill excluded CPAs so it really does not directly apply to me". He then said, "I understand that. I also know that you represent a lot of professionals and that you always have an opinion. Please let me know what you think". I thought about tort reform carefully, and then I answered, "I truly believe that any attorney who files 3 frivolous lawsuits in 10 years should be disbarred!".

The lobbyist and his friend, a politician, was stunned, then he appeared shocked. He said, "Maybe you do not understand, that is not what the bill is about". I asked, "Why not? I am sure that medical providers do not want the bad doctors practicing as "bad medicine gives all of the doctors a bad name". On the other hand, there are so many absolutely frivolous lawsuits against doctors, that they also need to be stopped. There needs to be some kind of tort reform against the attorneys too".

The lobbyist then said, "I'm sorry, but you are wrong. There are not very many frivolous lawsuits against doctors. In fact, I am not aware of one".

I then told him, "You are delusional. You are not listening to everyone and people who have directly told you otherwise. For example, in my own client base, I also told him that I had 7 doctors who had to move from the State of Washington over frivolous lawsuits. I described each and every one of the doctors, told him about the frivolous cases, told him how most of them (both men and women) were crying in my office over the frivolous lawsuit, and told him that all of them had to uproot their families over frivolous lawsuits". As it is now, I explained to him that I believed there is a shortage of good doctors. Over the next 20 years, I told him that I understood that there will be fewer and fewer doctors. This is related to not only the frivolous lawsuits, but also, medical reimbursements from the government (i.e., Medicare, Medicaid, Obama Care, etc.).

I found that when a professional was frivolously sued, their insurance companies tended to "force" the professional into a settlement. A common "net" result is the attorney gets paid, the frivolous complainant gets paid and the doctor's malpractice insurance increases so much that the doctor can no longer afford to practice in the State of Washington. There are two costs to this to the residents of the State of Washington. The first is that good quality doctors leave the state because of the legal system within the state. The second is that medical services can cost more in Washington to cover the costs of the doctors who do not move away, but are forced to pay the increased malpractice costs as a result of the frivolous lawsuits.

The lobbyist obviously had never really listened in the past. He ultimately apologized to me and admitted to me that he "did not know and understand the number of frivolous lawsuits and that the frivolous lawsuits were that bad until that moment, after (I) had explained my experience with him". I told him, "Thank you for saying that. However, I truly believe that you have been told over and over about frivolous lawsuits, you just haven't seemed to have listened until tonight!". The funny thing about this lobbyist is that I actually liked the guy. And, I believe we got along pretty well after that. Over the next few years, we were able to get to know each other better and better.

I believe that frivolous lawsuits happen all of the time. I also believe that the judges are very much aware of this, the lawyers are very much aware of this and the existing legal system allows this process to continue. In my opinion, this should not be allowed to happen. Frivolous lawsuits take time, take money, and worst of all, frivolous lawsuits take "a part" of a human being who is being wrongfully sued. I used to advise my clients that in my opinion that they could "expect to be sued at anytime for any reason, and sometimes, they can be sued for no reason at all". This practice of filing so many frivolous lawsuits needs to stop, and in my opinion, the attorneys responsible for filing the frivolous lawsuits need to be disbarred.

Search Your Conscience

When I entered the profession of being a CPA, I found that many of the older IRS auditors appeared to be more mature, learned, experienced, and shrewd. The older auditors also appeared to have a better handle on the intimate details in a taxpayers' accounting system. And one of these older auditors was especially indicative of that. I remember this auditor being wise, quick and very fair to work with. Such was the case in an audit with a restaurant client that I had that this auditor selected for examination.

This particular auditor had an extensive background and lots of experience in auditing small businesses. He had also been "around the block". In other words, he pretty much knew when the information he was presented was not proper or if a taxpayer was not being genuinely honest with him. He also had a very good handle on the income tax code. This could be trouble for any practitioner if the books were not in good shape or if there were pending theoretical issues. This auditor also had a very good personality.

Thank goodness, the bookkeeping system for this client was excellent. The company was a husband and wife business. The husband worked full time as the manager and the head cook. The wife did all of the bookkeeping, the internal financial statements and the payroll, including all business tax reports. They worked the restaurant full time and more. The restaurant was successful. And, as they became more successful, they did whatever they could to make the restaurant grow.

The clients who owned the restaurant were actually friends of mine. They ran a successful restaurant. And as they became more successful, they used the restaurant to help buy "toys" for the restaurant operation that were operated by the business. And the owners were willing to do whatever it took and comply with whatever income tax rules were necessary in order to write off these particular toys.

This meant that the toys were to be used only in the business and extensive and comprehensive logs would need to be maintained. The logs were maintained in a neat, orderly, thorough, and wonderful fashion. These were probably the best written logs that I had ever experienced. There was no question from reading these logs that the assets were used in the business.

However, the nature of 3 of the assets that required logs was that there could be substantial personal enjoyment. I found that this is not precluded if the assets were used in the business. And, some personal benefit had to be attributed to those assets; although, everything was well documented enough to show that the assets were used in the business.

This is when it was fun to have a good old wise auditor. At the end of the audit, the auditor told me that the books were as good as any he had ever seen. As to the 3 major "toys", he told me, "Please do not answer me right now; instead, sleep on it tonight and search your conscience. Call me back tomorrow with a fair amount of additional personal use that could be attributed to the owner's personal use".

Now that was just plain mean! On the other hand, it was clear that the toys were being used; albeit, for business purposes. And, at the end of the day, the taxpayers were benefiting, even in a small way. As I recall, I discussed this with the taxpayers and we offered and settled for $1k in additional tax, no penalties, no interest.

Sometimes it is better to make a good deal with the IRS than to try to make a great deal in tax court.

Years later, I was playing golf at my home course. As I was walking by one of our neighbor's homes, a familiar looking old retired guy walked out onto to the course and said, "Good to see you --- you SOB you!". Sure enough, this was the wise old and retired auditor. Seems he is my neighbor's uncle. We were able to laugh and catch up on a few things. I have fond memories of this auditor.

Do You Have Time to Look at Some Pictures With Me?

As mentioned, I was often asked to help other CPAs with certain ongoing consulting, expert witness and/or IRS audit issues. Such was the case with this example.

A local attorney who was well known to me and a local CPA who I had run in to from time to time, telephoned me and asked if I would help them as an expert witness in a "child support" case. From everything they said, the case looked to be quite "open and shut".

As background, they told me that the mother and the father were never married. However, they lived together for a few years and had a child together. So far, this was still not too complicated. And the attorney told me that the issue of child support hinged on what the father was making in his own small business. I understood from the income tax returns and the general ledger that this small business owner was earning about $3,200 per month.

I asked to see other records: bank statements, internal financial statements, financial statements filed with banks, I discussed the matter with the regular CPA for the company (who I knew), and I interviewed the father. My conclusion after meeting with everyone and looking through the records was that the father was earning about $3,200 per month.

The mother alleged that the father was making closer to $20,000 per month! I did not find this unusual when a mother is trying to maximize her child support; however, the difference just did not seem reasonable to me.

So, I prepared my affidavit for the court. The judge knew me and the attorney for the other side knew me. The court accepted my opinion and child support was awarded based upon the father's $3,200 per month in earnings. And, I thought "that was that".

Several months later, I received another telephone call from the same attorney and CPA. It seemed the father was being audited. When I learned who the auditor was, it was apparent to me that this was a "tax fraud" audit. The auditor and I had known each other for almost our entire professional careers. We both sort of advanced through our different professions and he was working in the tax fraud unit at that time.

Thankfully, he had a very good working demeanor, but, he also was very knowledgeable of the rules and regulations. And, he was fair. In other words, you do not want to make someone like this unhappy during the audit process. He can be your best friend or your worst nightmare.

Obviously, this CPA was "old school". He told me that the auditor was forced to work in the "shop" where it was sort of cold and they stalled the auditor as long as they could. Frankly, I told them that with respect to this auditor, that was probably not a good idea. Anyway, they showed me the audit requests and the final audit issues. As I recall, there were 8 theoretical issues and some substantiating documents that were needed. I explained to the attorney and the CPA that it appeared to me that the taxpayer would more than likely prevail on 5 of the 8 issues, but, 3 of them simply looked wrong to me and the taxpayer would probably owe tax.

I met with the CPA, spent considerable time getting through some of the reconciliations for the substantiating documents and generally prepared myself to assist them with this auditor. I scheduled an appointment with the auditor to go over the findings. I estimated that the auditor would be in and out of my office in less than 2 hours based upon the issues in the document request from the auditor and what the taxpayer, the attorney and the accountant had told me.

The auditor showed up at the agreed upon time. We had coffee and generally caught up on each other's lives since the last time we talked. Finally, we got to talking about the audit. I was somewhat surprised when he opened with, "Well I suppose you think you will prevail on 4 of the issues?". I responded, "Actually, I believe we will prevail on 5 of the issues". He smiled and said "OK". We did not even have to talk about the issues.

Then, he asked me how long I had known the taxpayer. I explained the background, the child custody case and my only meeting with the taxpayer. The auditor gave a mischievous smile and asked, "Have you ever been to his home?". I said, "No". He then asked, "Do you have time for some pictures?". This surprised me.

All of a sudden, the fraud auditor's "hat appeared" and he brought out a three ring binder of pictures that he had taken of certain assets of the father.

He showed me a picture of a brand new home. The auditor said, "This home is assessed at over $800k and is fully paid for". He then showed me pictures of some automobiles owned by the taxpayer, sea dos, ATVs, and a helicopter! He said, "These are also all owned by the taxpayer. Now, Chuck, all I need you to do for me and I can then close this audit and move on is to explain to me how a guy who makes $3,200 per month can afford to pay cash for all of this stuff!". In other words, not only had the taxpayer not reported his income correctly, but the "mother" of his child had met with the auditor to provide him as much information as he needed.

Regardless, I was a bit embarrassed and explained this to the auditor. I promised him that I would get back to him with an answer as soon as possible. I then telephoned the attorney, the CPA and the taxpayer and had them meet with me in my office. Frankly, I was disappointed with all of them. I believed both of the professionals knew that the taxpayer had mislead the court and filed improper income tax returns and I was unhappy with both of them for "setting me up".

My reputation had been used not only for purposes of the courtroom, but also, in trying to help make the auditor go away. I did not like that. However, the immediate concern was what to do for the taxpayer at the time. I sincerely believed that the 5 issues were won, but, the IRS was now pursuing income tax fraud. I did not believe I was the one that should continue representing this audit. Instead, I believed a well qualified income tax attorney should be involved. Then, if the income tax attorney needed my help, I could provide it. If not, the attorney was free to negotiate after this time.

So, the client, his CPA , attorney and I conference called a well known income tax attorney in the area. I explained what I believed had happened, including what I considered to be my excellent relationship with the auditor. The attorney asked me, "What do you think we should do?". I said, "Well the records are poor as they do not reflect what has gone on. So, the auditor is going to want to hear how much income tax is owed in my opinion. I believe we should try to offer about $150k in tax, and ask that there be no penalties". The attorney asked, "What are the chances he will take it?". I said, "Based upon my experience with this auditor, I believe there is a 90% chance the auditor will accept it and simply move on providing the taxpayer is "clean" in the future".

The tax attorney then said something that I did not anticipate, "So Chuck, what you are saying is there is a 10% chance that my client will be sent to jail if you make this proposal. I believe the risk is too high so I better take over the income tax fraud audit". I then transferred whatever I could to the income tax attorney's office and did not work on this audit after that telephone call.

About three years later, my wife and I were grocery shopping. As we got into the line to check out and pay for our groceries, the income tax fraud auditor got in line behind us. He had his groceries too. I had not seen him since the "$3,200 conversation".

We caught up on a few personal things and then he asked me why I resigned from the audit representation on that particular audit. He said, "I simply expected you to offer on behalf of the taxpayer something like $75k, and we would have agreed to it". I smiled and said, "I had not spoken to that taxpayer since I resigned. And, as I recall, my number at the time was more like $150k, why do you ask?". He then told me the guy was in jail now on tax fraud. I told him that was terrible.

The auditor said the attorneys seemed to get involved and made a legal "hullabaloo" and a complete mess of the situation. He said, they made it tough on the auditor. So, their client ended up in jail. He said he thought the total income tax, penalties and interest now was in excess of $1.5 million.

I believe this is an excellent example of how the legal system works with our income tax system. No one wins if you tick off the IRS auditor.

You're Screwed

Many years before this, the same auditor was an office auditor. That generally meant that the taxpayer being audited (or the taxpayer representative) would simply meet with an auditor at the IRS office and go over all of the questions. In this setting and format, I found it incredibly important to be well prepared for the office audit.

Simply stated, if you had everything that you believed the auditor requested and were able to answer all of the questions in one sitting, the chances of a clean audit report (or "no change") would increase substantially. I believe I had a very good track record with these. And, if a taxpayer did not have proper substantiation for a small expense, simply let the IRS auditor know at the time and move on. I did not believe a taxpayer ever wanted me to argue for an improper deduction. The result would normally be an increased fee and the denial of the deduction anyway. And, from time to time, many taxpayers simply lost their supporting documentation, did not have the support or simply made a mistake.

And, with the office audit, you were at risk to the "luck of the draw". In other words, there are different office auditors. The taxpayer or their representative will meet with the auditor assigned to the case. In this setting, one hopes to get one of the auditors in the 80%, but, statistically, once in a while you get one of the auditors in the 20%.

This particular auditor that I have referred to was definitely in the 80%. The taxpayer that was being audited in this case was a local Realtor who originally thought that he could represent his own audit. So, he initially telephoned the IRS to schedule the appointment. The good auditor answered the telephone. Each auditor had access to the others' calendar. While on the telephone, the Realtor asked some basic questions of what he was supposed to bring in.

The auditor on the telephone then asked "What is on your list that you received from our office?". And they went through the list. One of the items that the taxpayer was to bring to the audit was the automobile log for tracking mileage. The automobile log generally records all of the business miles driven. A separate log should be maintained for each separate automobile. One of the audit items that the Realtor seemed to be lacking was his automobile logs when he spoke with me. I stressed the importance of these to my clients.

However, the taxpayer continued to speak to the friendly auditor on the telephone. The auditor asked him what he did. The taxpayer answered that he was a Realtor. So, it seemed a reasonable person would understand that there should be at least one business automobile, as was the case with the auditor. However, remember this auditor was one of the 80%.

The auditor then asked the taxpayer who his audit meeting was to be scheduled with. When the taxpayer told him, the auditor paused and then said, "With respect to the automobile log, you're screwed!". The taxpayer had gotten one of the 20% to conduct his office audit, and the auditor in the 20% was a real stickler for automobile logs.

Later that day, the taxpayer telephoned me and informed me that he was being audited. He asked that I represent the audit.

A Man With A Gun

Different auditors serve different roles from time to time. This particular auditor was a criminal fraud auditor. I understood that he had recently moved into the area when we first met. He made it clear to me that he was a criminal fraud auditor and told me that he carried a gun.

The client that was being audited was a successful professional. The professional worked night and day when working. And, when not working the professional spent all of the spare time with his spouse. They had 4 different residences, no children and they enjoyed doing things together.

The spouse had inherited assets from a deceased father. Thus, enabling them to live a bit more comfortably than most people I have known.

Most criminal audits get started when someone tries to turn someone else in. I have experienced some of the referrals being quite genuine. And sometimes, there are simply malicious referrals to the IRS. And, if one can tell the story just right, then someone whom they do not like may have to suffer through a criminal audit.

As was the case with this audit. However, just to be certain, I interviewed both the husband and wife and asked if they had any fears about criminal prosecution for failure to report what was alleged to be quite a bit of income. Neither of the spouses seemed concerned. This made me feel a lot better about my representing this examination.

We gathered all of the requested documents for the audit prior to the auditor arriving at our office. It was my goal to provide the auditor the requested information and convince the auditor that "he had the wrong guy" so to speak.

And the auditor showed up as scheduled. He seemed a bit tense or maybe a little bit too much "IRS Corporate" in the manner he was talking to me. So one of the things I routinely did was to talk to the auditor while I showed the auditor to where they would be working. I opened the back door to our office and pointed to a picnic table and then told the auditor, "We have reserved this table for you today to do the audit".

With that, I noted his body language. He was not phased a bit. That can be a good sign. So, I laughed and said that I had a private office set up for his examination and took him to the office.

Once inside, he explained that he was conducting a criminal investigation of the taxpayers and began asking routine questions. This seemed to be a "lifestyle" audit. That is, the taxpayers appeared to be "living it up"; albeit, one of the functions of this audit was for him to probe for unreported income. I tried to dismiss his fears and told him, this is a very successful professional couple with no children. Not only are they successful themselves, but in addition, they received a substantial inheritance.

Frankly, I believe it is important to give the auditor enough general information to help the auditor to be able to form a favorable opinion of the taxpayer. Then, the auditor said something that tried to put me on notice. He said, "You have a great reputation in working with the IRS. I understand that you are friends with many of the auditors. Let me make this perfectly clear, I am not here to become one of your friends". I guess he needed to get the "testosterone" out a bit. I simply responded, "Well, I am being paid to become one of your friends. When this is over, let's see who wins!". Again, he did not show much emotion.

We went over many of the audit items in his document request. One of the items was substantiation of an item from about twenty five years earlier. The taxpayer had sold the item during the tax year being audited and the auditor wanted proof, including a canceled check. Generally, receipts are just as good as a corroborative tool. But the auditor was insistent that he was going to demand to see the original canceled check for this item that was 25 years old.

So, it was my job to convince the auditor that all was OK with or without a canceled check from 25 years earlier. After all, how many people would keep a canceled check for 25 years. So, I tried to change the subject. I asked him, "How good are you with you gun?" I explained to him that my mother was from England and that we were raised without any guns. He perked up and pointed across the street to the sidewalk and told me, "From here, I could put a bullet between your eyes with my handgun using either hand".

"Wow", I exclaimed. "I guess you can just write up the audit however you want and I will sign it!". He said, "No, I can't do that, I just want to see all of the requested documents". With that, I presented him with an original canceled check from 25 years earlier.

At the conclusion of the examination, the auditor seemed convinced that whomever "turned these taxpayers in" were just being vengeful or jealous. And, by the conclusion of the audit, I had helped him enroll his young daughter in a local soccer program. The taxpayers gained the right outcome and I gained a new friend.

During the audit I learned that this auditor was a very nice individual that had become a single parent. A lot was going on in his personal life and he had lots to think about. And, we became good acquaintances during this audit process. He is definitely one of the 80%.

Wild About Harry

Sometimes the funniest things happen in the course of an audit. And sometimes the auditor may be auditing one business and actually endeavoring to learn about another business. Generally, these auditors are much more specialized and experienced than the normal and customary auditor. As was the case with this memory.

A client telephoned me and let me know that he was being audited by the IRS. The audit was fairly routine; however, I learned that the taxpayer never paid the income tax owing. Thus, the audit was also a collection matter. In other words, the auditor also was there to collect the outstanding income taxes from the client.

I met with the auditor and she was a very sharp and knowledgeable person. It was obvious that she had substantial experience in collection matters.

The first item of business was the income tax examination. And, the auditor wanted to interview the taxpayer. It is unusual that I would allow such a meeting; however, the audit issues were not complicated and totally verified and the taxpayer was sophisticated enough to get along with just about anyone, including this auditor. So, the taxpayer and I met before the auditor arrived and reviewed the income tax file.

We then reviewed the application to allow the taxpayer to enter into an installment agreement with the IRS to pay the delinquent income taxes. These applications are somewhat complex and the application is normally accompanied by an explanation as to how the taxpayer will be able to pay the delinquent balance. In addition, there are pages and pages of supporting documentation.

The auditor arrived and met both the taxpayer and me. I was surprised that the examination portion of the meeting only lasted a short period of time. The auditor indicated that she was satisfied that the supporting documents were sufficient to corroborate the requested information.

She then commenced the installment agreement application, supporting documentation and the resultant negotiations as to whether or not the proposed installment agreement would be acceptable. During this portion of the interview, I found that it was important to listen carefully to the IRS representative, answer completely and in this case, the taxpayer was present and presented an articulate and fair summary of what happened to cause the delinquency.

She then told me that she understood that I had experience in a particular income tax area and needed to ask me a question unrelated to this taxpayer. The auditor then asked a question that concerned tax "theory" and I tried to help her through the thought process of that particular subject. She was thankful. I also told her that I had some supporting summaries in my office concerning her question. Frankly, it was my experience that if you could help an auditor in an unrelated matter, that was good for the existing engagement. In other words, the auditors are only human, and if you can help them, the quid pro quo is that more often that not, they will also work diligently to complete the matter at hand that I was concerned about.

The IRS representative appeared satisfied and began a casual conversation. Then, she looked at me, smiled, and asked if I knew a particular person (a local business man). By then, the taxpayer and I had learned a little bit about the representative and her background and experience. The question was uncomfortable as the question was asked about someone that both the taxpayer and I knew. Because of the manner the question was asked it seemed that she knew or should have known that both of us knew this other person.

Granted, the other person was a high profile local businessman. The taxpayer acknowledged that he knew the individual. Then she asked me again. I looked at her and said, "Somehow, I believe that you already have researched whether or not I know this individual". As the other person was also a client, that was pretty much all I could think of to say. She then asked, "What can you tell me about that person?". I said, "Nothing at this time".

She then asked, "Do you know if he gambles?". I thought about this and felt uncomfortable with the question as I did not know one way or the other. And answering the question may show that I may have known and did not want to answer the question. I did know this individual, not well; however, we did dine together from time to time. He never gambled while he was with me. The question was simply a bad question. I said, "I can not answer the question without talking to him and asking him the same question, then authorizing me to talk to you". She acknowledged that and told me she appreciated that.

She then said, "Do you know if he is a pool player?". I said that I had never heard of him ever playing pool. She then asked, "Do you know his brother?". I said, "No, but I have heard that he is a very good pool player". She then told me that she had a book whereby an under cover IRS agent had traveled with some professional pool players across the country. She said that he wrote a book about the experience. She explained one of the people that the under cover agent traveled with was the other businessman's brother. The under cover agent was gathering information as to the cash business of the pool player. The under cover agent then wrote a book concerning his travels.

She then explained there is an entire chapter in the book that the under cover agent dedicated to the businessman's brother. She said the chapter was called, "Wild About Harry" and offered to give me a copy of the book in exchange for the aforementioned tax theory answer that I had already provided to her. I took the book. The chapter was hilarious. I do not know if the book was accurate, but it was funny.

CHAPTER FIVE - PROFESSIONAL CONDUCT AND ETHICS

Most people believe that CPAs are the most ethical of all professionals, I certainly do. I found that any ethical conduct is only as good as the value system that each of us learn growing up. I do not believe you can teach ethical behavior.

As an example, the CPA is thought of by many to be the conduit between the publicly traded company and the Security and Exchange Commission (SEC) to help protect the public trust. The CPA is also thought of by many to be the buffer between the taxpayer and the Internal Revenue Service (IRS). This level of trust and respect demands supervision and self policing of our own credential. For the most part, I believe this happens. However, in my experience, I have unfortunately witnessed instances whereby our profession could have or should have acted more swiftly to protect the public trust and to protect unsuspecting individuals who relied upon their CPA. In addition, I have learned there are some pretty smart people out there who take advantage of the CPA relationship.

Sometimes I believe there may be political motivations for actions and/or in-actions by our State Boards of Accountancy (SBOA). For instance, the SBOAs generally issue and police the CPA licenses in the areas the SBOA would have jurisdiction. The SBOAs generally work hand in hand with the National Association of State Boards of Accounting (NASBA). These organizations are the "holy grail" so to speak of our profession. The ultimate public trust must be maintained by theses organizations who are given the responsibility to do so. In my opinion, this responsibility trumps the politics and silliness of the licensing authorities when they somehow "look the other way" or if they are slow to respond for any reason.

If a member is suspected of doing something wrong or unethical, it is generally the SBOA who would try to remedy the situation, unless there are "other circumstances". The SBOAs have a difficult task. It is their responsibility to enforce the rules. To maintain the CPA credential at the highest level, the responsibilities or the SBOAs must be adhered to at all costs.

To me, NASBA is the national holy grail organization for all CPAs. NASBA has a difficult task. NASBA helps identify the current issues facing the profession. These issues are not only for the CPAs, but also, the lawmakers and regulators. However, this responsibility must be maintained while simultaneously keeping the high level of ethical standards that the public expects from CPAs.

The AICPA and state societies are more or less the "fraternal" organizations of the CPAs. In other words, the latter are voluntary organizations. The AICPA sets forth ethical and auditing standards for the profession. I had the opportunity to serve on the AICPA Council. This was an honor and something I look back on with great memories. An overwhelming majority of the Council members, in my opinion, endeavor to increase the public trust and improve the profession.

However, I found there were questionable or dishonest CPAs in public practice. Granted this is a small number as compared to the total number of CPAs; nonetheless, I believe there is more that can be done to help police the CPA profession.

Let's Get Along

Sometimes, I learned the above organizations do not get along. I witnessed this first hand when I sat on the National Council of the AICPA. My first AICPA meeting was not a pleasant one. To briefly describe the time period, the CPA profession had recently received well deserved bad press from such alleged accounting failures as: ENRON, World Com and others. This does not mean that the CPA profession failed. Please note that there are pretty smart people at the top of the big companies who generally know the accounting rules "equal to or better than their auditors". However, I found that our legal system and the press like to hold the wrong people accountable from time to time.

And, in the past, the stewardship function and fiduciary duty of the officers of these public corporations was to protect the shareholder and enhance the value of the company. However, over the past couple of decades, that trend has diminished. In its place seems to be a battle between the legal system and trying to operate a business for the benefit of the officers running those large companies. In its place is also a battle for 50% or more of the American people not to pay taxes. Concurrently, many people want the big companies and the wealthy to pay more and more taxes. In its place is the feeling of a general frustration of corporate executives to gain fair contracts with many of the unions. In other words, there are real struggles going on that are really not "CPA problems".

As a segway, ask yourself what the average union members are getting that the average American does not get? For instance, the benefit packages, such as health care and retirement, are extraordinarily more costly than the average non union workers. Specifically, the union retirement plans are under funded by many of the large companies, some say by billions of dollars. This is also true for the governmental authorities, except this shortage may be in the trillions of dollars. The scheduled cost of the payments to the retirees simply cannot be maintained under ANY set of assumptions. I understand that the average governmental retired employee will retire at more than $75k per year in retirement and health care benefits; however, the average American on Social Security and Medicare retires on average at about $28k per year. Therefore, the benefit issues are worse than just social security and medicare. Nonetheless, these benefits are the "elephant in the room" that no one will discuss for both political and auditing reasons.

So, the corporate executives have given in to the unions. In my opinion, the executives see the writing on the wall. The executives know that the companies will die a slow death because of these ever increasing unfunded benefits. Accordingly, what do the executives do? Easy. The executives appear to be taking what they can get today! The executives pay themselves millions and millions of dollars (sometimes billions) per year. I guess they figure they may as well get theirs and let the chips fall where they fall, after they are gone. The rationale seems to be "let the next generation deal with it". Well, if it is not dealt with today, there may not be a next generation as we want to perceive it.

Is it reasonable to think that these corporate executives and hedge fund managers make thousands of times more than the average American. Is it reasonable to think they are worth it? Who allowed this to happen? Why does it go on? Who will stop it? In other words, can there be legislation (excuse me, these same executives generally know one or more of the members on the supreme court) or do we need a constitutional amendment to limit the total compensation of these people? Should the SEC simply step in and stop this insanity?

As a solution, why not consider a base amount of eligible compensation for these executives? If the companies do not show a profit, they lose any right to a bonus or stock options that year. Sure they may deserve bonuses. However, the key is how much can their bonus be? In my opinion, their average bonus as a percentage of base pay should not be more than the average percentage increase in shareholders' value (in the shareholders' value of stock). This would exclude the executives' shares of stock. In addition, the executive's average bonus should not be more than the average employee's annual bonus as a percentage of total compensation. For hedge funds, the bonus cannot be more than the average percentage increase of the investors' portfolios. Compensation is simply too high to many of these individuals. Who allowed this to get out of control? Why not tie the executive compensation to what their responsibilities should be; that is, the success of the companies they work for?

As an example, why not limit the base compensation package of the executives to a multiple of 25 times the average employee's base compensation package, including benefits? And, this is indexed to the average employee's base salary, including benefits. Neither the executive nor the hedge fund manager should receive more. Frankly, I am puzzled that a public company or similar entity can rationalize the "value" differential using any set of circumstances to this small class of officers or directors to their employees' detriment. And by the way, this form of compensation based results will help equalize the tax base and help stabilize the fragile economy. This is because that if more and more citizens pay income tax, the budget deficit will not grow as fast as it has, all other things being constant.

At the same time, the unions have to understand, both governmental and non governmental, that their retirement system and benefit packages are a complete bust! Admittedly, the union pension plans and benefit packages are great for the perception of the workers. The problem is THEY ARE NOT AFFORDABLE and their expected benefits will bankrupt the governmental authorities and related businesses, not to mention many of the insurance companies who have insured many of those retirement benefits.

To begin the fix on this, the unions need to do what the average American company has done. That is, go to a PROFIT sharing (cash) based retirement system, a 401(k) plan and/or a cash balance plan. In that way, employers can fund "based upon profits". If we allow the companies to accrue a liability that everyone knows is not attainable, then we are consciously allowing these governmental entities and companies to fail. The politicians know it, the unions know it, the executives know it, and this is another elephant in the room. Nonetheless, our profession has historically chosen to "look the other way" when disclosing these unfunded liabilities at actual amounts. Recently, there have been some changes to the amounts that are recorded on financial statements concerning pension accruals.

Rather, in years where companies are more profitable and years where the respective governmental authority has a surplus, additional amounts could be paid to fund retirement and health care plans for those then currently working. Additional amounts could also be paid to health savings plans of those employees then currently working. And, in bad years, difficult decisions will need to be made, little or nothing can be funded. A plan like this forces everyone to operate on a level playing field. That is, everyone has a goal and a reason to try to make their employer become more efficient, more profitable and a better place to work. What could possibly be the downside to something like this type of plan? Everyone has to become accountable.

And like the average American, everyone, including union workers, becomes at will employees. Simply stated, if you are not productively working toward the common goal of the business or governmental entity, you are at risk of losing your job. Who ever allowed this to change to a tenured system anyway? As an example, if you were going for brain surgery, do you want the oldest employee doing the surgery or do you want the best surgeon doing the work? Many times this may be the same. Often times it is no longer the case. This is because when "risk reward" is taken out of the mix, the recipe simply will not work.

I know of a governmental agency that has a tenured union employee who does not do any work. She simply "plays on her computer" every day. I was told that it was easier to allow her to not work than to try to terminate her through the bureaucracy of the union system. In addition, I understand the "wink wink union retirement" calls for a percentage of final average pay being used as the base for retirement. And in those final years, the union worker happens to get tens of thousands of dollars of additional "overtime pay". Everyone seems to know that this unfunded benefit is up to $2 million PER PERSON. Common sense would dictate not working these employees overtime in the last few years. No prudent person would allow it. However, this union loop hole is bankrupting many pension plans. They know it, the workers know it and the practice is being allowed to continue. This is garbage. There are so many other areas of waste that should be fixed. Who has the ethics and fortitude to knowingly do what is right?

In fact, I had one retired governmental employee who I really liked. He was a long term client. He had 4 governmental pensions, including social security. These pensions totaled about $175k per year! He openly explained to me how the system worked for him and that he knowingly took advantage of the system during his working life to maximize his retirement benefits. I do not deny that he did not work; however, it is unbelievable how much more this union employee can make by taking advantage of the "system", or at least the expected behavior of the system.

Ethically, everyone knows that this current system will not work. Too many people are making money from the current system. This includes the union bosses, the union workers, the executives, the politicians and the decision makers who are all profiting as long as the system is not fixed. At some point in time, everyone should have to justify why they did not change the broken system. However, to do that, these same people need to not be so greedy. Is that possible in the American lifestyle? Should these individuals need to reasonably enhance their companies, increase profits, increase shareholder wealth, increase retirement benefits, or have regular established "global achievements" in order to get paid?

Why not tie politicians' and union bosses' salaries to the success of their organizations? And, all liabilities would be required to be shown at today's values, including the unfunded retirement and health care benefits. Then, if the respective governmental authority or respective organization is not making money, the corporate executives', the politicians' and union bosses' salaries are rolled back to a level as to when money and stakeholder value was being enhanced. Isn't this the requirement for all small business owners to make money? When risk reward is taken out of this mix, I believe there is too strong motive to only protect themselves. This possibility needs to be removed from the mix.

I wandered a little bit back there. So, back to AICPA Council. The President of NASBA was a "sole practitioner", the year I was appointed to council . That is, he did not work for an international accounting accounting firm. He did not work for a large governmental authority, a major university, a large not for profit, or a Fortune 500 company. He worked for himself. He owned his own small accounting firm and still made time to be President of NASBA. This time commitment was huge. Upon meeting him, it was evident to me that he was a highly ethical individual.

During my first AICPA council meeting, I remember that the President of NASBA sat at one of the head tables of the AICPA with some prominent CPAs from the AICPA. When it was his turn, he went on stage and delivered his speech. As I recall, his speech was highly critical of the CPA profession and how the AICPA knowingly or unknowingly allowed some of the so called audit failures to happen. Remember, this individual, the President of NASBA, is also a CPA. His presentation was from his heart and based upon what he considered to be the highest ethical standards. It was clear that many of the top AICPA individuals did not like his tone and his conclusions. Nonetheless, they were his opinions based upon his experience. Simply stated, for his speech and presentation to be right, the AICPA may have had to have been wrong in some of its practice and ethical interpretations. The crowd was stunned to say the least. There was no applause when he left the stage. He made a difficult point in front of an audience that is highly respected. He made this difficult point in front of an audience that is partly responsible to fix the problems that he was discussion with a lot of passion.

As he returned to his table and sat down, EVERYONE else got up and left the table where he was sitting. The AICPA members sharing that table left him to sit by himself. Apparently this was to try to "punish" him, like a 5 year old in trouble. Frankly, I thought that was a bit odd and that it was rude behavior. At the very next break in our meeting, I made it a point to go over and to sit with him and talk to him.

I understood he was looking for the "greater good" of our profession, without question. And, it was during this discussion I learned that he was a sole practitioner. He had no personal experience in publicly traded companies and he never intended to gain experience in publicly traded audits. He seemed to me to be genuine, ethical and doing the absolute best he could. His service to NASBA came at a high price to him. He gave thousands of hours to NASBA. There was really no one to "hold all the balls up" for him at his office during his service. He impressed me.

I remember I attended that particular AICPA conference alone (without my spouse). I was invited to a private reception in the suite of the then Chair of the AICPA and I was allowed to bring a guest. So, I brought the President of NASBA as my guest.

It seemed childish to me that the two organizations (AICPA and NASBA) could not get along in my opinion at that time. Upon entering the private reception I immediately and rightfully sensed everyone in the room moving away from us. That did not stop me. I introduced him to everyone I knew from the AICPA. Frankly, it has been my experience that volunteers trying to do the right thing always rise to the top. I could see people warming up to my new friend from NASBA. By the end of the evening "all was well". And, I am proud to say that the relationship of the organizations today (as I am writing this) is also better. I took a big chance and it seemed to pay off for the greater good.

Which brings me to being President and Chair of the WSCPA. Before taking office, it was clear that the WSCPA and our own SBOA did not get along or work together. In fact, I do not believe the former directors of the WSCPA and the SBOA could even talk civilly together; although, they were both very nice to me. I liked both of them and I believe I got along with both of them. Nonetheless, it was a disaster from the onset and one that I looked forward to trying to fix. Concurrently, upon entering the office as President and Chair, there were 16 ongoing legal cases between the State Attorney General (through our SBOA) and our WSCPA membership. Our legal counsel had provided an estimate to the WSCPA as to our cost to help defend these 16 members. The matters had been ongoing for quite some time with regards to a couple of the WSCPA members without resolution through the "legal process".

On the other hand, I knew the new Director of the SBOA and we scheduled a time to meet for lunch. During the lunch, we were able to discuss numerous issues, including these 16 cases. Over a couple of hours we managed to cut through all of the red tape and get these members their CPA licenses properly returned. I initially believed we had done the right thing.

At my next WSCPA board meeting, our legal counsel was in attendance. Frankly, I had almost forgotten about the meeting with the SBOA director. There were many things going on at the WSCPA and I also had my normal "day job". The aforementioned members were already back to work as their licenses had already been restored by the new SBOA Director. I had other things to do and I forgot to tell our legal counsel of the favorable result to our members. 12 of the 16 had personally thanked me for being able to settle their cases so quickly.

I was more interested in the 16 professionals and helping them to help support their families and get back to work than I was in the legal process. When I announced at the board meeting that the 16 cases had settled, instead of a thank you from the legal counsel, I was accused of "the unauthorized practice of law". I looked around the room at my board. I thought of the 16 people that were back to work. I thought about the next correct move in the board meeting. I made my decision. I immediately excused our legal counsel. Our board later decided we did not need our legal counsel present at any additional board meetings that year.

Anyway, at the beginning of my Presidency, I sensed "same old same old" behavior between different professional organizations. In other words, many of our own board members were not speaking positively of our SBOA. Some of this begins with what I call "corporate culture". That is, what is the allowed behavior of your own board and leaders of your own organization? It seemed to me to be a "class warfare". That is, each side at the time seemed to treat the other as inferior (i.e., Harvard/Princeton, Republican/Democrat, Hatfield/McCoy, etc.). At least this was before my year as President and Chair. At my first board meeting I simply requested that no negative words would be said about the SBOA or any other professional organization. Concurrently, we had a new director at the WSCPA and the governor appointed a new director to the SBOA. It was a priority for me that these organizations began a new era, that is, I wanted them to get along.

Luckily, I knew both new directors and quite frankly, it could have been easy to allow the old behavior to perpetuate. However, that did not seem to be in the best interests of our profession. I was there for our profession, plain and simple. So, one of my missions was to allow these two "personalities" to get along. I carefully picked my words when I spoke to members of the WSCPA and the SBOA. I encouraged mutual participation at CPA events. I even drove the new SBOA director to his first WSCPA networking event. I wanted to try to control what was going on and to patch up what I considered to be childish differences. Well, mission accomplished once again.

A personal memory from that year was that I was questioned by each of the new directors to tell them something about the other. I knew both of these individuals and believed they would get along. I also was aware that they were to meet at an upcoming professional meeting. My response to each of them was the same. "Nice guy, have a beer with him and you will get along". Nothing more, nothing less. They met and they got along as I expected they would. Again, mission accomplished.

During my active tenure with the WSCPA board, one of my most rewarding experiences was serving as the board liaison between the WSCPA Professional Conduct (Ethics) Committee and the WSCPA Board of Directors (BOD). Everyone that served with me on that ethics committee did not have a "personal agenda". All of them seemed to want to do the right thing for the membership, without exception. Many of them were not as "experienced" with "forensics" and the "legal system" as I was. So, I believe I was able to enlighten many of the members of the ethics committee as to "life in the trenches" and exercising common sense. Imagine, this was another professional committee that I was fortunate enough to serve, and all of them had the same goal. It was a wonderful experience for me.

For instance, the population at large might file a complaint against a CPA to our ethics committee. I had many experiences concerning the population filing complaints with the ethics committee. I believe it has become too much of a common practice for a former client to try to "use the profession" to delay paying a CPA's bill for services rendered. For instance, on several occasions I noted former clients reporting an alleged "ethical issue" to the ethics committee. Coincidentally, the former client had a "large outstanding bill" that it refused to pay to that same CPA. Generally, the scenario is: CPA performs accounting, CPA does not get paid, CPA demands payment of bill and/or resigns --- then the former client files a complaint, files a malpractice suit or simply acts as a 10 year old spoiled child. This was not always the case, but it certainly was the case in a majority of the cases I was presented while serving on the ethics committee.

I found that the ethics committee gets many of these types of complaints. In addition, so do the court systems. I believe these types of frivolous complaints should be easily identified and then accordingly dismissed by the ethics committee and/or the court system. However, there is potential money to be made in keeping some of the frivolous cases alive (by the attorneys) and also dismissing some that should not be dismissed. In cases that I assisted with, I tended to call the complainant (and their attorney in some cases) and discuss the matter with them. Without exception, their attorneys had advised them to file the complaint. It seemed if our ethics committee performed an investigation and found any wrongdoing, the complainant would get our services for free.

On one hand, there is nothing wrong with someone wanting an independent opinion when it is the right thing to do. However, during my tenure on the committee, not one of the complainants could tell me specifically of any wrongdoing by their CPA prior to filing their complaint with our committee. Instead, in a super majority of the cases presented to me, it all seemed to me to be "about the non payment of the fee". In my service as an expert witness, I was also referred many cases. I never accepted a malpractice case against a CPA when it seemed to me that the complainant simply did not want to pay the outstanding fee. It seemed to me that each and every time I was referred into a case (and some by the WSCPA) the problem was more often than not about non payment of a fee.

That is not to say that I never found CPAs that I believed to be in the wrong. In my experience, I have reported CPAs to our ethics division and/or the SBOA on numerous occasions for what I perceived to be real ethical violations. Without exception, none have been actively or properly pursued by the SBOA because of my complaint. Instead, the reaction was always a puzzlement to me. The first began when I was working for another CPA firm. A client of the firm came in to see the "partner in charge" of the office. That partner happened to be out of town at the time. So, the client asked to speak with me about what he thought was a theft. Here is my first experience in turning in a CPA for alleged theft.

Turning in Your Boss

As background, the partner in charge of the office had put together several real estate partnerships with his clientele and he also participated in other transactions with certain clients of his firm. This client had invested in one or more of those. The reason for this client's visit was because he had received a notice from a lender that concerned one of the partnerships with this CPA. I understood from the client that the partnership was somehow "behind in its mortgage payment". I listened intently to the client; however, I did not say anything at that time. Instead, I promised to look into the matter for him and get back to him as soon as possible. The partner was out of town and on vacation when the client had come in to speak to me.

After the client left, I simply went into the partner's office. I was aware that he maintained the books for his partnerships and investments all by himself. And I was not expecting to find anything negative anyway. In those days, I recall all the old black general ledgers that he used for these investments were neatly on the credenza behind his desk. I went through the general ledger in question and "was surprised" as to what I believed I was looking at. It was unbelievable. Bottom line, it appeared that someone I knew, trusted and respected may have been a part of some impropriety. Rather than tell the client that at the time, I elected to wait for the partner's return (a day later) and ask him about the transactions that appeared odd. After all, it could be that there was a rational explanation.

When the partner returned, I went into his office and shut his door and asked if I could speak to him. He nodded affirmatively. I mentioned that the client had come into the office and asked about a mortgage on a particular partnership. He immediately looked up and said, "What did you tell him?". I said "I could not tell him anything at the time". He said, "So what did you do?". I said, "I looked inside the general ledger". He became all flushed in the face and looked up and said, "What did you find?". I said, "That is exactly why I need to talk to you". He smiled and said "thank you", that he was "really busy" and "would look into it and get back to me later that afternoon". We did not even talk about it at the time. I went back to work and waited for his response. He said there was a "simple explanation". I believed him at the time.

Actually, when you trust someone, you do not think anything more about it. And I did not think anything more about it until he called me into his office later that afternoon. I expected an explanation; instead, he terminated my employment. This shocked me to no avail. In this case, he was a thief and I got fired for finding it! He warned me about telling anyone about this. In other words, he threatened me about telling the truth. If I told anyone, I could be sued. It is really odd how our legal system works to protect the criminals anymore.

The truth be told was --- the reason my reading the books and finding the mortgage was such a surprise is simple. This partnership was NOT supposed to have a mortgage, and therefore, it was not supposed to have a "mortgage payment". As it turned out, the CPA had borrowed on the building without permission from the other partners and without their knowledge.

To go on, I later learned that the CPA had borrowed funds inside a number of other partnerships that he controlled the books on. I understood this included his own CPA firm. As an example, I understood that the CPA firm had taken out a Small Business Administration (SBA) loan for a new computer acquisition. Simultaneous with the close of that loan, a series of other loans and/or leases were funded almost simultaneously on the same computer equipment (the same collateral). As I recall, the other partners in the CPA firm indicated they had no knowledge of the "additional" transactions or the subsequent borrowings.

And, I understood other types of transactions were used to take advantage of older people. Remember, a CPA has a public trust that other credentials simply cannot attain. That public trust is the responsibility of each and every licensee. At the time, different retirees were selling their homes. This CPA saw an opportunity. That is, the CPA would go to the retiree and offer them "full price for their home, nothing down, and 12% interest, unsecured, if they carried the note". There were several of these transactions also. Everyone wants to believe in the American dream, that they will get something for nothing, that a mysterious "big brother" will "give them money" or give them more than they should reasonably expect. It generally does not happen. But, greed is a nasty personal sin. By the way, he simultaneously, mortgaged those same properties at closing. In other words, he took cash at each closing from these transactions and the sellers only received a "promise to pay". Ultimately, I understood the unsecured notes were lost by the original home owners and the missing cash was unaccounted for that was derived from the mortgages.

All told, as I understood it from the State Securities Division, the irregularities were in the millions. I did not know the security rules at the time. I also did not recognize, until then, the absolute conflict of interest this was for a CPA to invest with his clients. That is, finding investments and bringing your clients into them with you. A CPA is highly respected and trusted. A CPA is in a position of trust and this should not be compromised. I never thought a CPA would do that to his clients, friends and/or colleagues.

I believe I did the right thing. I went to an attorney, explained to him what had happened and I let the attorney do the reporting of the irregularities to the SBOA. The SBOA did nothing at that time. Once everything was reported to the securities division, it did not take long for them to do the right thing. Frankly, the disgruntled aforementioned client had already told others about this. The mutiny was beginning against this CPA. And once the lawsuits began against the CPA, it was not long until the CPA firm simply unwound and filed for bankruptcy protection. However, damage was being continued to be done against some very good people because of the actions of the CPA and the SBOA did not act at the time. They told me that I had a conflict of interest in reporting this matter to the board and let the CPA continue in business. Unbelievable!

As it turned out, the person whom I referred to above as the "new" director of the SBOA (years later) was the then Chair of the Professional Standards Committee when this was reported through my attorney. There was another director at the SBOA at the time, someone I respected. This same mess was concurrently reported to him as director of the SBOA at the time. I was disappointed in their actions and in their non actions at the time. 5 years went by without either accounting entity sanctioning, admonishing or punishing the CPA. I was told at the time that their investigation showed that I was a "sour graped former employee". Seems the CPA was a popular guy around town and no one could believe (or wanted to believe) the actual truth. Sort of like the pension issue above! Everyone could see the white elephant in the room, no one wanted to act. Was it a popularity contest or was it fear of legal recourse?

Concurrently, the State Securities Division had launched an investigation into this CPA for securities fraud, embezzlement and other issues as I recall. I worked closely with the Securities Division to help them protect the innocent investors. Frankly, I was impressed by their "stepping up" to do the right thing. Many of the investors had contacted them trying to get some sort of retribution. In the end, the Securities Division seemed to come up with the right answer.

As a result of the Securities Investigation, the CPA was sentenced to jail time. It was only then that the SBOA stepped up and took away the license of this individual. In the mean time, many more individuals were harmed. I believe our SBOA should have reasonably acted more quickly. Was it Politics? Popularity? Regardless, their behavior was wrong in my opinion.

Bad Apple

As another example, years later, our firm had an employee who was not working out. Although he came to our firm with very high recommendations: client problems, fee problems and creative accounting seemed to be a reoccurring theme in our office. He did not generate any business for our firm, or very little if any at all. His ethics were always suspect to me. I remember one Friday evening I was coming into the back door of our office as he was leaving for the weekend. He was taking 4 audit bags (extra large brief cases) with him out of the back door of the kitchen. Unfortunately for him, the timing was bad. I was just coming in that door from visiting a client.

I asked him what he was doing over the weekend with the audit bags. He began explaining to me that he was taking work home to get a head start on a particular client. Our firm policy was that client files were not to leave the office, except to go to the client's office. I simply picked up one of our audit bags, opened it and found it was totally full of office supplies. I then repeated this and found the same in all 4 audit bags! Needless to say, I was surprised at his actions. However, I should not have been given my intuition about his ethics. We had a brief discussion about his future with our firm.

It was not just the removal of office supplies from individuals like this that bothered me. They also brought other problems and issues to the office. They generally had other ethical issues surrounding them almost regularly. As an example, certain clients may believe they were being overcharged by their professional. To a client, being overcharged is close to having someone take something from them. This was the case with a client he was working on that I had served for about 15 years prior to that time. In all of that time, each and every month, the client had paid their bill to our firm without question, until this particular day.

As to the client, this was an account relationship that this particular client expected me to be involved in (the big picture stuff); however, they understood that a firm CPA would be helping them with their routine accounting and bookkeeping. Nonetheless, I was in charge of many similar accounts. I relied upon the firm CPA "in charge" to not only be on top of all of the client needs and services, but just as important, to bill for services rendered in a fair and reasonable manner.

This client telephoned our billing department and asked to speak to me about their bill. As I recall the fee was about $550 on the bill. Historically, the amount of the fee itself was not one of the larger bills to this client. For instance, their year end services were in excess of $10,000. However, something about the $550 seemed to have ticked off this client, albeit the telephone call to me. She explained to me the question that she asked of our in charge CPA. This was a fairly routine and easy question. She said that this CPA answered her question. And the client told me she expected a bill for the telephone call; however, she did not expect a bill to be any where near $550.

I thought about her comments and the many years of absolutely no questions or problems with their bill. It was clear to me that they were unhappy about something else too, not just the bill. I found that these telephone calls were a real test of "business acumen" for the CPA partner in charge of that particular client. Based upon my experience with what I considered to be very good clients, I simply responded to her, " do not pay anything as I was writing off all charges for that month. I am sorry they had any problems whatsoever with anyone from our firm". The tone of the telephone conversation immediately lightened.

As good honest people would, she politely objected and reminded me that she did receive services from our firm. I agreed that they had received services and reminded her of her loyalty for 15 years to our firm. I said that I was sorry for the services and needing to question our charges. I told her I would simply write off all of her charges for the month and that I valued her friendship and client relationship. She never forgot that and we continued to have that client relationship until the day that I retired. That particular CPA that initiated these charges simply did not seem to be fair either to the client or to me. I learned that after I researched what had been done.

In the end, that CPA decided to leave our firm. Frankly, we were glad to see him go. As it turned out, he went into law school and became an attorney!

Not long after he left for law school, our firm received a telephone call from the area he was attending law school. It seems he had applied for an income tax season job at a CPA firm in that area. As part of his job interview, we understood that he told them that he was "personally responsible for the success of our firm". The interviewer on the other side of the line telephoned our office to verify his employment and ask us a few questions. He initially was speaking to our managing partner. Later the managing partner came into my office and requested I join this conversation related to the former employee. The CPA on the other side of the conversation then restated to me that our former employee stated that he was personally responsible for the success of our firm. He then asked if I would respond to that. I scratched my head and tried to think of something that I could respond to as a former employer. All I could think of at the time was "I am not surprised he would say that". What else could I say?

And like a bad cold, the former employee returned to our area after law school and began soliciting all of our clients that he had formerly worked on while with our firm. He actually had limited success with these solicitations; however, a few of our clients did leave and transfer their CPA relationship to his new CPA firm. Over the years, I found the larger clients are generally loyal to their CPA firm. I believe the larger clients understand what is needed to help them with their businesses. Some of the clients we had actually terminated and a few others did begin using him for his services. However, they learned that they were getting more than they expected from his new firm. In addition to providing CPA services, our former employee (and now attorney too) began forming investments. He invited these individuals to invest with him in these investments. I found that it could be a conflict of interest to invest with your clients. And regarding his actions, does this sound like a possible ethical repeat of the above?

While his practice was forming and his investment invitations were going on, I was elected President of the WSCPA. Being recognized by your peers in this manner is a great honor to in our profession. However, in this case, I believe this former employee saw an opportunity to "advance his personal agenda and career" by using his former relationship with me. However, my parents did not raise a complete fool.

Our former employee unexpectedly showed up at our office one day and wanted to meet with me. I did not have time to meet with him. However, since he previously had worked at our office, he somewhat understood how our front office worked. He simply waited in the lobby until I appeared from my office between appointments. Unfortunately for me, he aggressively cut me off from a normal office traffic pattern that I used around our office. He approached me and said he wanted to talk to me. He stuck out a hand for me to shake and said he came in to see me to apologize for his prior actions. He tried to explain to me that he "had changed" and wanted me to know "how much he appreciated everything I had done for him". I did not believe him. Just the feeling of having him in our office again was getting a bit uncomfortable.

I simply shook his hand, said thank you and wished him well. He said "you do not believe me do you?". I could not help myself, and I said, "actually, I do not believe you. I believe you are here because you believe you can make money by somehow being here and getting me to somehow say nice things about you to different people in our profession". I was as polite as I could be and I asked him to leave the office. He kept talking, but I was strong. I walked away. He finally left.

As it turned out, many of our clients simply refused to become a client of his or become an investor with him (the lucky ones); however, a few people invested with him. It was not long afterward that we began receiving nervous telephone calls from our "former clients" and "current clients who invested with him". They all went into these investments with their eyes wide open. However, all of them had previous experience with the owners of our firm and our high ethical standards.

We learned he was being investigated (we were not surprised). I recall the conclusion of the bar association was that "his trust account" did not balance. As I recall, he immediately lost his license to practice as an attorney. Some time later, he lost his license to practice as a CPA. I believe most want to believe that CPAs would have reacted more quickly to help keep the public trust of our profession at a very high level. In this case, the bar association acted swiftly to protect the public perception of their profession and the integrity of the related legal trust accounts. Our profession did not react so quickly. I actually found this true numerous times throughout my professional career. Our own profession acts very slowly in these types of matters; too slowly in my opinion. And, we are not allowed to warn our clients of the suspicious ethical behavior or another CPA. It is so sad that our own legal system does not allow CPAs to properly warn people of the potential harm they can face with partnering with these types of other CPAs. If so, we faced serious repercussions to us from our licensing agency and the legal system.

In fact, his other behaviors in other areas of his professional life sort of put another type of black eye on our profession. This individual had become an instructor for certain continuing professional education classes (CPE) for the WSCPA. CPAs are required by law to attend a minimum amount of CPE; although, CPAs are generally free to pick and choose which classes to actually attend. Our firm had a policy of not attending any of his classes.

The director of the WSCPA knew we did not participate in his classes. Although she should have known something was going on, she never asked me about him until after he was disbarred and after he lost his CPA license. And, as stated above, we could not talk about him under the risk of a legal onslaught or repercussions from our own state board of accounting. We had to wait "patiently" for the system to deal with him, if that is possible. Upon the loss of his legal license and ultimate loss of his CPA license, she said to me, "you knew about him but you did not say a word". I simply pointed out, "you should have known when you knew we were not taking any of his classes". This was one of her favorite instructors as he had taken her under his wing. However, after thinking about it, she agreed with me.

Anyway, our CPA profession came to a cross roads with this individual concerning his scheduled CPE classes after it was known that he was in trouble with the law and with our profession. Whereas, he had lost his license to practice as an attorney and he had lost his license to practice as a CPA, a tough decision had to be made. It seems that the WSCPA had sold some future CPE courses. This suspended member was scheduled to instruct those courses that the CPA society had already received payment. So, a difficult decision had to me made. Would the WSCPA allow this individual to instruct, would the WSCPA find an alternative instructor, or would the WSCPA issue refunds? I disagreed with the decision at the time. A decision was made by the state society that allowed him to instruct the courses that had already been marketed. The CPA society kept the money. The profession may have been compromised by those actions.

Walk Away at the Right Time

One of the nicest thing about parents is that they love their children forever. As was the case with my mother. After my father passed away, I tried to do more and more for my mother. One of things that I assumed was that I would routinely take my mother to a regular weekly early morning doctor's appointment. My mother had a terminal illness. This was difficult to watch progress. Anyone who has watched a close family member deteriorate is one that I do not have to tell the difficulty that everyone close to the situation goes through.

Well, my mother was a typical parent. She never missed an opportunity to tell her doctor, in my presence, what a wonderful and knowledgeable son and CPA that I was. My mother was proud of me. She had to give up everything to legally immigrate with my father to the United States and she was so happy that I seemed to be doing well with my business. At the time, the doctor would smile and say thank you. I would smile and be a bit uncomfortable; nonetheless, my mother received great care from the compassionate doctor.

Within a month of my mother's passing away, her doctor, together with a few other doctors from that medical practice, left their old medical practice with several doctors to form a new medical practice with only a hand picked few of the doctors. Initially, they used another CPA firm for their professional services. This was the same firm used by the predecessor medical practice. Ultimately, they decided to break away from this old firm and find a new CPA firm that could properly represent the medical group and all of the individual practitioners.

Over the years, I found most individuals and businesses choose a CPA by word of mouth. These individuals and businesses generally go to people they know, respect and trust and ask them which CPA firm they use. And, I understand from their inquiries that my name kept coming up.

So, my mother's doctor telephoned me and told me what was going on and that their new group needed a new CPA. He told me that he had received several suggestions from his peer group to use me, not to mention all the times my mother told him about me (he remembered). That was memorable and cute.

I later met with the entire group of doctors, except for one "Jewish" doctor (as he was out of town at the time). The rest of the group decided to change to our firm and we began organizing their records. Later, the Jewish doctor returned from his vacation and he wanted to come into our office to interview me. He said he wanted to determine if he would use me as his CPA also. He was a great, professional and funny individual. And he confessed to me that he had little leverage concerning our conversation. He said the group had already changed to our firm; however, he kept emphasizing to me that he was a Jewish doctor. He then asked me why a Jewish doctor would want to use me? He was half serious and half trying to see my reaction.

I looked into his eyes for a determination as how I was going to answer the question. I knew he was humorous and also understood that he wanted my response to be honest and sincere. I also understood that this was going to be the beginning of a new relationship for us. I knew that I needed to make a connection with him. So, I said, "Another Jewish doctor from your geographical local area and specialty of expertise once told me, the only doctors that anyone should use are Jewish doctors. He is now retired". The new client's eyes lit up and said, "How do you know Dr. "so and so"?" (he knew who I was referring to and he had no idea that I knew this man). I told him that I could not tell him how I knew him. He asked how he could contact the retired doctor. I said that I would have the retired doctor telephone him to talk to him about our firm and myself.

Needless to say, the Jewish doctor was able to talk to the old respected and retired Jewish doctor about me. We made a great connection during that early meeting which was only facilitated by my old friend and retired doctor's comments to this new client.

Well, just as it was supposed to, the new medical practice was up and running. There were many hurdles to overcome as the medical industry was a tough industry to form a new practice at that time, especially for independently and physician owned medical practices. The accounting fees can be very lucrative from helping these practices with their accounting and income services. The accounting fees can also be proportionate to how well the CPA was able to get along with and interact with the client. This was no different when representing physicians. As was the case with similar businesses, there were many practitioners in this particular practice and many of those doctors had very different opinions.

As one thing lead to another, there were disagreements about how to practice among the different physicians within the medical group, so much so that 2 of the doctors left the group to form their own medical practice. After those doctors established their own medical practice they also wanted me to represent them as their CPA. This seems natural, but it can be a touchy situation as it may lead to the "appearance" of a conflict of interest. As expected, the managing physician from the initial group requested that our firm not represent the new medical group. They believed it would be a conflict of interest.

Wow. All of a sudden we had both a moral dilemma and an ethical dilemma. On one hand, it is standard and customary for CPA's to represent multiple businesses in the same industry. However, many "perceive" that this practice may in fact be a conflict of interest. They believe that even the appearance of the duplicity is a bad thing. So, a decision had to be made: would we continue to represent all of the doctors? If not, which doctors and medical group would we represent, the original company or the new company?

After careful consideration, I did not believe it was a conflict; however, I believed there was a perception that there was a conflict. And the group did not split amicably. Hence, we did not represent that latter group and we resigned from the representation of the individual doctor owners of that latter group. Probably not something that had to be done, but, it was the right thing to do.

The medical group that we had been representing was very happy in our decision. And although I did not continue to represent the other doctors, I did maintain a personal relationship with those doctors. I was sorry we could not represent them but I was convinced the decision was the best in these circumstances.

CHAPTER SIX – EXPERT WITNESS WORK

One of the services that I really enjoyed assisting with was expert witness work. As I stated earlier, I have testified from Alaska to Florida. I reviewed each case thoroughly prior to agreeing to accept the case. If the case were not one that I "believed in" or if it was a case that I thought had no merits, I would refuse to accept the case.

Such was the case on a reference to me from our WSCPA office to take a case as an expert witness. It began for me when I received a telephone call from an attorney and their client who was suing their prior CPA. I knew the attorney as he was well respected in the accounting community. They told me that they needed an expert witness for their case. They said that both of them had received references to me from different people and professionals. I therefore listened to them and asked them about their case.

As I understood it, the taxpayer had engaged the CPA to prepare income tax returns. The CPA had begun collection action for non payment of their bill. Then, this former client of that CPA firm had filed a malpractice claim against their prior CPA. I understood from them there were several allegations against the CPA in the complaint. I simply asked, "What do you believe the prior CPA did wrong and why". Their answer surprised me. I was told that they did not know. Instead they explained that they needed me to tell them what was wrong.

This puzzled me as to why someone would sue someone and not know if the other party had in fact done anything wrong. I asked them the remaining balance of the accounting bill. I then asked how much they had paid on the bill to date. I was told that nothing had ever been paid.

So I tried to summarize as follows, "So, I understand that you received income tax returns from your prior CPA and a bill for services rendered for them to prepare those income tax returns for you. You have indicated to me that you do not know if the CPA has actually done anything wrong. You have not paid anything to date and it appears that you filed your claim for alleged malpractice after your delinquent account was sent to collection. At first blush, this looks to me like you simply do not want to pay your CPA bill". Both the attorney and his client laughed and said, "that is probably what this case would come down to". I told them thank you for thinking of me for this case but in the circumstances I would have to decline accepting the case. I explained to them that in order for me to agree to take the case and testify on their behalf, that they would need to have a good case with good facts. From what I heard from them, neither the case or the facts seemed to be in their favor. My "gut" told me this was a bad case, and accordingly, I refused to work on the matter with them.

Prior to ending the telephone call, they reminded me that they had received the referral to me from our State Society of CPAs. Somehow, it appeared to me that they thought I would take their case regardless of the merits of the case. I said that the referral itself did not guarantee that I would take the case. However, in the back of my mind I was surprised that a CPA Society would make such a referral. Regardless, I refused the case and wished them well.

I understand that the case was later settled for a partial payment on the CPA bill. There was never any malpractice --- as expected.

Long Time Clients

This experience can probably be classified in multiple chapters. However, it appears fitting here because of the strategies imposed. Sometimes you just cannot deal with stupid.

I received a telephone call one day from an older gentleman, a doctor. His specialty is irrelevant to this experience. However, he told me that he founded a group many years ago and was getting ready to retire and needed my expertise. He said he would probably continue to practice another couple of years.

As I got to know this gentleman, I really liked and respected him. The client was smart, successful and wise. He was well liked by everyone in our office. Over the years, we became friends. And with many clients such as this, I was able to meet and get to know his family.

I had met many families over the years of many of my clients. This family was not unusual. Here was an elderly gentleman and he was very financially successful. I found that many of the "next" generation of children of successful people did not have the same goals and ambitions of the parents. This was especially true in cases when the parents themselves grew up poor or with little assets. They tended to give their children many of the things they wanted when they were children.

The family idiosyncrasies were not unusual; however, the best things I found that parents could give to their children was their undivided love and a great education. Even with these attributes, the children may still want (and sometimes expect) more and more money. Or alternatively, the children would not want to work and have some or all of their bills paid or subsidized by mom and dad.

During family meetings to discuss estate planning, it was clear to me that the children wanted more and more control of the assets. However, prior to finishing this part of the story, I will regress to what happened not too long after the doctor became a client of mine.

I asked him why he wanted to switch his long time CPA to me. He told me that his practice had used the same CPA firm for almost thirty five (35) years. That originally, there were 3 owners of the professional practice and 2 of the original 3 had already retired. The practice had brought in 3 additional younger owners. Now the practice was using the same firm, but a younger professional who was also an attorney. The doctor did not believe the CPA firm was looking out for everyone's best interest.

Incidentally, I was coaching one of my son's soccer team at the time. This will become important later in this story as one of the younger doctors in the group also coached soccer in the same league. We did not know each other well; however, we had met.

Bottom line, the doctor did not believe he was being treated fairly by the 3 "next generation" doctors in his practice. And he believed the former CPA firm was helping their side over his personal interests. Although I did not find that unusual for the CPA to be loyal to the "business", I thought the behavior of the other CPA firm was not proper in the circumstances, especially with regards to how this elderly gentleman was treated.

I asked the doctor what amount he expected from the practice for his interest when he retired? He showed me what the other 2 already retired doctors received. Although the practice had grown, he only wanted what the other 2 had received. On the surface, this sounded reasonable to me.

I indicated that I thought the best way to solve this was for us to meet with the CPA firm for the group and the doctor in charge of the group (the next generation). This was set up in the other CPA's office. I met my client at the door of the other CPA firm and we went in.

We were called into the meeting where the CPA and the other doctor had already been talking. I mentioned that I was thankful for the meeting and that I hoped all would proceed amicably. I said that I understood that the 2 of the original doctors had already retired and received the same amount. This was acknowledged by the other doctor too. I said that in view of the facts and circumstances, it did not appear unreasonable for my client to expect the same amount.

The other doctor sat and listened and the CPA for the practice said boldly, "I have represented this firm for the past many years. Let me also remind you that I am an attorney. As such I noted that there was no Buy Sell Agreement for the practice. As such I advised my client that your client is a minority shareholder and they do not have to pay him anything. However, to be courteous, we will pay him 25% of what he wants".

Although this was rude and unprofessional on many levels, the one that I was most sorry for was that this "founding" doctor. He had given the younger doctors their start in the profession. Without his careful attention, tutelage and overall administration skills and training, the younger doctors would not be where they were today. Now was their chance to do the right thing concerning the elderly gentleman and they simply did not want to do it. They wanted to exercise their "legal rights" as explained by their CPA.

So, I asked the other doctor, "Dave, how do you feel about what your CPA/attorney just said?". Dave said, "I believe our group wants to follow his advice". At that moment, I was so sorry for the older doctor. I was thinking, how can this be settled amicably? Is there another strategy that could be employed to help move this along?

So, I said, "Are you sure?". The other CPA said, "You heard him, he is sure". I looked at Dave once again and then said, "I am so much smarter than your CPA that you cannot begin to comprehend it. Let me ask you again, are you sure?".

The other CPA said, "I am insulted". I said, "You shouldn't be, because it is true".

With that, and as expected, the other CPA said, "Well, what can you do to help?". I said I can help him on a couple of levels. First is with the malpractice action against his firm and him personally. He shouted, "Malpractice?". I said, "Sure. You just said that you were an attorney and you represented this man for a long time and the medical group. And, you never advised your clients to enter into a formal Buy Sell Agreement. Strike one counselor".

He said, "What else?". I said "Absent a Buy Sell Agreement, I understand that my client can then transfer his stock to anyone or any entity, is that true?" The CPA/attorney said a bit more softly, "Well --- yes".

I went on, "For instance, we could donate the stock to a charity and take a 100% deduction of the value of the stock". The CPA/attorney replied, "With the current income tax rates, that only gives him 50% of the value though!".

I said that "I agreed, but that was double what they were already offering. And besides, absent a Buy Sell Agreement, I believe he can donate the stock to one of the wild religious organizations that may raise some alarm in the local community. And, I know the editor of our local newspaper who can run a front page story about your clients and their partnership with this wild religious organization. Strike two".

The CPA/attorney then said, "Well what else?". I said absent the Buy Sell Agreement that you failed to get for your own clients, they will probably sue you also. He yelled, "Why?". I said "It is my understanding that the only allowable shareholders in that form of medical practice were doctors, and since there was an improper transfer to a non doctor, that the corporation would cease to operate and be administratively liquidated and dissolved, thus causing each of his clients to also pay income taxes in addition to the corporation paying income taxes. Strike three".

The reaction we received was that they were stunned. They simply had not thought the issue through. In their greed, they simply forgot that the other party would try to optimize his own situation. They appeared to be in a position to "talk".

Instead, I then got up and asked my client to leave with me. We left and as we walked outside my client was really happy that we seemed to get the best of them. He told me he was very happy with the way the meeting developed. I reminded him that none of what I said was for anything other than posturing the other doctors in order for them to pay him a fair and reasonable price for his interest. I said that in my opinion the CPAs should not try to enter/disrupt this negotiation as long as the negotiations can go on.

He then asked, "Well, can I do any of the things you just said?". I said, "I do not know; however, I suspect if you drop by Dave's house this evening, he will be ready to settle with you".

By the way, my client settled with Dave that evening for slightly more than the other doctors received. Dave had a conscience and everyone were ultimately able to remain friends. I never forgot the demeanor or the chosen ethical behavior of the other CPA though.

As to the family, as I stated, the gentleman was elderly. Over the next few years, the children seemed to want more and more of his assets. The children solicited the support from his wife (their mother) in order to help them to get to their inheritance prior to the death of their parents. The retired doctor did not want to give any more than they had already been giving to them. In fact, his estate was sufficient to warrant a comfortable retirement for he and his wife. If he gave too much away, it would compromise his own retirement.

And during this time, it was evident that he was slowing down, both physically and mentally. He would look forward to coming into our office. We had a desk for him in our computer department. He would go "on line" and try to balance his month end banking and brokerage statements. He also liked to keep all of his books on the computer. He had several rental properties and other investments. And while he was in our computer room, he could ask for help from any of our staff in that department.

We never had anyone that was allowed access to our computer room before, and we never had another person allowed this access. He was just a nice guy that got along with everyone in our office.

This practice of him coming in monthly went on for a few years. During this time, he continued to slow; however, I never noticed any time that he was not able to manage his financial affairs. One day, his wife telephoned me to talk about her husband. She said that he was suffering from the onset of Alzheimer's and Dementia. And she was trying to take control of their assets together with her children once again. She asked me to meet with her and her husband. He agreed to the meeting; however, he did not believe that he was suffering from anything affecting his mental status. He made it clear that he trusted me. That was one of the incredible benefits of being a CPA --- meeting great people like this gentleman.

So we set up a meeting in our conference room with just the 3 of us. We began talking about their estate, their finances and their children. And during the meeting I witnessed something that I had never seen before. That is, he sort of "went away" mentally during the meeting. He did not know where he was for part of the meeting and he was unable to intelligently answer questions or participate in our discussion.

He finally "mentally" returned to the meeting. I had never experienced anyone with Alzheimer's or Dementia before. And he did not know that he had "left the meeting" for awhile. However, he trusted me and I began to explain to him what I had just witnessed. His wife was in tears watching this situation play out.

Ultimately, the retired doctor entered and Alzheimer's and Dementia facility. His wife and children seized control of the assets and began spending the assets while the doctor was still alive. Fortunately, the assets survived the doctor's stay in the medical facility. In the "alert" times, he was aware that his children had taken control of his assets. Unfortunately, those assets were not sufficient for the widow to live in the style that she had become accustomed before her demise.

After the doctor's funeral, one of the sons telephoned me. He said that he wanted thank me for helping his parents for such a long time. He said his father thought of me as his closest friend. He mentioned to me that he had been wrong to pressure his parents to give him additional assets while they were alive. For some reason, I interpreted his actions, by telephoning me, as something therapeutic for the son. He seemed to want some sort of "absolution" that I was unable to give him. Instead of saying thank you for calling, I told the son about what a great man that I believed his father was. I then asked the son, "How was your relationship with your father when he died?". I truly hoped that their relationship had improved. In the big picture, our memories of our relationships are all we have left after everything else is gone.

It is Cold in Alaska

I do not believe that business people divorce any more often than non business people. However, the financial issues are generally the same in either instance. For whatever reason, I found that if the couple is doing very well financially, they believed they could afford to break up. When they were struggling and working together to survive, I found they did not have the where-with-all to divorce. Hence, the struggling couples tended to be the least likely to divorce in my opinion. They seemed to have a common goal to get by for financial reasons in the latter example. As was the case with this divorce.

I was introduced to this client as I represented many similar businesses in the same industry. This gentleman worked for 30 years in the industry prior to becoming able to purchase a franchise for his family. He saved his money for 30 years and was finally able to qualify to purchase a franchise. The cost of the franchise was almost $1 million dollars. Please note that I found that in order to buy a franchise that these franchisees typically had to leverage all of their personal assets (house, retirement plan, etc.) to qualify to purchase a franchise. Even then, a lender would have to loan them the balance, the "lion's share" of the purchase price.

Within 3 days from the time the husband and wife moved and took possession of the franchise, the wife filed for a divorce. I understood that she believed she would be on "Easy Street" from other advice she had received. Her "friends" had told her that she would now be rich as they were small business owners of this franchise. And this was even before they had taken possession and control of the franchise. He came to me together with his attorney for financial advice concerning the divorce. He also wanted our firm to represent his franchise during and after the divorce. I never met his estranged spouse.

In preparing for any divorce and the related property settlement, it is important that the CPA looks at all relevant information. This includes all of the assets of any kind. I always tried to do this. And, I had valued dozens, if not more than a hundred, similar franchises in my practice as a CPA. Thus, I was aware of how the franchise was valued for the purchase price that was just paid. It seemed to be a normal and customary valuation. The valuations that I had performed were for similar buyers, similar sellers, financing, refinancing, and for other franchisees going through dissolution proceedings.

However, this dissolution action became more and more contentious. The attorney on the other side had a reputation for dragging the matter out for as long as possible and asking for too much money in the dissolution proceedings. Many discovery documents were requested by the "other side" and ultimately an expert was hired by the estranged spouse. That so called expert supposedly had both high credentials from the "bar association" and as a "CPA". His full valuation report for this matter was over six hundred (600) pages. The value that was concluded in his report was slightly more than $5 million (remember they just paid $1 million for the franchise in the same week that the couple separated). In my opinion, his report was total "garbage", but not a surprise, given what the courts will accept these days. This has always been a disappointment to me that the court system would allow such a valuation report as anything other than frivolous.

On the other hand, my report was about twenty (20) pages long showing in detail how the franchise was originally valued for the purchase transaction and why that valuation was still true for the dissolution proceeding. I also was able to show why the valuation was valued consistently with many transfers of similar franchises within the same system that I was familiar with. In fact, I had assisted on the buys side or the sell side with many similar transactions in that region.

As you can probably guess, the 2 sides did not agree to the valuation, and accordingly, off to court the parties went. On their side were also expert witnesses from 2 different national CPA firms acting as financial and income tax advisers to the estranged spouse. It was clear that the attorney representing the other side was certainly an "advocate" for the other side, probably too much of an advocate. He got lost in "his case", not in the merits of what he was doing in my opinion. Concurrently, the estranged spouse's attorney appeared to be completely blind to common sense and reasonableness.

During the court proceeding, one important part of the trial was "the incremental income tax rate" of the franchisee husband after the divorce. Simply stated, the incremental income tax rate on income is the percentage of income tax that would be paid on the increase in income, if any. The income tax tables showed a maximum income tax rate of 39.6%. However, that is not always the "incremental" rate. This is for many reasons because some deductions may be lost as well as certain tax credits as income increases.

I testified that my client's incremental rate was just over 50%. Under cross examination, the other attorney tried to embarrass me as he was trying to limit the incremental income tax to the Federal maximum income tax rate. He yelled at me, moaned and did a great acting job before the judge. He then presented me an income tax code and asked that I identify the tax tables. He then asked that I tell the court what the highest tax rate was in the tables. I said 39.6%. Then I said, "It is clear to me that you do not understand what an incremental income tax rate is. Please let me use your experts to explain". He unwittingly agreed.

I asked the attorney to give the book (Internal Revenue Code) to his experts. I then asked that his experts to "go to the blackboard" in the courtroom. I then gave them an "example case" for them to write on the board. I carefully chose each and every expense and income amount. I asked them to calculate the income tax on that amount, which they did correctly. I then changed one variable (more income) and asked them to compute the income tax on the additional amount of income. Their result came out to be 72%! Well, both the CPAs and the attorney were surprised. I said "Well maybe 72% in your illustrative case for the court today, but just over 50% in this dissolution proceeding". The ultimate decision of the court upheld my opinion for this portion of the proceeding.

I then testified as to the value of the franchise. Prior to that testimony, other testimony was heard from the highest ranking employee in the area for the franchise organization. He testified that I was probably the country's best expert on valuation of these franchises. He went on to say that I had helped with sales of dozens of franchises. In addition, he was personally aware that I provided related services for franchisees, including succession planning and estate planning. Frankly, it was humbling to hear someone speak of you that highly in a hostile courtroom atmosphere. It was also fun!

Next, their expert took the witness stand. He brought his "impressive" credentials and his valuation report. As I stated earlier in this book, our so called "professional" credentials seem to just add "fuel to the fire". This man was not an expert to me. However, he had the credentials. He was there to provide specific testimony that the other attorney wanted in my opinion. Nonetheless, he had credentials, he looked good in a suit and he made his first presentation under direct testimony in a careful and professional demeanor. As stated earlier, he valued the franchise at $5 million when the franchise was purchased for about $1 million 3 days earlier!

I had carefully reviewed his report for our client. And, I more or less found the report defective in too many ways to mention. I then wrote a series of questions to cross examine the witness expert with. The questions were more or less:

1   How many purchases of these franchises have you ever represented? Answer, none,

2   How many sales of these franchises have you ever represented? Answer, none,

3   How many franchisees have you assisted in succession planning? Answer, none,

4   How many franchisees have you assisted with estate planning? Answer, none,

5   Other than this case, have you ever represented a franchisee before in this industry? Answer, no,

6   Finally, would it surprise you to learn that $1 million is the highest price ever paid for one of these franchises in the history of the organization? Answer, yes,

7   So, how does that change your opinion of value and your prior testimony? Frankly, the guy stumbled.

And the judge could see that the "so-called expert" was not an actual expert, just a professional "paid assassin" that was highly trained to do just that. Ultimately, my valuation which was equal to the purchase price, was sustained by the court. This should not have been "rocket science".

By the way, $1 million was not the highest amount ever paid for a franchise; however, if you look closely at the wording of the question, the other expert obviously thought so. Sometimes a little honest trickery goes a long way! I call that "anchoring"; that is, give the other guy something to think about during his live testimony to see how he reacts. In this case, he did not react very well nor did he respond quickly enough.

This trial concluded in January in Alaska. I remember it being very cold and windy. I remember my vehicle sliding sideways while simply stopped because it was so icy. I had never been that cold before (or since) in my entire life. The final decision was beautiful though! It made everyone on the franchisee's side "warm and fuzzy".

Back to Alaska

I represented those franchisees all over the country from time to time. And the national franchiser would sometimes request that I assist in certain "problem" franchises. Sometimes, the problem was created by the franchiser Sometimes, the problem was a result of the franchisees inexperience or ineptitude. If the problem was inexperience, the operational side could be fixed by the franchiser and we could assist with the financial side.

From our perspective, the financial side could sometimes be assisted with assisting with a "global refinance". If payments were too high, a refinance could help. Sometimes the issue was profitability. If that were the case, then I was able to provide examples of other things that could be considered, together with the franchiser's help, to raise profitability and ultimately cash flow.

Sometimes, the franchiser simply was overly optimistic and due to no fault of the franchisee, the business was not profitable or the franchisee had exhausted all financial resources because of the franchiser's original estimates. If this were the case, the normal protocol would be to discuss with the national franchiser and if they agreed, certain accommodations could be made.

However, if the problem was ineptitude, as I said, you cannot fix stupid. Ultimately, in these circumstances the franchisee would need to be replaced by a more experienced or better franchisee.

In this particular case, it appeared that the original estimates of the franchiser were unreasonable or unattainable. Accordingly, the franchisee had exhausted all of his resources. In simple terms, he was broke. Refinancing and profitability were not issues. For whatever reason, certain individuals at the franchiser still wanted this franchisee to surrender the franchise. The result was litigation.

The ethical dilemma for me was what to do? On one hand the national franchiser asked me to help the franchisee. The national franchiser introduced me to this client. However, the national franchiser did not pay me any money nor were they ever a client at any time. Thus, a dilemma. Do I simply resign and let this poor franchisee lose everything he owned? The franchisee was the client, not the franchiser A tough decision had to be made.

I discussed this with the other owner in our firm and I also contacted the AICPA ethics division. Both agreed the "right thing to do" was to help this franchisee. And, everyone recognized that we may not get paid as the franchisee had no money. We also recognized that our representation of this franchisee could put us in a controversial and adversarial position with the franchiser We also recognized that the franchiser would spend and spend through the legal system in order to maintain its image. In other words, the franchiser had a reputation of making it very difficult to go to trial against it; regardless of the costs.

The funny thing is that the franchiser has a great image and I continue to this day to be surprised why this matter was allowed to get to a lawsuit. However, at the time, it appeared that it was the only recourse left to the franchisee.

I was then treated badly by the franchiser Although, all of our other franchisee clients appreciated our loyalty to this client (and fellow franchisee), the franchiser tried to make our decision to help our client difficult for our business too. Pressure was coming in from all angles.

By the way, over the years, I had met many corporate attorneys for this franchiser As was the case with this attorney working with the other "hired guns" for the franchiser This corporate attorney was one that I highly respected and I had known for years. I found it odd to be on the other side of him in a case such as this.

As an aside, if you are an expert witness, never list your telephone number in the telephone book. This is because process servers can serve you at your home if they are unsuccessful at your business in serving you. This is normally for such things as subpoenas for deposition or other things.

Normal protocol with experts, especially a CPA during income tax season, is to have the attorneys for the parties pick a mutually beneficial time to schedule a deposition. However, if the other side wants to be unreasonable, they will simply go out of their way from time to time to make the representation of our client difficult. This was certainly the case in this matter.

However, the other side finally got frustrated and I agreed to a scheduled deposition. I also agreed to drive seventy (70) miles to the deposition as 4 of the 5 legal firms for the other side (that is right, they hired 5 different groups of attorneys, including their own in house counsel) were at or near to the area chosen for the deposition at the time. I also let them know my schedule, that I was also coaching soccer for my one of my son's teams, and that I would have to leave by 4 PM to make it to the soccer game on time.

This should not have been a problem because we began the deposition at 9 AM; however, there was a relentless strategy to try to trick me on my testimony. All of the attorneys took turns and they all asked the same questions; however, they used different manners to ask the questions. And, the deposition dragged on and on and on. Finally, I looked at my watch and it was slightly after 4 PM. I stood up and apologized and told them I would return the next day, but "per agreement and I had to leave".

The senior and most experienced trial attorney then yelled at me "Sit down!". I said "Or what?". The trial attorney then told the court reporter to go "off the record". In other words, to quit typing what he was going to say to me. I asked her to keep going. I said, "This is exactly our agreement. I have a bunch of 10 year old children waiting for me and we had already discussed this and agreed to my leaving at 4 PM." I reminded them "I came under verbal agreement and without a subpoena. This was because I was trying to do the right thing and to help move this matter along".

With that, the trial attorney said, "OK you SOB, here is a subpoena for you --- you have now been served, I am not done with my interrogation of you, so sit your a$##$ down".

I casually looked at him and said, "You are from Alaska and in Alaska you have Burroughs. We are now in Washington and we have counties". He said "What is the point?". I said that he had just served me "Outside of the county where I reside, so I cannot even return tomorrow, I will return in 5 days. If I returned in less than 5 days it may violate my client's interests". With that, I left. All 5 attorneys for the franchiser were sitting there in disbelief as I walked out.

My client's attorney followed me down the elevator laughing and said that he was proud of the way I acted and then told me that he was intimidated by the other attorneys (our client could only afford one attorney from a small legal firm). He asked me what to tell the attorneys as he really wanted to get back to Alaska the next day also. I asked him what he believed was best for his client. He said that coming back the next day would be the optimum solution. I agreed, but under one provision. He asked "What?".

I said, "Telephone the trial attorney about 10:30 PM and let him know that he had finally talked me into it". I wanted them to contemplate having to leave town the next day and return at a mutually agreed later time. I figured that the lead and rude trial attorney should "stew for a while". He laughed and agreed. The deposition concluded the next morning.

In my experience, these types of matters can be settled by mutual agreement, by a trial, or by something referred to as a settlement conference. Such was the next step. Everyone met in Alaska for the "next round". This included the franchiser's corporate counsel, which I thought was a good thing as I had known him for many years.

However, at the time, I was under the misconception that a settlement conference was a conference whereby people tried to settle things. This was my first experience with a settlement conference, such as this, and I learned that was not the case.

Instead, our side initially entered the judge's chambers to meet with the settlement judge without the other parties. The judge was a very nice man who seemed experienced with these types of matters. The judge had recently broken his foot and I remember his foot being elevated on his desk when we came in. The judge had a quiet demeanor, certainly good for a settlement.

After we presented our position to the settlement judge, we left his chambers and the other side then met with the settlement judge. Then the judge calls in each side without the other side and concludes "there will be no settlement". Well, go figure! Lots of money was spent in getting everyone there, in this remote location, and there was no reasonable chance this matter was going to settle. And, I knew that our client was living day to day on his expenses and that he could not afford for the matter to proceed to trial.

So, I explained that to the judge, the critical nature and timing of the finances for the franchisee and my thought that a settlement conference was just that, a "conference with the parties to settle things". I asked if both parties could be brought into the same room to talk and try to work this out? The judge said "that is really unusual when the parties are this far apart". I still asked. The judge checked with the other side and we all met together later that day.

I then learned that many of the other attorneys wanted to "exercise some of their testosterone". In other words, they went first talking about the merits of their case. Although they were skilled trial attorneys, they had little experience with this franchiser But they said what they said and they said it loud, rudely and threatening. It was pretty intimidating to listen to the ramblings. The corporate attorney for the franchiser did not speak. He listened intently to what his attorneys were saying to us. We listened intently and did not interrupt. They were pretty intimidating and incredibly rude about the case. From what they were saying, they gave our client little or no hope of success in the matter.

Other than the client, I was the only non attorney in the room. However, when it was "our turn", my client's attorney asked me to speak instead of him as I was familiar with the facts and circumstances. I agreed.

Rather than address all the attorneys, I simply looked at the franchiser's in-house legal counsel and then I began to speak, "Dave, you and I have known each other a long time. You know I would not be here if I did not believe there was a good reason. My client's attorney is obviously out gunned here this morning. My client cannot afford this whole ordeal. You know that. He has invested everything he ever owned into this franchise and now he has nothing. This parade of "Bozo's" that you have hired is pretty intimidating".

With that, the lead trial attorney began to rudely interrupt me and argue with me. In my opening remarks, I was simply being slightly less rude than he was in his original remarks. However, I looked at the lead trial attorney in the eye and said "Sit down!" (remember the deposition), "I did not interrupt you and you will not interrupt me. Is that clear?". The judge interceded and told him, "Sit down Bill, I want to hear what Chuck has to say".

With that I continued, "Dave, you and I are the only ones in this room that will understand what I am about to say. The others may be well qualified attorney; however, they do not have the experience that you and I have with this franchise organization. In my opinion, they will not be able to find a believable expert, certainly not one that I believe could contradict my testimony. This is a David versus Goliath claim and if it goes to trial, Goliath will lose". I then explained our position in detail with what we would use for trial and the amount of probable damages that the franchiser may owe to my client. I went on to say, "Dave, you do not have to say yes or no at this time. I would like to break for lunch and give you the opportunity to confirm everything I just said with those you need to speak to in your organization". He agreed. With that, we broke for lunch.

During lunch, I advised my client that if he could get back his investment in his franchise, to "take it and run". That is, instead of the total amount of estimated damages, if he could get the franchiser to offer him his original investment that he should agree. I said that I doubted that he could afford to get his case to trial and there was a huge risk of loss. I said the risk of loss was not necessarily in the merits of the case in my opinion, but the risk of loss was because the franchiser would do all things possible to extend the case, increase the expense to him and try to keep the case from getting to a jury trial. His attorney said that he understood and agreed with me at the time.

We reconvened the meeting with the franchiser's attorneys in the judges chambers after lunch. The franchiser in house counsel, Dave, was in a more amicable mood after lunch. He said he reviewed everything with everyone and would allow our client to walk away with nothing.

In other words, the franchiser would drop their claim for a couple of hundred thousand dollars, but our client would leave dead broke. An improvement, but not something that he could live with. As I said during lunch, I believe the franchiser would return the original investment.

I said to him, "Thank you Dave. We are making progress. However, that is not enough". I went back into the chronology of what happened that brought this matter to litigation and what I understood that other franchisees had typically received in similar circumstances. I then said, "In my opinion, this is a David versus Goliath case. If David makes it to trial, you will lose a lot of money, certainly more than you have to pay today. And you will save potentially hundreds of thousands of dollars in legal fees. Today is "let's make a deal" day and you have the opportunity to do the right thing and get this matter behind all of us".

Even though Dave was an attorney, he understood that and the potential cost and risk to his franchiser He thought about it, and offered the franchisee's original investment, plus interest! I again said "Thank you", and looked at my client. This was even more than I believed my client would receive in the settlement conference, and potentially, in the entire matter. My client and his attorney whispered to me, we talked a bit, and then my client told the judge, "Absolutely not!".

I was both surprised and shocked. This is exactly what we wanted (and more) going into the conference. And the risk of proceeding was too high in my opinion. However, for whatever reason, the client said no. As we left the settlement conference, the corporate counsel put his arm on my shoulder and looked at me like "what happened?". I could only shrug.

Ultimately, and as I thought, this case never made it to trial. The client ran out of money as expected and the attorney working for the client simply could not bring the case to trial. The franchiser aggressively litigated and asked for an incredible amount of discovery in the matter leading up to the trial. The client lost everything.

Greed can be a very harmful and deadly sin.

Closing Remarks

During my career I encountered what I believed was both unethical and ethical behavior from CPAs, other professionals, clients and others. It seems to me that one can do the right thing almost their entire life. Once they get caught for doing the wrong thing, that is generally what they are remembered. This is unfortunate, but true.

And one "bad apple" can have a lasting impact on anyone or any business associated with a perceived wrong thing. Thus, it is important to a professional's success to always try to do the right thing. This is very big picture stuff.

I was blessed to have an unbelievable family while growing up, life experiences, different part time jobs during my early years, a great college education, a super job upon graduation, great mentors, great friends, and great clients.

One person seemed to stand above and beyond all the rest. The day after I turned in one of my former bosses for embezzlement I was looking for a job change. That very next day I met the man who would become my business partner since 1983 (and still ongoing). He was the managing partner of our CPA firm. He is the embodiment of what one expects from a trusted professional.

Although we did not always agree (and still do not always agree), we trusted each other since we got into business together. Each and every detail of our business that I did not like having to do; somehow, those were exactly the parts of the business that he excelled. In addition, he handled all of those responsibilities in a highly professional and ethical manner. Every person who came into contact with this partner left with exactly the same feeling.

Accordingly, I am ending this book with a big heart felt thank you to my friend and partner, John Strader. I would not have been successful without John and I recognize that.